COLLEGE STUDENTS IN THE UNITED STATES

THE JOSSEY-BASS HIGHER AND
ADULT EDUCATION SERIES

COLLEGE STUDENTS IN THE UNITED STATES

Characteristics, Experiences, and Outcomes

Kristen A. Renn
Robert D. Reason

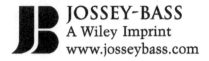

JOSSEY-BASS
A Wiley Imprint
www.josseybass.com

Published by Jossey-Bass
A Wiley Imprint
One Montgomery Street, Suite 1200, San Francisco, CA 94104-4594—www.josseybass.com

Consulting Editor: John Schuh

Jossey-Bass books and products are available through most bookstores. To contact Jossey-Bass directly call our Customer Care Department within the U.S. at 800-956-7739, outside the U.S. at 317-572-3986, or fax 317-572-4002.

Wiley publishes in a variety of print and electronic formats and by print-on-demand. Some material included with standard print versions of this book may not be included in e-books or in print-on-demand. If this book refers to media such as a CD or DVD that is not included in the version you purchased, you may download this material at http://booksupport.wiley.com. For more information about Wiley products, visit www.wiley.com.

Library of Congress Cataloging-in-Publication Data
Renn, Kristen A.
  College students in the United States : characteristics, experiences, and outcomes / Kristen A. Renn, Robert D. Reason.
      p. cm.
  Includes bibliographical references and index.
  ISBN 978-0-470-94720-3 (hardback); ISBN 978-1-118-41550-4 (ebk.); ISBN 978-1-118-41844-4 (ebk.); ISBN 978-1-118-43355-3 (ebk.)
  1. College attendance–United States. 2. College students–United States. 3. Education–Demographic aspects–United States. I. Reason, Robert Dean. II. Title.
  LC148.2.R44 2012
  378.1'619–dc23

                              2012030724

Printed in the United States of America
FIRST EDITION
HB Printing   10 9 8 7 6 5

CONTENTS

PART THREE: OUTCOMES   171

LIST OF FIGURES AND TABLES

Figures

Tables

PREFACE

Higher education in the United States in the twenty-first century is exciting, daunting, and compelling. The goal of increasing the proportion of the U.S. population that goes to college and earns a degree is central to national higher education policy (Obama, 2009b). Participating in the global knowledge economy by attracting increasing numbers of international students is another goal that serves the interests of public policy and individual institutions (Altbach & Knight, 2007). A central mission of the student affairs profession entails understanding and supporting the success of this increasingly diverse student population (American College Personnel Association, n.d.; National Association of Student Personnel Administrators, n.d.). Administrators outside student affairs, as well as policymakers in the public sector and others, are concerned about improving student learning and degree attainment. As former student affairs administrators and current faculty in higher education graduate programs, we think a lot about what professionals need to know about college students and their experiences to achieve these missions.

For decades, student affairs and higher education graduate programs in the United States have included courses on "The American College Student." Perhaps the mythical "American college student"—we will call him John—still exists: a full-time student who came directly to college from high school, John lives in the residence halls, works on campus ten hours a week, and takes a full course load that has him on track to graduate in four years with a bachelor's degree from a selective public university. John is white, Christian, heterosexual, middle class, and without disabilities, the quintessential "American college student" of big-man-on-campus lore. We argue that given changed and changing demographics and environments, it would be a mistake to produce a text on the "American college student." Certainly, educators must still attend to the thousands of "Johns" (and, more often, "Janes"), but the majority of undergraduates in the United States *are not like* John. They engage in nonlinear attendance patterns; go to community colleges; take courses (or entire degrees) online; attend for-profit institutions; come from underrepresented racial, ethnic, and religious groups; speak a first language other than English; work between high school and college; work thirty-plus hours a week *during* college; are international students; raise families; negotiate accommodations for disabilities; or do not complete their intended educational goals. They barely resemble John or Jane, except in their desire to improve their lives through higher education.

We wrote this book, *College Students in the United States,* to account for contemporary and anticipated student demographics and enrollment patterns; a wide variety of campus environments (such as residential, commuter, online, and hybrid); and a range of outcomes including learning, development, and achievement. We organize the book around Alexander Astin's Inputs-Environment-Outputs (I-E-O) framework (1993b). Student demographics, college preparation, and enrollment patterns are the "inputs." The transition to college and campus environments is the substance of the "environment." Student development; learning; and retention, persistence, and completion are the "outputs."

The enduring I-E-O framework provides both a useful organizing frame for the book and a meaningful component of the book itself. No matter how much students and campus environments change, the I-E-O model offers an approach to describe, explain, and explore students' experience in U.S. higher education. We build on this foundation by providing relevant contemporary information and analysis of students, environments, and outcomes. We also provide strategies for readers to project forward in anticipation of higher education trends and to develop skills to update knowledge as needed in a world in which understanding "college students in the United States" is an ongoing project. By consolidating foundational and new research and theory on college students, their experiences, and student outcomes in the United States, we aim to provide educators and students themselves with knowledge to inform policies, programs, curriculum, and practice.

FIGURE 0.1 ASTIN'S I-E-O MODEL

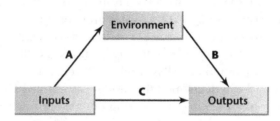

Source: *Assessment for Excellence* (p. 18), by Alexander W. Astin, 1993, Phoenix: The Oryx Press. Copyright 1993 by The Oryx Press. Reproduced with permission from the American Council on Education.

Astin's I-E-O Model

Astin (1977, 1993b) proposed a framework for understanding how college affects students. Although he had worked on these ideas for several years, his iterations of the model in the 1977 book *Four Critical Years* and the 1993 book *What Matters in College? Four Critical Years Revisited* remain foundational sources for understanding studies of college students. In the most basic formulation, the framework lays out a longitudinal model that incorporates inputs (I), the college environment (E), and outputs (O) (see Figure 0.1).

According to the I-E-O model, students enter college with a collection of input characteristics (such as gender, race, academic ability, and learning style) and measurable attributes (for example, interest in public service, inclination to seek out interactions with diverse others, political viewpoints). Precollege environments (family and school, for instance) and college environments (including courses, peers, living arrangements, and interactions with faculty) can be measured according to a number of factors of interest. Then researchers and educators can examine a variety of outputs, more commonly called "outcomes" today. The I-E-O model implies a longitudinal perspective—it follows a student from before college until, ideally, graduation and beyond.

Importantly, the I-E-O model considers the effects of both inputs and environments on outcomes, as well as the effects of inputs on interactions in the environment. It provides a framework for understanding that some input characteristics—for example, high school GPA—may have as much or more to do with outcomes—such as persistence from the first to the

[handwritten margin note: Breaks down what goes into I-E-O Model]

second year—than anything that happens in the college environment. As well, the I-E-O model provides a framework for examining how such input characteristics as motivation for learning or social interaction may interact in the environment to cause a student to, for example, choose to live in a residential college or a fraternity house, both of which have consequences for outcomes (Pascarella & Terenzini, 1991, 2005).

When Astin developed the model (see Astin 1970a, 1970b, 1977, 1991, 1993b), student outcomes assessment was not as well developed a field as it is today, and he noted that there was an overabundance of studies claiming causal relationships between college environments and student outcomes, without accounting for student inputs. One reason for these overreaching causal claims lay in the reality that higher education settings do not lend themselves easily to experimental designs with random assignment of participants to intervention and control groups. Astin thus developed the I-E-O model "to address the basic methodological problem with all nonexperimental studies in the social sciences, namely the nonrandom assignment of people (inputs) to programs (environments)" (Astin & Sax, 1998, p. 252).

For example, if a vice president of student life wants to know about the effects of residential college (RC) participation on student motivation to learn (see Jessup-Anger, 2012), she cannot simply measure fourth-year students who participate in an RC and compare their motivation to that of fourth-year students who do not participate. Such factors as precollege characteristics (high school GPA, SAT score, first-generation status) and who signs up to participate in such a community in the first place (students seeking involvement in learning, for example) may be related to an outcome, such as motivation, as measured years later. In addition, she cannot simply compare the fourth-year students to first-year students in the RC; the samples do not account for variations in motivation to learn that the separate groups of students may have on entry, or other factors that may facilitate or impair their full engagement in the RC experience. The I-E-O model calls on the vice president (or, more likely, her staff) to measure motivation to learn at the beginning of the first year (input), aspects of the RC (environment), and motivation to learn of the *same* group of students in their fourth year (outcome).

A more ideal research design would include a matched sample (for example, students with similar background characteristics) of first-year students not in the RC, whose motivation could then be compared in the fourth year to that of the group of RC students. The vice president could then determine to what extent any observed gains in motivation to learn of the RC students would have happened even if they had not participated in the RC. Such designs are, unfortunately, too rare, owing perhaps to a predominance of convenience sampling in student affairs research. But when enough same data are collected from enough people, results similar to those of the pre-post, matched sample design can be achieved through statistical means, allowing researchers to make claims about the effect of specific experiences (for example, participating in a diversity course) on specific populations (such as students of different racial backgrounds).

The archetype of I-E-O research is the Cooperative Institutional Research Program (CIRP), located at UCLA's Higher Education Research Institute (HERI). Founded by Alexander Astin and now led by Sylvia Hurtado, HERI has for over forty-five years collected data about college students and their experiences. Of course, the research questions one can answer are limited by the data that have been collected. Still, there are hundreds of studies published out of this valuable research resource (see www.heri.ucla.edu/research-publications.php). The I-E-O model is at the center of it all.

Certainly HERI's longitudinal CIRP surveys and data represent a type of "gold standard" in research on the impact of college on students, but the I-E-O concept provides a guiding framework for studies of many types. Qualitative studies of student learning and development that follow a longitudinal approach can provide rich data about how environments act on and with students to influence outcomes. Institutional research outside of the CIRP surveys can track student inputs and, for example, curricula, to point to meaningful experiences during college that seem to produce differential outcomes. The I-E-O model is a fairly intuitive framework that reminds researchers to look at characteristics of incoming students and features of the environment when examining a range of outcomes. We discuss the I-E-O model as a framework for outcomes assessment in more detail in Chapter Nine.

Purpose of the Book

We wrote this book to bring together in one place essential information about college students in the United States in the early twenty-first century. Synthesizing existing research and theory, we present an introduction to studying student characteristics, college choice and enrollment patterns, institutional types and environments, student development, persistence, and outcomes of college. We intend this text to be a starting point for graduate students and others who seek a foundational understanding of the diversity of students and institutions in the United States. We include discussion points, learning activities, and further resources for exploring the topics in each chapter. We assume that some readers—perhaps those who will work most closely with college students—will seek additional depth in some topics. Other readers—perhaps those who will work in areas of higher education outside student affairs—may find the book adequate to meet their needs as administrators or policymakers.

Organization of the Book

Because the I-E-O model provides a "wrap-around" framework for examining college students in the United States, we found it a useful way to organize this book. The book can be read in I-E-O order, or readers may find it useful to read selected chapters in some other order. As already noted, the interactions in the environment connect the input characteristics to output measures. These concepts can be understood as separate but closely related; indeed there are entire cottage industries of scholarship in each area (inputs, environment, outputs). Scholars working in different traditions (including qualitative or quantitative) approach the relationships among inputs, environment, and outputs differently, though we have chosen a fairly straightforward organization for the book that leads from precollege to college choice, enrollment patterns, transition to college, college environments, student development in college, retention and persistence, and student outcomes.

Part One, Inputs, begins with Chapter One, in which we provide an overview of the diversity of students attending two-year and four-year institutions. Chapter Two outlines the college choice process, that is, how students decide whether or not to go to college and then what college to attend. Chapter Three describes student enrollment patterns, including the nonlinear, stop-and-start "double dipping," "stopping out," and "swirling" patterns that are increasingly common.

Part Two, Environments, describes the student experience from the transition to college onward. Chapter Four explains the transition to college and what is known about the ways that the transition varies across student demographic groups. Chapter Five describes and applies an ecological lens to understanding institutional types, campus climate, and other aspects of the campus environment. Chapter Six includes holistic and ecological approaches to college student development, including self-authorship. Chapter Seven highlights key student development theories in the areas of cognitive, moral, and psychosocial development, including racial, gender, and sexual orientation identity development models.

Part Three, Outcomes, describes what happens to students as a result of attending college. Chapter Eight addresses critical elements of student retention and persistence, which are necessary but not sufficient for student success and degree completion. Chapter Nine describes specific student outcomes in several areas (including cognitive, moral, civic, and identity development as well as self-authorship) and general approaches to assessing student outcomes. Chapter Ten synthesizes the I-E-O approach to understanding our new vision of "the American college student" under the more inclusive description of "college students in the United States" in the twenty-first century.

At the end of each chapter we offer discussion points directed at implications for students, for institutions, and for policy and national discourse. These questions are intended to serve as starting points for discussion. They might also be useful to some readers as prompts to consider before and during the readings. We also provide one or more learning activities in each chapter as starting points for instructors to help students connect theory to practice. Finally, we provide additional resources, often online sources, for further exploration of the topics of each chapter. We sought stable Web sites that are likely to remain reliable sources of information over time, even as their content is updated by the sites' owners. We hope that the discussion points, learning activities, and additional resources provide instructors, students, and other interested readers with ways to connect theory and knowledge to higher education practice and policy. To begin that process, we invite readers to consider the following questions while reading the book:

- What assumptions do you hold about college students in the United States?
- What do you want to learn about college students, environments, and outcomes?
- How will this knowledge improve your contribution to higher education?
- In a time of rapid change, how will you continue to stay abreast of changes in college students, environments, and outcomes?
- What groups of students or types of institutions are missing from this book? How will you identify new populations coming to college and

create learning environments that support their success? What new institutional types—or changes to existing types—will emerge to meet their needs?

- What student outcomes can and should higher education institutions demonstrate to various stakeholders (for example, students, families, and members of the public)? How can they do so?

Acknowledgments

Arriving at the final manuscript of a new book provides an occasion for reflection and gratitude. We undertook this project at the invitation of our colleague and friend John Schuh, a scholar and educator whose work we have both admired throughout our careers. We appreciate his encouragement, mentoring, and editing. As we progressed from proposal to drafts to final manuscript, the book took on a life of its own and we came to rely on one another, our colleagues, our students, and our families, as we worked to fulfill our vision of what *College Students in the United States* could and should be. We thank them for their wisdom, insight, and patience.

A few people deserve particular mention here. At Michigan State, doctoral student G. Blue Brazelton committed untold hours to searching literature, managing and formatting references, and composing end-of-chapter matter. Karla Loya, Penn State University doctoral student, and Chad Kee, Iowa State University doctoral student, participated in all facets of the writing process as well. Karla and Chad were instrumental in the completion of Chapter Two of this book. We deeply appreciate their hard work and hope that the experience has contributed in some way to their learning.

In addition, Kristen thanks colleagues and students at Michigan State, who since 2001 have provided an optimal environment in which to think, write, and teach about student affairs and higher education. I also thank my former colleagues in the Office of Student Life at Brown University for the foundation they provided for my continued work in the field. Particular thanks are due to mentors Tamie Kiddess Lucey, Robin Rose, Mark Nahorney, and Karen Arnold. New perspectives on higher education emerge as my nieces and nephews embark into it; I thank them for letting Aunt Kristen be nosy and ask lots of questions. I see them throughout this book. My sister, Amy Renn, continues to teach me about the important work of student support services at for-profit institutions. I thank my partner, Melissa McDaniels, for reminding me that much of higher education exists beyond what happens in student affairs, and much of life exists beyond what happens in and at work. Finally, I thank my friend and colleague Bob for undertaking this project with me and being such a great collaborator.

Robert thanks colleagues, friends, and students at Penn State and Iowa State Universities, who informed and pushed my thinking on the students in American higher education. I must provide special acknowledgment to my mentor, colleague, and friend Pat Terenzini, who during my nine years at Penn State University nurtured in me a of love of learning, a pride in precision, and an appreciation of high-quality research within the broad literature that is higher education. Early in our relationship, Pat reminded me that "sometimes you must say 'no' to the good, so you can say 'yes' to the great." Writing this book with Kris was certainly "the great," and I appreciate the opportunity to work with and learn from her. Finally, I must thank Andra, Elliot, and Ava, who gave of their time to allow me to complete this project, but did not let me forget what was most important.

It is a true joy to engage deeply in a topic that engenders one's passion, a topic that is both interesting and important. Certainly the study of college students in the United States—who they are, what they experience, and how they learn—is such a topic for us.

ABOUT THE AUTHORS

Kristen A. Renn is professor of higher, adult, and lifelong education at Michigan State University. Her areas of research and teaching lie in student development, student affairs, and campus environments. Dr. Renn holds a bachelor's degree in music from Mount Holyoke College, a master's degree in educational leadership from Boston University, and a doctoral degree in higher education from Boston College. She started her professional career in student activities at Wheaton College in Massachusetts and worked for ten years as a dean in the Office of Student Life at Brown University. Dr. Renn has published extensively on the topics of mixed-race college students, LGBTQ issues in higher education, student leaders in identity-based organizations, and new professionals in student affairs. She has extended her work on college students in the United States to consider international contexts for creating learning environments, including a multinational study of women's colleges and universities. Dr. Renn's contributions to scholarly and professional communities of practice in student affairs and higher education include editorial roles with the *Journal of Higher Education, Academe,* and the *Journal of College Student Development,* and leadership in the American College Personnel Association (ACPA), the Association for the Study of Higher Education, and the American Education Research Association. She is an ACPA Senior Scholar.

Robert D. Reason is an associate professor of student affairs and higher education at Iowa State University. From 2003 to 2011 he was an associate professor of education at Penn State University, where he also held an appointment as senior research associate in Penn State's Center for the Study of Higher Education. Dr. Reason holds a bachelor's degree in economics from Grinnell College in Iowa; a master's degree in counseling and college student development from Minnesota State University, Mankato; and a doctoral degree in higher education from Iowa State University. Dr. Reason studies college student outcomes, including how institutional policies, practices, and climates affect these outcomes. Dr. Reason has been particularly interested in first-year student outcomes, completing two national studies of first-year student outcomes (with Patrick Terenzini) while at Penn State University. His research has been published in the *Journal of College Student Development, Research in Higher Education,* and the *Review of Higher Education.* He currently serves as director of research for the Core Commitments Initiative for the Association of American Colleges and Universities, as a National Association of Student Personnel Administrators Faculty Fellow, and as an ACPA Senior Scholar.

COLLEGE STUDENTS IN THE UNITED STATES

PART ONE

INPUTS

CHAPTER ONE

CHARACTERISTICS OF COLLEGE STUDENTS IN THE UNITED STATES

A hundred years ago, eight and a half percent of American seventeen-year-olds had a high school degree, and two percent of twenty-three-year-olds had a college degree. Now, on any given weekday morning, you will find something like fifty million Americans, about a sixth of the population, sitting under the roof of a public-school building, and twenty million more are students or on the faculty or the staff of an institution of higher learning.

LEMANN, 2010

The current generation of college students not only is the largest ever but also has been called "the most racially and ethnically diverse in this nation's history" (Debard, 2004, p. 33). Data provided by the National Center for Education Statistics (Aud, Fox, & KewalRamani, 2010; Snyder & Dillow, 2009) certainly support these claims. Snyder and Dillow report a 32 percent increase in total enrollment over just the last ten years. Between 1976 and 2008 all racial and ethnic groups saw enrollment increases, with the sharpest increases in the Hispanic and Asian American and Native American Pacific Islander populations[1] (Aud, Fox, & KewalRamani). These trends are expected to continue through the next decade, with growth in college enrollment by students from traditionally underrepresented racial

---

[1]When referencing social identities and groups of students throughout the book we use contemporary, inclusive, and specific language whenever possible. As is often the case, however, when reviewing the work of other authors we use the language they have used. When reviewing U.S. census data, we use the federal government's language.

and ethnic groups outpacing the growth by white students (Hussar & Bailey, 2009).

Data on college-going trends suggest student diversity also continues to increase in areas beyond race and ethnicity. This generation includes more openly gay, lesbian, and bisexual students, and more religiously diverse students, than ever before (Bryant, 2006; Lucozzi, 1998). Financial aid data suggest that more students from lower-income families are enrolling in postsecondary education. The College Board (2009) reported that over 6.1 million college students received a Pell Grant in 2008–2009, up from 3.9 million students in 2000 (King, 2003). Certainly the tough economic times of the late 1990s and early 2000s have had some effect on the number of Pell Grant recipients, but the trend toward higher college-going rates by lower-income students is undeniable.

This increased diversity of students has the potential to lead to increased learning for all, as students learn to manage cross-difference interactions and improve interpersonal relationships (Hurtado, Dey, Gurin, & Gurin, 2003; Milem, 2003), if postsecondary educators can effectively prepare students for such interactions (Allport, 1979). In this chapter we review enrollment trends for higher education in the United States, paying special attention to those trends that have resulted in an increasingly diverse student body. Further, the chapter details projections of college enrollments for different student groups that will, by all accounts, continue to diversify the student population into the next decade.

In the following sections, we have chosen to present groups of students as distinct, both to simplify presentation and for ease in comprehension. We readily acknowledge the inherent limitations of this approach as well. Current models of how students' various and multiple identity statuses affect their higher education outcomes and experiences reveal that a nuanced understanding of the intersection of various identities is needed (see Torres, Jones, & Renn, 2009). Wherever possible in this chapter we highlight intersections of identities, as these intersections affect an understanding of who is coming to higher education, and we strongly encourage the reader to look for these intersections. Although it is true, for example, to say the college-going rates of Latino/a students have increased substantially in the last decade, acknowledging that much of this growth is driven by women (Latinas) is both more accurate and nuanced. For those readers who wish to explore more deeply the demographic trends presented here, we draw attention to the list of resources at the end of this chapter.

One final caution is necessary: when studying college enrollment data and rates, readers should be aware of the populations on which numbers are being reported. Different studies use different population definitions, which is particularly important to know if the college-going rates of specific populations are being reported. For example, some studies report college enrollment data only for traditional-age college students (students ages eighteen to twenty-four). Data based on the U.S. Census Bureau numbers are likely to reflect this age range (Fry, 2011; Heckman & LaFontaine, 2007). We draw heavily from census data for the discussion in this chapter. Finally, readers should pay careful attention to whether enrollment figures reflect total enrollment (which includes undergraduate, graduate, and professional students) or just undergraduate enrollments. Throughout this chapter, we highlight the different populations reflected in the data we present.

Trends in College Enrollment

The United States has seen growth in the number of students enrolling in higher education. The National Center for Education Statistics (NCES) reports that between 1998 and 2008 the number of students enrolled in higher education increased from 14.5 million to 19.1 million, a 32 percent increase (Snyder & Dillow, 2009). Undergraduate students made up the vast majority of enrollments: 16.3 million undergraduates were enrolled in 2008 (Aud, Hussar, et al., 2010). NCES projections suggest that the number of students enrolled in higher education will continue to increase over the next decade, reaching an estimated 20.6 million students in 2018 (Hussar & Bailey, 2009). Much of this growth is driven by populations of students who have been traditionally underrepresented in higher education.

Overall Undergraduate Enrollment

We turn our focus now to undergraduate student enrollments. Because undergraduate students constitute the vast majority of total postsecondary enrollment, the trends in undergraduate enrollment follow—and dictate— the trends mentioned briefly earlier. Undergraduate student enrollment has been increasing over the last forty years and is expected to continue (Aud, Fox, & KewalRamani, 2010). Between 2000 and 2008, for example, total undergraduate enrollment increased 24 percent. Overall undergraduate enrollment is expected to continue to increase over the next decade, growing to an estimated total of 19.5 million students in 2020.

Although all sectors of American higher education are experiencing growth in undergraduate enrollment, that growth is not evenly distributed (Aud, Fox, & KewalRamani, 2010). Private two- and four-year institutions saw a 44 percent increase in enrollment between 2000 and 2008, whereas public institution enrollment increased by 19 percent. Much of the growth in the private sector is driven by growth in enrollments at for-profit institutions. Although the *rate* of increase at private institutions is higher than the *rate* of increase at public institutions, it is important to note that public higher education still enrolls the larger number of undergraduate students (12.6 million students in 2008). Projections indicate that public institutions will continue to educate the majority of students for some time.

Enrollment growth at four-year institutions outpaces enrollment growth at two-year institutions (Aud, Fox, & KewalRamani, 2010). Since 2000, four-year institution enrollment has increased almost 31 percent to a total of 9.4 million undergraduate students in 2008. During the same period, enrollment in two-year institutions increased 19 percent, to a total 7 million students. Both the four-year and two-year sectors of higher education are expected to continue to grow over the next decade. By 2019, four-year institution enrollment is projected to increase 50 percent over 2000 enrollments to 10.8 million students. Similarly, two-year institution enrollment is projected to increase to 8.2 million students in 2019, a 39 percent increase over 2000 enrollments.

Racial and Ethnic Diversity

Enrollment trends related to the racial and ethnic diversity of college students in the United States show an increasing proportion of students of color on college campuses. The growth has been driven by both changes in the demographics of the U.S. population, which is becoming much less white, as well as changes in the college-going rates of several racial and ethnic groups, particularly Latino/a students (Pryor, Hurtado, Sáenz, Santos, & Korn, 2007; Snyder & Dillow, 2009). The distribution of racial groups across the United States is not geographically even, so many of the trends described in this section do not apply to all institutions equally. For example, the Hispanic population made up 16.3 percent of the total U.S. population in 2010 (up from 12.5 percent in 2000), but approximately 41 percent of Hispanic census respondents reside in the western United States, and only 9 percent reside in the Midwest (Ennis, Ríos-Vargas, &

Albert, 2011). Growth in enrollment of Hispanic students, therefore, will be greater in institutions in western states.

The percentage of white students in higher education has decreased over the last several decades. In 1976 white students represented 82 percent of all college students; in 2008 white students made up 63 percent (see Table 1.1; Aud, Fox, & KewalRamani, 2010). Although the overall percentage decreased, the total number of white students actually increased by 34 percent over the same period. Compare the growth in the number of white students to a 560 percent growth in the number of Asian American and Native American Pacific Islander students and a 496 percent growth in Hispanic students, and a picture of greater diversity begins to unfold. During the same period the total number of American Indian and Alaska Native college students increased by 151 percent, and the total number of African American college students increased by 141 percent. This growth continues; according to a report by the Pew Hispanic Center (Fry, 2011), Hispanic student enrollment jumped 24 percent in a single year—from fall 2009 to fall 2010.

Students from different racial and ethnic backgrounds tend to enroll in different sectors within higher education, with students of color more highly represented at two-year and for-profit institutions (Aud, Fox, & KewalRamani, 2010). For example, in 2008 black students accounted for approximately 11 percent of all students in public four-year institutions, but 14 percent of students at public two-year institutions, and 27 percent of students at for-profit institutions. White students, however, are more likely to attend four-year, nonprofit, and private institutions. White students make up almost 69 percent of students at private, nonprofit institutions; only 59 percent of students at public two-year institutions; and 52 percent of students at for-profit institutions.

Another way to compare enrollment rates at two- and four-year institutions is to look at the proportion of a group enrolled at each type. Examining enrollment in this way reveals that Hispanic students were the most likely group of students to attend a two-year institution (Fry, 2011). A 2011 report by the Pew Hispanic Center, which focused exclusively on younger students ages eighteen to twenty-four, reported that over 44 percent of all Hispanic students in the United States who fell within that age group in 2010 were enrolled in two-year institutions. Approximately 35 percent of black students in the same age group were enrolled in two-year institutions. Asian American students were the least likely to be enrolled in two-year institutions, with 25 percent. Slightly over 27 percent

TABLE 1.1 ENROLLMENT BY SEX AND RACE

	1976		2000		2008		Percentage Change, 1976 to 2008
	Total Enrollment	Percentage of Enrollment	Total Enrollment	Percentage of Enrollment	Total Enrollment	Percentage of Enrollment	
Total Undergraduates	9,418,970	100.0%	13,155,393	100.0%	16,345,738	100.0%	73.54%
Women	4,521,106	48.0%	7,380,175	56.1%	9,300,725	56.9%	105.72%
Men	4,897,864	52.0%	5,775,218	43.9%	7,045,013	43.1%	43.84%
African American and Black	943,355	10.0%	1,548,893	11.8%	2,269,284	13.9%	140.55%
American Indian and Alaska Native	69,729	0.7%	138,506	1.1%	175,552	1.1%	151.76%
Asian Pacific Islander	169,291	1.8%	845,545	6.4%	1,117,865	6.8%	560.32%
Hispanic	352,893	3.7%	1,351,025	10.3%	2,103,524	12.9%	496.08%
White	7,740,485	82.2%	8,983,455	68.3%	10,339,216	63.3%	33.57%

Source: Adapted from Aud, Fox, & KewalRamani, 2010.

of eighteen- to twenty-four-year-old white students were enrolled in two-year institutions in 2010.

American Indian and Alaska Native students are a smaller, and often overlooked, population in U.S. higher education. In 2006 American Indians and Alaska Natives accounted for approximately 1.5 percent of the total U.S. population, concentrated primarily in the western United States (Aud, Fox, & KewalRamani, 2010; DeVoe & Darling-Churchill, 2008). That same year, American Indian and Alaska Native students made up less than 1 percent of all students in U.S. higher education (DeVoe & Darling-Churchill). Although this underrepresentation is problematic, trend data suggest that the total enrollment of American Indian and Alaska Native students has doubled since 1977.

Finally, a growing number of college students identify as multiracial (Shang, 2008). Jaschik (2006), citing findings from the 2000 Census—the first year individuals were allowed to check more than one box on the demographic question about race—reported that about 40 percent of the 6.8 million people who identified as multiracial were under the age of eighteen. Data from the Cooperative Institutional Research Program, which has been tracking the number of multiracial students for over three decades, reported consistent growth in the percentage of college students who identify as multiracial (Pryor et al., 2007). In 1971, for example, 1.3 percent of college students identified as multiracial; in 2006, 7.3 percent identified as such. Coupled with the census data reported by Jaschik, these trends suggest that the percentage of multiracial college students will continue to grow.

International Students

An emphasis on globalization in higher education, and the global aftermath of the terrorist attacks in 2001, has increased attention on international students studying in the United States and U.S. students studying abroad. The percentage, but not the total number, of international students within the total population of U.S. students declined in the years immediately following September 11, 2001. Almost a decade after the terrorist attacks, international student enrollment in U.S. institutions has begun to increase again (Aud, Fox, & KewalRamani, 2010). The downturn after 9/11 notwithstanding, trend data suggest that international student enrollment in U.S. institutions has increased from about 1.6 percent of total students in 1970 to slightly over 3.4 percent of students in 2008. International student enrollment is not evenly distributed across graduate and undergraduate students, however. The majority of international students enrolled in higher education in the United States are enrolled in graduate programs; international students make up approximately 10.5 percent of all U.S. graduate students (Aud, Hussar, et al., 2010; Planty et al., 2009). By contrast, international students make up only 1.6 percent of undergraduates.

The majority of international students studying at U.S. institutions come from six countries, with India, China, and South Korea accounting for about 40 percent of all international students in the United States (Planty et al., 2009). Students from India, China, and South Korea represent 15, 13, and 11 percent of international students, respectively. Japan, the fourth-most-represented country among international students, accounts for only 5 percent of students.

Sex Differences in Higher Education

Women became the majority of all students in American higher education in 1979, when they accounted for approximately 51 percent of all students (Snyder & Dillow, 2009), and have been a "stable majority" ever since (Pryor et al., 2007, p. 4). By 2008, the percentage of women students had increased to 57 percent of the total undergraduate population, although this percentage was down from a high of 57.4 percent in 2004 (Aud, Hussar, et al., 2010). As is the case for almost all groups we have examined, the total number of women students has been generally increasing. For example, there were 7.4 million undergraduate women enrolled in higher education institutions in 2000; in 2008 the total number of women had increased to over 9.3 million.

Obviously, because the proportion of women represented among undergraduate students has increased, the proportion of men had to have decreased over the last decades. Based on trends of actual enrollment patterns over the last forty years (Freeman, 2004; Peter & Horn, 2005), it is reasonable to expect that total enrollment for women, and perhaps proportional representation of women undergraduates, will increase. This prediction has raised concerns among scholars and popular media about the condition of education for boys and men in the United States (Kellom, 2004; Lamport & Bulgin, 2010). Although the total number of men enrolling in higher education in the United States continues to increase (Freeman, 2004; Hussar & Bailey, 2009), the rate of increase has been considerably lower than that of women. From 2000 to 2009, for example, the undergraduate population of men grew about 31 percent, whereas the growth for women undergraduates was closer to 35 percent (Aud, Hussar, et al., 2010). Although this discrepancy could be an artifact of women, particularly Latinas (Peter & Horn, 2005), catching up, the call for greater attention to men's achievement in higher education is well heeded.

LGBT Students in Higher Education

Although data tracking the enrollment of openly lesbian, gay, bisexual, and transgender (LGBT) college students are difficult to find, many higher education professionals agree that more students are arriving on college campuses already open about their sexuality and gender expression (see, for example, Beemyn, 2005). Estimates of the proportion of college students who identify as LGBT vary widely, and only one national survey—the Harvard College Alcohol Study (HCAS) (Wechsler, 2005)—currently asks a question about sexuality. A recent national study surveyed transgender individuals (Beemyn & Rankin, 2011) but does not make any inferences about transgender college students. Without more information specifically about LGBT college students, current understanding presented in this subsection must be viewed cautiously; these are, at best, estimates.

Part of the problem with tracking students by sexual orientation is definitional; researchers struggle to find ways to operationalize the definitions associated with sexual identity (Black, Gates, Sanders, & Taylor, 2000). Many surveys rely on questions about sexual behavior. The HCAS survey, for example, asks respondents if they have ever engaged in same-sex sexual behavior. Just because a student has engaged in same-sex sexual behavior does not mean that the student is, or would identify as, lesbian, gay, or bisexual (Dilley, 2005). Carpenter (2009), in reporting data from HCAS, correctly discusses "same-sex behaving" (p. 697) men and women, rather than labeling these individuals as gay, lesbian, or bisexual. This critique notwithstanding, the data coming from HCAS are the best currently available.

Using the data from HCAS, Carpenter (2009) reported that 1,800 of the 15,000 college student respondents to this survey (12 percent) over the course of four years indicated that they had previously engaged in same-sex sexual behavior. In a study that allowed students to self-identify as gay, lesbian, bisexual, or transgender, however, Gonyea and Moore (2007) reported that only about 6 percent of respondents identified as such. Although these two studies allow some understanding of the proportion of LGB and transgender students on college campuses, they also highlight some of the methodological and definitional issues involved in identifying these students.

Because HCAS was administered three times between 1997 and 2001, the data also provide some insight into enrollment trends for LBG students. The proportion of "same-sex behaving men" increased from 3.3 percent in 1997 to 4.7 percent in 2001. Similarly, the proportion of "same-sex behaving women" increased from 3.7 in 1997 to 6.2 percent in 2001. These percentages appear to align with findings from other surveys that use similar definitions (Black et al., 2000). Again, however, because it is likely that the proportion of "same-sex behaving" students is different from the proportion of students who identify as LGB, these trend data must be understood cautiously and interpreted narrowly.

Although researchers often conflate lesbian, gay, and bisexual with transgender, it is important to note the distinctions between sexuality, gender identity, and gender expression. We discuss these distinctions in more detail in Chapter Seven. Briefly, sexuality relates to whom one finds physically or sexually attractive. Gender identity and gender expression relate to how one identifies and presents oneself in terms of masculinity and femininity (Bilodeau & Renn, 2005). In a national study of the climate for LGBT students in higher education, Rankin and her colleagues (Rankin, Weber, Blumenfeld, & Frazer, 2010) allowed respondents to identify as lesbian, gay, bisexual, or straight (sexual identity), but also as men, women, transmasculine, or transfeminine (gender identity). Respondents also presented themselves as masculine, feminine, or other (gender expression). Although the within-sample differences these researchers reported provide some insight into the diversity within the LGBT community, the higher education community still has little understanding of the number of LGBT-identified students.

Family Income Differences Among College Students

The U.S. higher education student population is becoming more bifurcated when it comes to family income, as the median parental income of incoming first-year students continues to rise (Pryor et al., 2007) at the same time as financial aid, and student loans in particular, allow students from lower-income families to attend college at higher rates (Knapp, Kelly-Reid, & Ginder, 2010; Knapp, Kelly-Reid, & Whitmore, 2006). Unfortunately, an enrollment gap still exists for lower-income students, even after accounting for academic achievement (Fox, Connolly, & Snyder, 2005). Academically talented students from lower-income families are less likely to attend college than equally talented peers from higher-income families.

In general, students at four-year colleges and universities appear to come from families with higher annual incomes than those of community college students (Pryor et al., 2007), even as the total number and percentage of students receiving financial aid at all institutional types continues to increase (Knapp, Kelly-Reid, & Ginder, 2010). Over three-quarters of undergraduate students at four-year institutions received some form of financial aid in 2007, although these numbers must be understood in relation to the general health of the economy at the time. As one might expect, the percentage was highest at the highest-cost institutions—private, nonprofit four-year institutions (85.3 percent). The percentage was lowest at the public two-year institutions (61.2 percent), which makes some sense given that these institutions have the lowest tuition, but is surprising given the high proportion of lower-income students who attend such institutions (Provasnik & Planty, 2008; U.S. Department of Education, 2010).

Slightly under three-quarters of undergraduate students worked at least part-time in 2008; however, the relationship between income level and work might not be as most observers would assume (U.S. Department of Education, 2010). Students from the lowest income levels did not report working the most; in fact, students from middle income levels were most likely to work and to work more hours than students from other income levels. On the one hand, about 68 percent of students from the lowest quartile of family incomes reported working, with about 20 percent working full-time. On the other hand, 70 percent of students in the middle two quartiles of income reported working, with 36 percent working full-time. The effects of limited amounts of need-based financial aid are likely the reason for these counterintuitive relationships.

As one might expect, students' hours worked per week varied based on the type of institution attended; approximately 22 percent of students attending four-year institutions worked full-time (thirty-five hours or more a week), whereas 42 percent of students attending public two-year institutions worked full-time. Similar variance in hours worked is found when the data are examined by race. With the exception of Asian American students, the total percentage of students who worked (full- or part-time) did not vary much by race or ethnicity; approximately 64 percent of Asian American students reported working in 2008 compared to 73 to 75 percent of other racial and ethnic groups (U.S. Department of Education, 2010). A greater percentage of African American students, however, worked full-time (39 percent) in relation to other racial and ethnic groups.

Adult Students

There is little agreement within higher education research about how to define "adult students." Enrollment trends indicate that the assumption of an eighteen- to twenty-two-year-old college student is anachronistic (Donaldson & Townsend, 2007; Horn & Carroll, 1996); definitional ambiguity means that a clear picture of enrollment trends for adult learners is difficult to find. Donaldson and Townsend, for example, present widely varying enrollment figures depending on whether "adult" is defined as "older than twenty-four" or "older than twenty-five." Further, higher education researchers have paid little attention to the experiences of adult learners within higher education, as is the case with many nonmajority populations (Donaldson & Townsend; Pascarella & Terenzini, 2005).

Horn and Carroll (1996), using a very broad definition of adult students as "older than typical" (p. 6) that included some students who might not otherwise have been defined as adult learners, estimated that "older than typical" students constituted about 60 percent of undergraduate students in 1992, up from 54 percent in 1979. Their definition includes students who delayed enrollment after high school for at least two years. Twenty-year-old first-year students were included in these numbers, even though these students fall within the age range for "traditional-age" college students.

The National Center for Education Statistics uses a more conservative definition of adult learners—students twenty-five years of age or older. Using this definition, adult learners totaled approximately seven million students in 2007 (Hussar & Bailey, 2009). Hussar and Bailey estimated a 25 percent enrollment increase for students ages twenty-five to thirty-four, and a 12 percent increase for students over the age of thirty-five. Snyder and Dillow (2009) estimated that adult learners will constitute about 40 percent of undergraduate enrollment in 2019.

Adult learners are often included in discussions of other "nontraditional students," including students who are financially independent, are parents themselves, or are married. Unfortunately, these other nontraditional characteristics are often used euphemistically in lieu of "at-risk" categories (Choy, 2002; Horn & Carroll, 1996). Given the increasing number of adult learners enrolling in higher education, especially with the increases in returning student veterans discussed in the next subsection, higher education must find ways to address the needs of this population and decrease the risk that they will leave college before achieving their goals.

Returning Student Veterans

The Serviceman's Readjustment Act of 1944 (commonly known as the GI Bill) was one of the most influential pieces of higher education legislation of its time. Bennett (1966) reported, for example, that by 1946—only two years after the implementation of the GI Bill—over 70 percent of all male college students were veterans, taking advantage of the benefits of the bill. With the number of college-age men and women currently serving the military, the Post-9/11 Veterans Educational Assistance Act of 2008—the Post-9/11 GI Bill—promises to have a similarly powerful influence. The Post-9/11 GI Bill and the Yellow Ribbon Campus Campaign, which allows institutions of higher education to waive up to half the cost of attending that is not covered by the Post-9/11 GI Bill benefits, provide powerful incentives for veterans returning from service to enroll in higher education.

The United States Department of Veterans Affairs (VA) received over twenty-five thousand applications for benefits through the Post-9/11 GI Bill program within two weeks of opening the application process in 2009 (U.S. Department of Veterans Affairs, 2009a), portending the future demand for higher education among returning student veterans. Kotok (2008) estimated, based on data released from the VA, that by 2007 more than 270,000 post-9/11 combat veterans had claimed education benefits through the Post-9/11 GI Bill and were applying those toward degree programs. By September 2009, the VA had ruled over 200,000 applicants eligible for benefits and provided over $50 million to returning veterans (U.S. Department of Veterans Affairs, 2009b).

Enrollment patterns of student veterans will be unpredictable (Rumann & Hamrick, 2009). Although a significant number of young adults graduate from high school, enlist in the armed services, and enroll in college on the completion of their duty, contemporary military and homeland security strategies mean this linear trajectory may not be true for most student veterans. Rumann and Hamrick (2010) noted that the heavy reliance on National Guard and reserve personnel for armed conflicts requires many current college students to interrupt their enrollment for a period of time to deploy. Many returning student veterans, therefore, are likely to be reentering college after a sudden disruption, hoping to begin approximately where they left off prior to deployment. This enrollment-to-service-to-enrollment pattern adds to the complex transition issues already faced by student veterans (Rumann & Hamrick, 2010). As of 2009, only 22 percent of those colleges and universities with veteran services had developed expedited reenrollment processes for returning veterans (Cook, Young, & Associates, 2009).

Student veterans will require support in multiple forms as they transition into higher education (Cook et al., 2009). As stated previously, sudden disruptions in enrollment will require colleges and universities to negotiate ways to support the successful return of current students, with minimal disruption to their academic progress, at the same time as they prepare for an influx of new students who are returning veterans. Student veterans often perceive higher education environments as hostile and antimilitary (DiRamio, Ackerman, & Mitchell, 2008). Further, student veterans, particularly those who have seen combat and those who are closer to traditional college age, are at higher risk for stress-related illnesses (Seal, Bertenthal, Miner, Saunak, & Marmar, 2007). Similarly, student veterans are faced with role incongruities as they renegotiate a student identity while often maintaining a soldier identity (which can be a more acute issue if the student is in the National Guard or reserves and faces the possibility of redeployment) (Rumann & Hamrick, 2010).

First-Generation College Students

First-generation college students are difficult to define and difficult to count, but they remain a large and important segment of the undergraduate college student population in the United States (Davis, 2010). There is little clear consensus on what proportion of college students constitutes first-generation students, although many researchers point to a National Center for Education Statistics report (Nunez & Cuccaro-Alamin, 1998) finding that 43.4 percent of first-year students in 1998 held first-generation status. Davis, in his recent book on first-generation college students, suggested the 43.4 percent estimation might actually be low. Davis used a secondary calculation of data presented by Choy (2001) to estimate that more than half of all first-year students in 1992 were first-generation students.

As with some other groups discussed in this chapter, the difficulty in counting first-generation students relates to a difficulty in defining what it means to be a first-generation student. The most common and accepted definition appears to be a student for whom neither parent (or guardian) possesses a four-year degree (Davis, 2010), but there is not widespread consensus. Inkelas and her colleagues (Inkelas, Daver, Vogt, & Leonard, 2007), for example, defined first-generation students as those "for whom both parents or guardians have a high school education or less and did not begin a postsecondary degree" (p. 404). This definition is more conservative than Davis's definition and would exclude students whose parents began a postsecondary degree regardless of whether they finished (a group Davis's definition would include). The National Center for Education Statistics (for example, Nunez & Cuccaro-Alamin, 1998) uses three categories to classify students, providing a compromise for the discrepancy just noted: (1) first-generation students, (2) students whose parent or parents have some postsecondary education, and (3) students whose parent or parents have at least a four-year degree (Davis, 2010).

Regardless of the definition used, higher education researchers generally understand that enrollment patterns for first-generation students and the experiences they have once enrolled in higher education are different from those of non-first-generation students. First-generation students also are much more likely to begin their higher education at a two-year institution (Davis, 2010). They are also much more likely to experience difficulty in transitioning to college (Inkelas et al., 2007), and much less likely to engage in activities believed to support academic success and persistence (such as interacting with faculty, studying, and attending workshops) (Pascarella, Pierson, Wolniak, & Terenzini, 2004; Terenzini, Springer, Yaeger, Pascarella, & Nora, 1996).

Students with Disabilities and Mental Health Concerns

There is a widely held belief that the proportion of students with disabilities and mental health issues on college campuses is growing. The Americans with Disabilities Act (ADA) and increased sensitivity to issues of access have certainly made college attendance a greater possibility for more students who identify as having a disability, although the reality of greater proportions of students with disabilities attending college varies by type of disability. Evans and DeVita (in press) found that, much like many of the groups discussed in this chapter, students with disabilities represent a heterogeneous group. Not only do students with disabilities identify within each of the racial, ethnic, sexuality, and socioeconomic groups discussed earlier but also the differences in disabilities experienced by these students add to the diversity within this student group. Students with physical disabilities (for example, mobility impairments) are likely to be the most recognizable for student affairs and higher education professionals, but students with less visible or invisible disabilities, such as learning disabilities and mental health issues, make up this group as well.

According to the United States Department of Education (Snyder & Dillow, 2011), 11 percent of undergraduates in 2007 reported having a disability. This number was the same as the percentage of students reporting similar disabilities in 2003, indicating that this population of students is growing at a rate similar to the rate of total undergraduate population growth. The Department of Education definition is, however, limited to students who report learning disabilities or one of several physical disabilities (such as deafness or mobility impairments). Looking deeper into these statistics reveals that certain groups of students are more likely to report having a disability than other groups of students. Specifically, white students, older students, and student veterans are overrepresented among students with disabilities, compared to their representation in the overall undergraduate student population.

Although the Department of Education report (Snyder & Dillow, 2011) provided an overview of students with disabilities on college campuses, the narrow definition excludes an important category of students: students with mental health concerns. It is not uncommon to hear higher education professionals discussing the "increase" in the number of students with mental health issues on college campuses, often using an increased use of college counseling services as evidence for such an assertion. No longitudinal research exists to support this claim. Recently, however, the Center for Collegiate Mental Health (CCMH, 2012) was established to begin tracking the use of and outcomes associated with college counseling centers.

CCMH, since its inception in 2008, has collected standardized data from approximately 140 college counseling centers. Although it is premature to make judgments about trends in college student mental health, it will eventually be possible to do so. For now, the CCMH data provide a snapshot of mental health issues on campus. In the baseline year of 2008, 19 percent of students seeking mental health counseling at a campus facility had received counseling prior to enrolling in college (CCMH, 2012). Thirty-two percent of students reported serious thoughts of suicide, but the most prevalent issues presented by students included social anxiety and academic distress.

Although research related to the "increasing" numbers of students with disabilities is not available, readily accessible demographic data demonstrate that higher education professionals must be sensitive to and understand the issues of this diverse group of students. Partially in response to this need, helping skills have been identified as an essential competency of student affairs professionals (American College Personnel Association

& National Association of Student Personnel Administrators, 2010; Reynolds, 2009).

Attitudes and Beliefs of Current College Students

The previous section focused on sociodemographic characteristics of college students. We turn now to the attitudes and values of today's college students. Obviously, students do not enter college as "blank slates"; they come with attitudes, beliefs, expectations, and motivations that influence how they experience college. Much has been made of the belief that this generation of college students is different from any generation that has come before it. Howe and Strauss (2000, 2003), coining the term *Millennial Generation,* have asserted that students of this generation were treated as special and sheltered by their parents; have a sense of confidence in their interactions with authority; are conventional, team-oriented, and achievement-oriented; and experience a great deal of pressure to succeed. These characteristics combine to give the current generation of traditional-age college students (those born between 1980 and 2002) a set of shared values that are very different from those of the generation that immediately preceded them (those born between 1965 and 1980) (Debard, 2004).

Perhaps the most comprehensive longitudinal database of trends in students' attitudes and beliefs is housed at UCLA's Higher Education Research Institute: the Cooperative Institutional Research Program (CIRP). Since 1966, UCLA researchers have administered the CIRP instruments to incoming first-year students on thousands of college and university campuses (Pryor et al., 2007). The CIRP Freshman Survey gathers data on students' characteristics, attitudes, values, and behaviors. The consistent, longitudinal approach to this data collection allows for a comprehensive understanding of trends over time. In recognition of the fortieth anniversary of the CIRP project, Pryor and his colleagues (2007) compiled these trends into a monograph titled *The American Freshman: Forty Year Trends, 1966–2006.* This section highlights some of those findings and explores more deeply the trends identified by the UCLA researchers.

Religion and Spirituality

Even a cursory review of published literature in higher education reveals increasing attention being paid to students' spirituality and spiritual development as outcomes of college, outcomes that many researchers believe have been neglected (see, for example, Astin, Astin, & Lindholm, 2011). Descriptive data published by UCLA's Higher Education Research Institute demonstrates that college students may be refocusing on issues of spirituality at the start of the twenty-first century (Pryor et al., 2007). Although some of the research on students' spiritual development was completed prior to 9/11 (Jablonski, 2001), researchers point to the existential crises arising out of the terrorist attacks as well as general characteristics of Millennial Generation college students as precipitators of a renewed emphasis on spirituality (Braskamp, 2007; Nash & Murray, 2010; Parks, 2011).

Higher education scholars draw important distinctions between spirituality and religion that members of the general public, who may use these terms interchangeably, may not recognize. Astin and his colleagues (2011) summarized the scholarly difference between these two concepts. *Religion*, according to these authors, involves "adherence to a set of faith-based beliefs (and related practices) concerning both the origins of the world and the nature of the entity" (p. 5) believed to have created the world. Religion involves membership in a like-minded community, drawn together by shared doctrinal beliefs. Spirituality, by contrast, is not bound by adherence to doctrine and is conceived of, in the higher education literature, as *bigger* than religion. *Spirituality* is the term often used to refer to students' search for meaning in life (Braskamp, 2007). According to Astin and his colleagues (2011), spirituality involves "the values that we hold most dear, our sense of who we are and where we come from, our beliefs about why we are here" (p. 4). Similarly, Nash and Murray (2010) characterized spirituality as the search for purpose in life and have, along with Dalton (2001), linked the search for spiritual purpose to the search for vocational purpose among college students.

In 2003 researchers at UCLA's Higher Education Research Institute implemented a seven-year study of how the college experience affects students' spiritual development (Spirituality in Higher Education, 2010). The findings, reported in a 2011 book by Astin, Astin, and Lindholm, indicated that engagement with religious institutions and practices among college students has decreased, whereas a search for spiritual meaning has increased. Of particular note, Astin and his colleagues found that students' inclination to engage in a spiritual quest, defined as actively searching for meaning and purpose in life, grows significantly during the college years.

The findings of the Spirituality in Higher Education (2010) study are supported by trends documented by UCLA's CIRP project (Pryor et al.,

2007). In reviewing data from a forty-year period, Pryor and his colleagues noted that the high mark for religion and spirituality among college students was the late 1960s, when the first-year student survey began. Over 80 percent of all entering first-year college students between 1967 and 1970 reported that developing a meaningful philosophy of life was an essential or very important outcome of college; in 2005 only about 46 percent of entering first-year students placed the same importance on developing a meaningful philosophy—although we must note that the 46 percent finding in 2005 is up from the findings in the 1970s and 1980s. The recent upswing in students' emphasis on developing a meaningful philosophy, combined with findings of other spirituality-related CIRP items, provides empirical support for the belief that college students in the twenty-first century are returning to a quest for spirituality.

The increasing search for spirituality by college students does not mean that students are not also engaging with religion. Although Astin and colleagues (2011) reported that religious engagement decreased over the course of their study, it is important to note that initial data were collected a few semesters after the 9/11 terrorist attacks. It is conceivable that religious activities were high following 9/11, inflating the baseline measure in this study; a decline in religious activities over time seems logical and predictable. The reported time spent in prayer or meditation by first-year college students has remained relatively stable since the question was first asked in 1995 (Pryor et al., 2007), although the proportion of students reporting no time spent in prayer or meditation increased slightly between 2003 and 2005.

Research conducted prior to 9/11 highlighted active engagement in formal religious activities among college students (Cawthon & Jones, 2004; Hill, 2009). Hill pointed out that although religious participation declines during college, the decline cannot be attributed directly to college attendance. Further, Hill found that college graduates participate in more religious activities than do individuals who did not attend or did not complete college.

Empirical research findings related to college students' search for spiritual meaning and religious participation are, at best, mixed and are certainly related to contemporary events. General trends indicate a decreased emphasis on religious engagement, with a concomitant overall increase in spirituality. This general trend is supported by much of the contemporary research on students' spirituality (Astin et al., 2011; Nash & Murray, 2010). It is also tempered by findings that the decrease in religious involvement seen during college (Hill, 2009; Pascarella & Terenzini,

2005) might be short-lived. Certainly, the importance of spirituality, whether coupled with religious practices or not, during the lives of traditional-age college students is supported by student development theories that suggest a search for meaning occurs normally during this stage of life (Evans, Forney, Guido, Patton, & Renn, 2010; Jablonski, 2001; Parks, 2011). Spirituality and religion are likely to remain important topics for college students and those of us who study them for some time to come.

Political Attitudes

College students in 1990 complained, "Our generation hasn't had any defining moment to really galvanize us" (Levine & Cureton, 1998, p. 138). Levine and Cureton painted a picture of college students in the 1990s who focused their political activism on local, campus issues related to financing higher education, multiculturalism and diversity education, and administrative policies that directly affected their lives. Of course, 9/11 provided the current generation with a "defining moment," but did it change the focus of their political involvement? Two wars, the constant threat of international terrorism, and an economic recession certainly offer reasons to look beyond local issues.

In an update of Levine and Cureton's 1998 study, Levine and Dean (2012) found that current students were still acting on local issues but had begun to contextual these issues more broadly. Levine and Dean used the "Occupy Movement" as an example of this phenomenon. Students engaged in the Occupy Movement were generally acting on issues of immediate concern to them (for example, cost of college and financial aid), but discussed these issues as part of the larger economy (for example, tax reform and income inequity).

CIRP trend data (Pryor et al., 2007) indicate that the current generation of college students is more politically polarized than any other in the past thirty years. Increasing percentages of incoming first-year students indicate that they are either "conservative/far right" or "liberal/far left" rather than "middle of the road" (p. 28) politically, although college students do not seem to adhere to any political ideology dogmatically. According to Pryor and his colleagues, "Conservative/far right and liberal/far left students are more polarized on abortion and gay rights, and less polarized on issues to do with the use of affirmative action in college admissions and the legalization of marijuana" (p. 31). Although there has been a slight decline in the number of students self-reporting as liberal since the election of President Barack Obama (Pryor, Hurtado, DeAngelo,

Palucki Blake, & Tran, 2009), longer-term trends suggest that political polarization will be a constant on college campuses for some time to come.

Attitudes Toward and Experiences with Civic Engagement

Beliefs about the importance of community service are a subsection of political beliefs that appear to transcend party affiliation or ideology. Community service and service learning have also become pedagogical tools for educators hoping to instill civic and democratic values in college students (Colby, Ehrlich, Beaumont, & Stephens, 2003; Kuh, 2008). Although Millennial Generation students have been criticized as being self-absorbed (Levine & Cureton, 1998), data suggest that these students both value community engagement and actively participate in their communities. Dey and Associates (2009) found that 93 percent of students responding to a survey supported the notion that "contributing to a larger community should be a major focus" (p. 3) of a college education. This belief strengthens as students progress through their education, with seniors indicating stronger support for this assertion than first-year students. Findings from CIRP data support the conclusions of Dey and Associates: over the last two decades the percentage of first-year students indicating that there was a very good chance they would engage in volunteer work during college increased from 17 percent to 31 percent (Pryor et al., 2009).

Attitudes Toward and Experiences with Diversity

College has long been assumed to be a liberalizing force when it comes to attitudes about diversity (Pascarella & Terenzini, 1991, 2005). Pascarella and Terenzini have reported that attending higher education appears to move students toward more progressive attitudes and beliefs about gender roles, race and ethnicity, and homosexuality (see Chapter Nine for more detailed analysis of the effects of college on students). Recent trend data also suggest that students are entering college with what would be considered more liberal attitudes toward these topics, although this phenomenon does not apply to all issues (Pryor et al., 2007).

In general, contemporary college students are less likely than previous students to believe that racial discrimination is a major problem in the United States (Pryor et al., 2007). Compared to the early 1990s, when about 12 percent of incoming students believed that racial discrimination was no longer a problem, almost 20 percent of students indicated that racial discrimination was no longer a problem in 2005 and 2006. On a related trend, fewer students indicate that helping to promote racial understanding is an essential or very important goal of a college education. In 2006, for example, only 34 percent of students reported that promoting racial understanding was an essential or important goal, a slight uptick from a low of 29.7 percent in 2004, but certainly on a generally lower trend since the early 1990s.

The finding that current students are less likely than students from previous generations to believe that racial discrimination is a major problem is difficult to interpret with any degree of certainty. It very well could be, as some might argue, that this finding indicates a lack of sensitivity to an ongoing problem in society. Levine and Dean (2012) concluded, however, that the multicultural divide between students that was so prevalent in the 1990s (Levine & Cureton, 1998) has begun to close. Although Levine and Dean did concede that current students lack an understanding of the historical context of racial issues in the United States and still engage in voluntary segregation on campuses, these authors found that students' beliefs and attitudes are less polarized by racial identity and that students are more likely to engage across racial and ethnic differences.

Trend data suggest that college students are becoming increasingly more progressive in their attitudes about lesbian, gay, and bisexual issues (Pryor et al., 2007). In 2006, 25.6 percent of students indicated it was important to have laws limiting same-sex relationships, compared to over 50 percent of students in 1986 and 1987. Similarly, between 1996 and 2006 the proportion of college students who believed that same-sex couples should have the right to legally marry increased from 50.9 percent to 61.2 percent. These trends suggest that college students are becoming more open and accepting of LGB people, although a closer look at the data reveals some clear trends related to gender. Men were more likely to believe that it was important to have laws prohibiting same-sex relationships (33.4 percent in 2006) and less likely to believe that same-sex couples should have the right to marry (52.9 percent in 2006) than were women (19.3 percent and 67.9 percent in 2006, respectively).

Conclusion

Students entering colleges and universities in the early years of the twenty-first century are certainly "the most racially and ethnically diverse in this nation's history" (Debard, 2004, p. 33). Enrollment trends suggest that students are diverse in manifold sociodemographic categories, including sex, race, ethnicity, sexuality, and socioeconomic status. Students also bring with them experiences, attitudes, and beliefs that further complicate the landscape of higher education. The recent military actions have increased, and will continue to increase, the number of student veterans attending colleges and universities. Further, the political polarization and subsequent discord of the larger society is evident on U.S. campuses. On a positive note, students enter colleges and universities today more committed than ever to understanding diversity (Levine & Dean, 2012) and engaging with the larger society through voluntary service (Dey & Associates, 2009).

We leave this chapter with a reminder of the caution with which we began: treating a student as a product of a single identity group, without a complex understanding of how multiple identity groups intersect and individual differences manifest themselves to influence students' experiences, is dangerous and ill-advised. This caveat does not mean that the information reported in this chapter, separated as it was for ease of reading and comprehension, is not useful to higher education professionals. As we continue through this text, exploring how the student "inputs" presented in this chapter affect the "environments" and ultimately the "outcomes" of college, readers will begin to see how understanding the sociodemographic characteristics and attitudes and beliefs of college students can inform policies and practices.

Points of Discussion

Implications for Students

- What are the implications of changing demographics for students' experiences and learning during college?
- How does the location of a higher education institution affect the relationship between changing demographic characteristics and student experiences?

Implications for Institutions

- How do institutions meet the needs of an increasingly diverse student body? What are the possible financial implications of providing the necessary support services?
- What role should institutions of higher education have in influencing the sociopolitical attitudes of college students?

- Given that with greater diversity comes the potential for greater conflict, what responsibilities do institutions have to avoid possible conflicts or facilitate learning during conflict? How might higher education administrators do this?

Implications for Policy and National Discourse

- What are the policy implications (positive and negative) of allowing students to self-identify and check all boxes that apply on survey items related to race and ethnicity?
- What is the role of federal and state governments in supporting the educational pursuits of returning student veterans?
- Is it appropriate to ask students to report sexual identity on federal forms or on institutional application materials? What are the possible implications of doing so?

Learning Activity

- Identify an institution you would like to explore; it can be one you attended, your current institution, or one at which you hope to work someday. Explore the data concerning student characteristics available on the institutional Web site. Think about how the institution displays this information and what questions are left unanswered by these available data. Using the information available in this chapter and data from other Web sites, determine how well the institution's student population represents the general population of the region in regard to demographic characteristics important to you.

Resources Related to Student Demographics

Higher Education Research Institute at UCLA (www.heri.ucla.edu /index.php)

Specific reports and projects of the Higher Education Research Institute at http://gseis.ucla.edu/heri/publications-brp.php include

- *The American Freshman: National Norms Fall 2011* (brief available free; full document available at a cost; www.heri.ucla.edu/tfsPublications.php)

- Your First College Year (full report of 2009 findings and summary of 2011 findings available free of charge; www.heri.ucla.edu/yfcyPublications .php)
- Spirituality in Higher Education (www.spirituality.ucla.edu/)

National Center for Education Statistics (http://nces.ed.gov/)

Specific reports and projects of the National Center for Education Statistics include

- *Digest of Education Statistics 2009* (http://nces.ed.gov/programs /digest/)
- *Projection of Education Statistics to 2018* (http://nces.ed.gov/programs /projections/projections2018/)
- Integrated Postsecondary Education Data System (http://nces.ed.gov /ipeds/)

Pew Hispanic Center (www.pewhispanic.org)

The Pew Hispanic Center is a project of the Pew Research Center (http:// pewresearch.org). According to its Web site, the Pew Hispanic Center is designed "to improve understanding of the U.S. Hispanic population and to chronicle Latinos' growing impact on the nation. The Center conducts social science research, including economic, demographic and public opinion studies." Much of the research presented by the Pew Hispanic Center focuses on college-going trends within the Hispanic population.

CHAPTER TWO

THE COLLEGE CHOICE PROCESS

Knowing what factors are most relevant when a prospective student makes a decision to attend college allows institutions to map out the key data elements involved. This map can then constitute the backbone of a comprehensive enrollment management information system.

CABRERA & LA NASA, 2000A, PP. 2–3

A student's journey from high school to college is more complex than it may appear on the surface. The college choice process comprises several decisions, including decisions about whether and where to attend postsecondary education, and is influenced by such factors as academic preparation and economic realities (Hossler, Braxton, & Coopersmith, 1989). In most cases the college choice process begins while the student is in high school, ideally well before the senior year (Hossler, Schmit, & Vesper, 1999). This decision-making process is linked to and affected by students' demographic characteristics as discussed in the previous chapter. It is also important to note that demographic and socioeconomic influences may prevent a student from viewing college as a viable option. When we refer to college choice, we are including students' academic preparation for college; searching for and gathering pertinent information; choosing to apply to one or more institutions; and, finally, enrolling in the institution of choice (Hossler & Gallagher, 1987).

Hossler and his colleagues (1999) categorized college choice models into four related groupings: (1) economic, (2) status-attainment, (3) information-processing, and (4) combined models. The economic and information-processing models share a rational analysis approach in which the cost of attending college is weighed against its perceived benefits. Both types of models are clearly derived from the disciplinary perspective of economics. However, information-processing models extend

beyond rational analysis to include social and cultural capital, and socialization. According to Bourdieu (1977), cultural capital is an accumulation
of knowledge possessed and inherited by privileged groups in society. This
knowledge allows for greater opportunities and resources, and access
to higher education. Similarly, status-attainment models "describe a
process that has acted to narrow students' possibilities since they were
born" (Hossler et al., 1999, p. 144). Combined models use both economic
and sociological lenses to explain the college choice process. One of the
most frequently cited combined models is Donald Hossler's own model,
which viewed college choice as a three-stage process: predisposition,
search, and choice (Hossler & Gallagher, 1987).

Alberto Cabrera and Steve La Nasa (2000b, 2000c, 2001) offered
another widely accepted college choice model that is empirically derived
from data gathered from students from lower socioeconomic backgrounds.
This model incorporates Hossler and Karen Gallagher's three stages
(1987), but it also describes the college choice process as the completion
of three tasks: becoming college-qualified, graduating from high school,
and applying for admission to a postsecondary institution. This chapter
explains and outlines the association between these stages and tasks, using
Hossler and Gallagher's three-stage model as an organizing framework.
After a brief overview of the history of college access in American higher
education, we explain the factors that influence—and tasks that make
up—the predisposition, search, and choice stages.

Brief History of Access and College Choice in American Higher Education

A detailed account of the history of access and college choice in American
higher education is beyond the scope of this chapter, but can be found in
the work of Kinzie and colleagues (2004), who examined fifty years of
trends related to college access in American higher education history.
Table 2.1 and the remaining paragraphs in this section provide a summary
of the major historical trends in postsecondary education as described by
Kinzie and her colleagues.

From the founding of the colonial colleges until the 1940s, access to
college was limited to a very homogenous group of students, allowing
admission predominantly to white males and members of the middle to
upper classes. The student preparation and application process, institutional structure for admissions, and attributes sought by students and

TABLE 2.1 ACCESS, ADMISSIONS PRACTICES, AND OTHER CONSIDERATIONS IN THE COLLEGE CHOICE PROCESS IN AMERICAN HIGHER EDUCATION HISTORY

Area of Change	1636–1940s	1950s–1970s	1980s–Present
Access	Mostly white male students from high and middle socioeconomic status	Increasing diversity in student body: more females, more students of color	Minorities; athletes; academically proficient, economically disadvantaged, adult and part-time, out-of-state, international, online students
Admissions office practices	N/A	SAT; open access, open-door policies, targeted marketing, active recruitment of students of color	Complex, computerized admissions processes, early decision, early admission deadlines, targeted financial aid (including loans)
Desirable institutional characteristics	Campus beauty, athletic reputation, president's reputation	Prestige, cost, location	Rankings, endowment
Percentage of high school students who entered college	Less than 20 percent	About 50 percent	Between 70 and 80 percent
Major influences on students' college selection	Parents, peers, reputation	Parents, peers, high school counselors, cost	Parents, peers, cost, rankings, prestige, financial aid
Catalysts, historical events	Founding of institutions	GI Bill of 1944, Higher Education Act of 1965, mandatory desegregation, 1972 federal amendments	Calls for accountability, decreased funding

Source: Adapted from Kinzie et al., 2004.

parents when searching for a college remained relatively stable until the mid-1900s. World War II had a profound effect on higher education, igniting particularly important questions about who would have access to postsecondary education. The war meant that fewer men were available to attend higher education institutions, opening more room for the admission of women (Kinzie et al., 2004). The GI Bill provided financial resources for World War II veterans to attend college; many of these veterans were the first in their family to do so (Thelin, 2011).

From the end of World War II through the 1960s, access to higher education for people of color and other traditionally excluded groups increased (Gelb & Palley, 1982; Levine & Nidiffer, 1996). Access to higher education for these underrepresented groups began to rise as federal student loans and grants became available in the 1970s and 1980s. The 1990s introduced a significant increase in the number of Latino/a students attending colleges and universities (Lucas, 1970), due to rising immigration and increases in college-going rates among traditional-age college students (Keller, 2001).

These later decades of the twentieth century brought a new focus on higher education management and practices related to enrollment, competition among institutions, and institutional rankings. Enrollment trends following the postwar years challenged institutional leaders to implement policies, practices, and procedures to remain competitive and meet the demands associated with a diverse population of students. Moreover, institutional leaders began to incorporate strategic marketing initiatives to promote enrollment. As the competition among universities with selective admissions increased, institutional rankings became more and more important among students as a deciding factor in choosing a college (Long, 2004).

The College Choice Process

The decision to attend college may seem to be individual, made by students and their families, but a comprehensive understanding of the process reveals several internal and external influences. We explore in this section the factors that influence students' decisions about whether to attend college and which college to attend. As mentioned earlier, many college choice models exist, but we use the Hossler and Gallagher (1987) model as an organizing framework for this chapter because it is comprehensive and well supported empirically and in practice. We therefore organize this discussion in three sections that correspond to Hossler and Gallagher's three stages: predisposition, search, and choice.

According to Hossler and Gallagher (1987), the task for students in the predisposition stage is to decide whether to continue education beyond high school and prepare to make this transition. Positive behaviors for students in this stage include choosing to attend high-quality high schools, engaging in college preparatory curricula, and seeking information about college costs and financial aid. Narrowing in on a specific higher education institution (or set of institutions) is not the task of the predisposition stage. In the search stage of the college choice process, students seek more information about colleges and universities. Information gathering in this stage results in the development of a set of institutions to which the students intend to apply. Finally, in the choice stage, students make enrollment decisions after evaluating colleges and universities, reviewing marketing and communication materials, and weighing subsequent acceptance from colleges and universities in the choice set. In the following subsections we examine individual and environmental factors that influence each of the three stages.

Predisposition

The predisposition stage involves students' decision to continue formal education beyond high school. Such demographic and background characteristics as parental involvement, socioeconomic status, high school culture, teachers' expectations, and interactions with college admissions staff influence the predisposition stage. We address the influences of each of these areas on the predisposition stage and student decision making in this subsection. Interestingly, in well-designed research studies, the effect of students' ethnic backgrounds fails to reach statistical significance in influencing enrollment rates, especially when socioeconomic status is included (Ekstrom, 1985; Jackson, 1976; Manski & Wise, 1983). Consequently, we do not include a stand-alone discussion of ethnicity as part of the predisposition stage. However, we acknowledge that ethnicity is an important point of consideration when addressing and seeking to understand the college choice process, especially among traditionally underrepresented students.

Parental Involvement Parents are the strongest influences in the college choice process (Cabrera, Burkum, & La Nasa, 2005; Hamrick & Stage, 2004; Hossler et al., 1999; López Turley, Santos, & Ceja, 2007). Having at least one college-educated parent increases the chances that a student will attend college (Cabrera & La Nasa, 2000b; Hamrick & Stage, 2004). Simi-larly, growing up in a household with both biological parents present has been found to increase a student's likelihood of applying, being admitted to, and attending a four-year college (Lillard & Gerner, 1999). Students with two parents or parents with higher education experience are more likely to receive information about the college choice process and to grow up with an unquestioned expectation of attending a higher education institution after graduation from high school (McDonough, 2004).

According to Bourdieu and Passeron (1977), cultural capital, enacted through a combination of parental education and access to information, has a direct correlation to parents' involvement in their child's secondary schooling. Lareau (1987) extended the work of Bourdieu and Passeron, positing that parents' educational capabilities; their understanding of teachers' role; and the availability of resources, such as guidance coun-selors and college information, had significant influence on parents' involvement in schooling. Parents' level of education increased their awareness of the role of teachers, the purpose of schooling, and the value of education. Thus children who have parents with higher levels of educa-tion benefit from greater parental involvement in secondary schooling as well as increased information about postsecondary education, increasing the likelihood that such students will continue on to college.

Socioeconomic Status Socioeconomic status (SES), which is related to levels of education and the number of parents in a household, has been found to be particularly important in the predisposition stage of the college choice process (Cabrera & La Nasa, 2000b; Hossler et al., 1999; McDonough, 1997, 2004; Niskey, 2007; Niu & Tienda, 2008; Perna & Titus, 2004). Family SES influences the opportunities a student will have to learn about the benefits and possibilities of obtaining a college education. Higher-SES students, for example, often benefit from attending schools with greater resources and access to highly qualified teachers as well as guidance counselors.

The college choice process is intertwined with socioeconomic status and cultural capital (McDonough, 1994). In the United States, local prop-erty tax is the primary means of funding primary and secondary public education. Students from higher-SES families who live in neighborhoods with higher property tax bases benefit from better-resourced schools and opportunities to take advantage of the cultural capital that comes from such schools (Kent & Sowards, 2008). Examples of these resources are music and arts programs, foreign language curricula, and Advanced

Placement (AP) courses. Conversely, students from neighborhoods with low property tax bases face limited funding support for neighborhood schools and are disadvantaged when it comes to availability of information and encouragement to attend postsecondary education. McDonough (2004) frames cultural capital as flowing from the educational credentials of parents to their children through students' access to information and opportunities.

Families with higher SES generally possess a greater amount of cultural capital than those with lower SES. This disparity is often maintained, as those people who have cultural capital benefit from the knowledge and networks created by this asset, whereas people lacking the capital—and who have the greatest need—struggle to gain access because of insufficient information, limited financial resources, and minimal social networks. In this way, family SES and cultural capital influence the predisposition stage, and the subsequent stages of the college choice process. Trying to explain why academically qualified high school students from economically disadvantaged or minority backgrounds did not take advantage of such opportunities as financial aid when applying to college, Zimbroff (2005) found that socioeconomic status was related to college aspirations, confirming previous research findings suggesting that students from lower socioeconomic backgrounds had lower aspirations (Cabrera & La Nasa, 2000b; Hossler, Schmit, & Vesper, 1999; Kirst & Venezia, 2004; Perna & Titus, 2004).

High School Culture The concept of cultural capital, as described earlier and defined by McDonough (1994), can also be used to understand the effects of the college-going culture of a high school. Family SES and neighborhood funding of public schooling influences the college-going culture created within a high school through a number of means (Hamrick & Stage, 2004; McDonough, 1994). Attending a "feeder" high school (one from which a significant number of graduates continue on to college studies) increases the chances that a student will attend college (Wolniak & Engberg, 2007). Students in these schools receive more, and more accurate, college information from high school teachers, counselors, and peers, which positively affects decisions to attend a postsecondary institution (Hamrick & Stage, 2004; McDonough, 1994; Zimbroff, 2005).

The positive effects of attending a high school with a college-going culture appear to be different for different groups of students. The college-going culture of a high school has a greater influence on men than on women (Wolniak & Engberg, 2007). Wolniak and Engberg also found that students without financial need were more positively influenced by a college-going culture than were those with greater financial need. Further, white students from higher socioeconomic status have more access to feeder schools than do students of color or students with financial need, perhaps indicating a possible double effect of race and SES.

Finally, as one might expect, attributes of a high school affect the quality of the postsecondary institutions its graduates select to attend (Wolniak & Engberg, 2007). Seniors from feeder or affluent high schools, regardless of class rank, tend to identify and apply to more prestigious colleges than do students from other high schools (Niu & Tienda, 2008). The college-going culture is woven into students' experiences and expectations.

Educators' Expectations of Students Education professionals' (for example, teachers, counselors, and school administrators) expectations of students have been shown to be a major influence on students' academic achievement and their process of deciding to pursue postsecondary education. Expectations among education professionals include their perceptions about who can be academically successful, which has an effect on students' self-perceptions and potentially influences students' decision to pursue formal education after high school (Rist, 2000; Zamudio, Russell, Rios, & Bridgeman, 2011). Higher expectations on the part of teachers, counselors, and school administrators create a foundation for high school students' predisposition to pursue further education.

College Admissions Staff College and university admissions officers influence the predisposition stage through marketing and recruitment efforts, and by providing students with suggestions, recommendations, and overall guidance (Kinzie et al., 2004; McDonough, 1994). McDonough (2004) argued that admissions officers have shifted from being educators to being marketers because of increased competition for students. She suggested that changing understanding among admissions personnel of students as clients, and students' (and parents') perception of college services as commodities, have changed the role of admissions officers. Further, she contended that "the ever-growing number of college selection guidebooks, software, videos, laser disks, as well as coaching and counseling professionals' services" (McDonough, 1994, p. 443) have almost replaced admissions office personnel and made the predisposition stage feel like a transaction and less personable. Still, the role of admissions offices in stimulating predisposition to college persists, even if it has shifted noticeably from guidance to marketing.

Search

Once students decide to continue formal education beyond high school, they enter the search stage of the college choice process. The primary task of the search stage involves gathering information about colleges and universities. Where students get information about postsecondary education and institutions dictates this information's accuracy and credibility. Students with relatives who attended college may find it easier to understand the search, choice, application, and admissions process because they receive more accurate information (McDonough, 2004). Summarizing existing research, Cabrera and La Nasa (2000c) indicated that

> in general, more affluent students, compared with their less-well-off peers, rely on several sources of information (including private counselors to guide the process), are more knowledgeable of college costs, are more likely to broaden the search to include a wider geographical range, tend to consider higher-quality institutions, and have parents who planned and saved for college expenses. (p. 9)

The result of information gathering during the search stage is a short list of salient institutions (Cabrera & La Nasa, 2001). This list of institutions is informed by data concerning available financial aid, tuition costs, policies, and potential debt (Paulsen & St. John, 2002). Individual student characteristics and socioeconomic status, and the quality of a student's college preparation, play a role in determining the availability of information, the quality of sources of information, and the list of potential institutions. Although we address individual characteristics first in this section, much research on the college choice process suggests that socioeconomic status may be the most influential factor at the search stage.

Individual Characteristics Such individual factors as academic achievement, gender, race and ethnicity, language of origin, parental income and educational levels, location of residence and high school, and extracurricular participation interact to affect the college search stage (Shaw, Kobrin, Packman, & Schmidt, 2009). Moreover, high school rank; entrance exam scores; ability (physical, mental, academic, other); and first-generation status have been found to be important factors to consider in regard to the college choice process.

Individual perceptions and values are also part of the college choice process. For instance, on the one hand, female high school seniors tend to perceive postsecondary education as an investment, and are more likely than their male peers to develop better plans to attend college and to complete admissions applications (Kleinfeld, 2009; López Turley et al., 2007). On the other hand, male high school seniors are less likely to view college as an investment, and are more likely than females to pursue technical training, take time off from school, or find interest in securing "implausible 'dream jobs,' such as designing videogames, owning a recording studio, directing movies, or becoming music stars" (Kleinfeld, 2009, p. 178).

As they gather information,

> many [academically] good students needlessly limit the number and types of institutions during the search stage. They may mistakenly eliminate an institution which is potentially a good choice due to a lack of awareness of the range of institutions as well as accurate information about institutions. (Hossler & Gallagher, 1987, p. 215)

Students' access to knowledgeable people and good resources is crucial during the search stage as they interact with institutions, make decisions, and develop their choice set of colleges.

Students' race and ethnicity influence their college choice process. For instance, African American students make the decision to go to college later than other groups (Hossler et al., 1999). Further, although mentoring by teachers or other adults while in high school is influential to most students, it has no effect on Hispanic students (Hamrick & Stage, 2004). Race and ethnicity may influence the types of institutions students deem realistic to include in their final list. As might be expected, African American students are more likely than any other group to choose Historically Black Colleges and Universities (HBCUs), and Hispanics are more likely than other students to choose Hispanic-Serving Institutions (HSIs) (Freeman & Thomas, 2002). Students from other racial or ethnic groups might be less likely to include HBCUs and HSIs in their final list of salient institutions.

Socioeconomic Status Socioeconomic status is an influential factor in students' decision about where to apply to college (Cabrera & La Nasa, 2000b; Hossler et al., 1999; McDonough, 2004; Niskey, 2007; Niu & Tienda, 2008; Perna & Titus, 2004). Students consider the cost of different institutions and eliminate institutions they deem too expensive. In some cases, this process discourages students from continuing their education altogether, causing them to revisit the decisions they made during the predisposition stage of the process. Moreover, students from higher socioeconomic status have more choices because they are more likely than students from lower socioeconomic status to be enrolled in a college preparatory track (Kirst & Venezia, 2004), and they have greater access to information (Cabrera et al., 2005).

Students from lower SES tend to have access to less information and fewer resources and knowledgeable people than do students from higher SES, limiting their search stage decisions (Cabrera & La Nasa, 2000c). Cabrera et al. (2005), for example, found that 76 percent of high school seniors from higher-SES backgrounds applied to four-year institutions; only 21 percent of high school seniors from the lowest socioeconomic status backgrounds applied to four-year institutions. Similarly, Plank and Jordan (2001) found that students' SES had a major impact on the probability they would apply to and attend a two- or four-year institution. In addition, students from higher-SES backgrounds are also more likely to consider, and ultimately enroll in, out-of-state colleges and universities (Perna & Titus, 2004).

Choice

The choice stage is the final step in the overall college choice process. During this stage students examine the colleges and universities included in the list of possible institutions they identified during the search stage. Having decided to further their education, gathered information about various colleges and universities, and focused in on a short list of salient institutions, students must now make a final choice about which institution to attend. This section examines institutional characteristics, college and university rankings, financial aid, socioeconomic status, and public policy as influences during the choice stage.

Institutional Characteristics of Colleges and Universities When students consider which college to attend, the variety of institutions from which to choose can be overwhelming (see Chapter Five for a discussion of institutional types). U.S. colleges and universities are public, private, or for-profit; focus on liberal arts curricula, professional curricula, or research and scholarly preparation; and offer two- and four-year degrees in person, online, or in hybrid formats. Institutional missions of some institutions, specifically community colleges, Tribal Colleges and Universities, comprehensive universities, HSIs, and HBCUs, focus on access for traditionally underrepresented student groups. Some students will also give consideration to proximity, prestige (sometimes based on public rankings), or financial aid offerings (Perna & Titus, 2004).

College and University Rankings College rankings have been both heavily used and widely criticized by the public and by those within higher education (Bastedo & Bowman, 2011; McGuire, 1995). Although rankings might not provide an accurate description or evaluation of college quality, they strongly influence students (and their parents) in their college choice process (Hossler & Foley, 1995). There have been efforts to explain and improve the use of rankings (Cremonini, Westerheijden, & Enders, 2008; Zimbroff, 2005), but for now they provide students with an at-a-glance ordering of institutions by type, field, or area, which ultimately may influence students' decisions about which institution to attend.

Socioeconomic Status and Financial Aid Institutional and state financial aid affects students' choice of postsecondary institution. Unfortunately, students and family often are not informed of their financial aid package or other sources of aid until after students are admitted (Heller, 2006). Following admission to an institution, students may receive merit-based or need-based aid—or a combination of merit-based and need-based aid. Certainly these awards allow students and parents to consider more prestigious and more expensive institutions than might otherwise be realistic, closing the access gap for students from lower socioeconomic status (Perna & Titus, 2004). Merit-based aid is intended to motivate and enhance the educational performance of students who are planning to pursue postsecondary education (Henry & Rubenstein, 2002). However, merit-based aid tends to reward students who would have otherwise been able to afford higher education, redirecting aid from those who are more financially needy (Heller).

Institutions with enough resources to offer more institutional aid can attract higher-quality students through the use of differential combinations of grants, loans, and work-study employment (McPherson & Shapiro, 1998). Harvard University, for example, offers full tuition assistance for all admitted students whose parents make less than $60,000 per year (www.fao .fas.harvard.edu/icb/icb.do). Other resource-rich institutions have followed suit, instituting similar policies to support lower-income students. Although such policies might limit the number of lower-income students admitted to an institution, the wealthiest of institutions can offer need-blind admissions, whereby students are admitted regardless of financial need (Tilghman, 2007).

These policies could provide opportunities for well-prepared, lower-SES students to attend some of the most prestigious institutions. Yet a report from the U.S. Department of Education's National Center for Education Statistics (Woo, Choy, & Weko, 2011) concluded that the emphasis on using financial aid to make college more accessible for lower-income students has dissipated over the first decade of the twenty-first century. These authors found that by 2008 the percentage of students receiving merit-based aid had overtaken the percentage of students receiving need-based aid. This shift seems to indicate that financial aid may now be more accurately seen as a recruitment tool for attracting desirable students rather than a means of helping lower-income students afford a college education.

Regardless of the important policy implications of various types of aid included in students' financial aid packages, the overall complexity of financing postsecondary education adds to students' anxiety during this choice stage, with higher anxiety for those prospective students with the least amount of knowledge and cultural capital (McDonough, 1994). Some students will be admitted and be able to matriculate with little concern about financial need; other students must make decisions after carefully considering the cost of different institutions, various financial aid packages, and their ability to pay for their education. Still other students may be scared off entirely by the complexity of the decision and the potential debt associated with funding higher education in the United States.

Public Policy Public policy related to direct appropriations to higher education institutions, tuition, and financial aid to students, as well as policies related to K–12 education funding and curriculum, influence what college or university a student chooses (Perna & Titus, 2004). Decisions about curriculum and funding in the K–12 system affect academic preparation, which in turn enables or limits students' access to institutions with selective admissions. Institutional policies concerning admissions requirements are another factor in the choice stage; if a student does not meet an institution's requirements, he or she is unlikely to consider applying or attending.

Public policies pertaining to college access tend to be directed at alleviating disparities related to students' SES or sociodemographic background characteristics (for example, affirmative action policies) or directed at rewarding meritorious academic achievement during high school (for example, Georgia's HOPE Scholarship and Florida Bright Futures scholarships). Scholarships aimed at rewarding academic achievement in high school are often based on the goal of keeping the brightest students in state for higher education (and, ideally, beyond). These types of scholarships have demonstrated mixed results (Niu & Tienda, 2008). The Texas "top 10 percent" policy, in place since 2002, guarantees admission to state universities for the top 10 percent of seniors from Texas high schools. The policy seems to be working in increasing access to prestigious institutions in the state. Even students who fall within the top 10 percent of graduating classes from resource-poor high schools are including prestigious universities in their application pools, but *only* when the students have received a scholarship offer from these institutions. Niu and Tienda concluded that students' socioeconomic status continued to influence college choice decisions even as this policy opened doors for more underrepresented students to attend prestigious public institutions in Texas.

Heller and his colleagues (Heller & Marin, 2001; Heller & Rasmussen, 2001) found that merit-based scholarships, like Georgia's HOPE Scholarship, do not further equity in college access. These researchers concluded that students who received Georgia's HOPE Scholarship were already likely to attend (and be able to afford) higher education, concluding that the resources might be better spent to support students less able to pay for higher education. However, Zhang and Ness (2010) found that merit-based scholarship programs may indeed achieve their secondary goal of keeping high-achieving students in state. These authors found that such state policies increased first-year student enrollment in in-state institutions and decreased the number of students leaving a state for higher education. As public policy related to merit- and need-based aid evolves, a clearer picture of the role of these policies in the college choice process may emerge.

Conclusion

The college choice process is complex, and given the ongoing changes in the higher education system, this complexity is only likely to increase. As competition for students becomes fiercer and the costs associated with higher education continue to rise, higher education institutions will need to find new and creative ways to attract students. Although it would be easy for higher education professionals to confine their thinking to the final stages of the college choice process—focusing on using a financial aid package to make a particular institution more attractive than a competing institution—college choice models and the information presented in this chapter suggest this approach is too narrow. The college choice process begins much earlier. Finding ways to improve the flow of information, particularly to lower-income students, at the elementary, middle, and secondary school levels would improve the process for students who are making decisions about whether to pursue higher education and which institutions to attend.

It is clear that socioeconomic status exerts a major influence on each of the three stages in Hossler and Gallagher's college choice model (1987). The influence is both direct and indirect. Directly, socioeconomic status influences the type, price, and quality of higher education institutions students deem realistic. Indirectly, socioeconomic status influences almost all other factors in the college choice process. Access to accurate information, a component that is key to the successful completion of the search stage of this process, is affected by the resources available to students either through high school teachers and guidance counselors or through parents and peers. Students' SES is directly related to the quality of the high school they attend and to the likelihood that their friends and family will have access to information.

Points of Discussion

Implications for Students

- How do students, particularly students from lower-SES backgrounds, gain access to college information?
- What factors should most heavily weigh into the decision to attend college for prospective students? How do higher education professionals make sure these issues are at the forefront of the decision-making process?
- How might students' individual sociodemographic characteristics (for example, race, ethnicity, and sex) interact to influence the college choice process at the three stages—predisposition, search, and choice?

Implications for Institutions

- What is the role of admissions staff at colleges and universities in supporting the college choice process among traditionally underrepresented students or students with less access to college information? How must current practices change to improve this role?
- How can institutions ensure that faculty and staff are trained to address the complex issues presented by students entering postsecondary education with limited preparation?

Implications for Policy and National Discourse

- How might the influx of traditionally underrepresented and underserved students into higher education (discussed in Chapter One) begin to change college choice models?
- What characteristics of public policies would be most beneficial to improving the college choice process for lower-SES students? For other traditionally underrepresented students on college campuses?
- What role might community colleges play in the college choice process? What policies might encourage the use of community colleges as "ports of entry" into higher education?
- How can federal, state, and local governments work together with schools, teachers, and parents to expand knowledge about the college choice process for students?
- How can schools, teachers, and parents work together to establish local and government policies that promote awareness about postsecondary education?
- How can policymakers who wish to increase postsecondary participation rates focus their efforts on families who have less experience with formal education at all levels?

Learning Activity

- Reflect on your path to college, answering the following questions: When did you know you would attend college? Who was most influential in your decision to attend college, and in your choice of what institution to attend? How did you learn about the colleges you considered? What role did finances, or financial aid, play in your decision?

Now compare your own experience with the process described in this chapter. How was it different? How was it similar?

Resources Related to College Choice

Pell Institute for the Study of Opportunity in Higher Education (http://pellinstitute.org)

Specific reports and project information are available concerning the following topics:

- College representation
- High school dropouts
- High school status completion
- Equal education opportunity

Postsecondary Education Opportunity Topics List (www.postsecondary.org)

Specific reports address the following topics, among others:

- College participation rates
- Income by educational attainment for families
- Tuition and fees
- Unmet financial need

U.S. Department of Education (www.ed.gov)

This site houses reports, projects, centers, and topics of the U.S. Department of Education, including

- College Affordability and Transparency Center (http://collegecost.ed .gov/catc)
- State spending charts (www.ed.gov/college-completion/governing-win)
- Financial aid (www.studentaid.ed.gov)

CHAPTER THREE

STUDENT ENROLLMENT PATTERNS

The traditional "linear-matriculation" image of the college student still influences policy formulation and educational practice at all levels, despite the reality that the majority of 18- to 24-year olds, not to mention older students, do not experience a college education in a linear fashion.

BORDEN, 2004, P. 12

During speeches on the difficulties of assessing outcomes in higher education, a senior scholar with whom one of us worked would often tell the story of his staff assistant. His staff assistant at the time was completing her undergraduate education. What made her story noteworthy was that she was taking courses at four institutions during one academic year. She was enrolled in a course at a local four-year college (the institution from which she would eventually graduate), a course at a local community college, a traditional correspondence course from another institution, and an online course from an online-only university. At the time, around 2003–2004, this story was not common, but neither was it unique. And, in the intervening decade, the situation has become less rare.

Although this scholar was highlighting the difficulties of outcomes assessment—the staff assistant was a "dropout" at three of four institutions, but ultimately achieved her goal—his story focuses on the changing enrollment patterns of college students. The assumption that students graduate from high school, enroll the next fall in a bachelor's-degree-granting higher education institution, and graduate from that same institution about four years later is anachronistic. An examination of the enrollment patterns of current college students is much more complex; even focusing on the differences between part-time and full-time enrollment is too simplistic today. A complete understanding of college student enrollment patterns must take into account full-time and part-time enrollment, as well as concurrent enrollment in multiple institutions (double dipping), serial transferring between institutions (swirling), and interrupted enrollment patterns (stopping out). It is also important to note that enrollment patterns differ by race and ethnicity, socioeconomic status, and first-generation status, and that the different enrollment patterns relate to differential outcomes.

In this chapter we describe the most common contemporary student enrollment patterns and provide evidence of the prevalence of each. It will become clear that the current story of college enrollment patterns is one of student mobility and the portability of college credits (McCormick, 2003). After describing the various enrollment patterns and how student and institutional characteristics affect them, we briefly examine the implications of increased student mobility for student outcomes, as well as for institutional and public policy.

Traditional and Emerging Enrollment Patterns

When considering the enrollment patterns of college students, many people think about what Choy (2002) described as the traditional route—enrolling in a four-year college or university immediately after graduating from high school and maintaining continuous, full-time enrollment at the same institution until graduation four years later. A slightly less traditional pattern, although one that seems fairly reasonable, would include a student's beginning her college career at one institution, perhaps a two-year community college, and transferring to a second institution, likely a four-year college or university, to complete more in-depth study and receive a bachelor's degree. Similarly, those who are familiar with higher education also recognize that students enrolling on a part-time basis or in distance or online education programs have become increasingly common—perhaps to the point of even being considered "traditional." In this section, we expand the definition of traditional enrollment patterns to include others that have been prevalent in higher education for some time: transfer, reverse transfer, part-time enrollment, and distance and online enrollment. We also contrast these traditional enrollment patterns with some that are emerging or are less common: swirling, double dipping, and stopping out.

Traditional Enrollment Patterns

The emphasis in recent years on "nontraditional" enrollment patterns should not lead one to believe that more "traditional" patterns of enrollment have disappeared. To be sure, some students enter postsecondary education, especially at four-year institutions, as full-time students immediately following graduation from high school, maintain continuous full-time enrollment, and graduate from that institution about four years later. Further, some other enrollment patterns are prevalent enough to have reached an arbitrary threshold for moving from emerging to traditional categorization. This section explores full-time and part-time enrollment, transfer and reverse transfer, and distance and online enrollment.

Full-Time and Part-Time Enrollment The definitions of full-time and part-time enrollment are relatively consistent in the literature, perhaps because of the importance of this distinction for financial aid eligibility. Many, if not most, institutions and researchers use the U.S. Department of Education (2011) definition of a full-time undergraduate student as a student earning at least twenty-four credits in an academic year, or twelve credits per academic semester. As Adelman (2006) pointed out in an extended discussion of the variables included in his study of enrollment patterns, what constitutes part-time enrollment is ambiguous. Generally, however, part-time enrollment is considered anything below full-time enrollment (that is, fewer than twelve credits during an academic semester).

The number of undergraduate students enrolling on a full-time basis has been increasing over the last decade, a trend that is expected to continue over the next decade (Hussar & Bailey, 2009). In fact, estimates by the National Center for Education Statistics suggest that increases in full-time enrollment will slightly outpace increases in part-time enrollment. Hussar and Bailey have estimated that the number of students enrolled full-time will increase 15 percent between 2007 and 2018, reaching almost thirteen million full-time students by 2018. By this estimate, therefore, in 2018 undergraduate students enrolled full-time will constitute about 63 percent of all undergraduate students, a proportion that remains unchanged from 2008 (Knapp, Kelly-Reid, & Ginder, 2010).

In fall 2008 slightly over 37 percent of all undergraduate students in either four-year or two-year institutions were enrolled part-time (Knapp et al., 2010). This simple statistic, however, masks very distinct differences between the two-year and four-year sectors of higher education. Of the approximately 9,400,000 undergraduate students enrolled at four-year institutions, slightly fewer than 2,000,000, or 21 percent, were enrolled as part-time students. By contrast, approximately 58.7 percent of undergraduate students (4,166,000 of 7,101,000) enrolled in two-year institutions in 2008 were part-time.

Transferring Between Institutions Adelman (2006) defines transfer as a "migration that is formally recognized by system rules, a sequential movement from a *de jure* status in one institution to a *de jure* status in a second (or third, or fourth)" (p. 62). Implied in this definition is that the student establishes himself or herself at the transfer institution; it "is not a short visit" (p. 62), but rather an extended stop along the way to the student's goal. Transfer also implies that credit hours generated at one institution are formally moved (that is, transferred) to a different institution.

Definitional disagreements about what constitutes transfer, and the multiple ways in which transfer students can be classified, hinder agreement on how common transfer behavior really is in higher education (Roksa, 2009). Most simply, higher education researchers recognize transferring as the movement between two institutions, normally horizontally between two similar institutions (for example, two four-year institutions) or in an upward fashion from a two-year to a four-year institution (Adelman, 1999, 2006). Unfortunately, the simple definition does not always suffice. Both Adelman and Roksa, for example, classify students as "transfer" students only if they have completed a minimum number of credits at their original institution, classifying those who complete fewer than ten or twelve credits at a college as "transient." Further, students' educational intentions often influence whether researchers count them as potential transfer students (Roksa, 2009). These types of definitional difficulties make comparisons across studies, and widespread agreement about the prevalence of transferring, difficult.

There is widespread belief that the amount of transferring between institutions of higher education has been increasing and becoming more complex. Adelman (2006), in a longitudinal study of students' transfer behaviors, found a 10 percent increase in the amount of transferring from community colleges to four-year institutions between 1999 and 2006. Although these data do not clearly indicate how many students transfer, Adelman's finding reinforces an understanding that transfer behavior is becoming more common. In this analysis, among students who completed at least one transfer during their college career, about 32 percent completed a horizontal transfer between four-year institutions, and 24 percent completed an upward transfer from a two-year to a four-year institution.

Transferring between institutions, even transfers from two-year to four-year institutions, has long been assumed to be a negative indicator of degree completion (Pascarella & Terenzini, 1991, 2005), although this assumption may not hold when the various forms of transfer behaviors are compared (Adelman, 2006; Roksa & Calcagno, 2010). After controlling for several confounding variables, especially students' academic preparation and educational goals, the occurrence of either a horizontal or upward transfer was found actually to increase the likelihood of a student's ultimately receiving a bachelor's degree. As Adelman was quick to point out, however, these findings must be understood with some caution, as *any* student who begins at a community college *must* transfer to a four-year institution to earn a bachelor's degree—it makes sense that such a transfer increases those students' likelihood of earning a bachelor's degree. This necessity is changing slightly as more community colleges, such as several in Florida, begin to offer bachelor's degrees. It should be noted, and will be addressed later in this chapter, that attending multiple institutions, a third variable in Adelman's study, was actually negatively associated with degree completion (indicating that "swirling" between institutions might be less effective than formal transfer behaviors).

Reverse Transferring Another form of transfer behavior worth noting is reverse transferring—the transfer from a four-year institution to a two-year institution. Similar to the difficulties in agreeing on the amount of transfer behavior generally, drawing a conclusion about the amount of reverse transferring that goes on is "nearly impossible" (Goldrick-Rab & Pfeffer, 2009, p. 102). Goldrick-Rab (2006) found that 15.5 percent of students who began at a four-year institution completed at least one reverse transfer. This type of transfer was more common among students from families with less-educated parents and among students who struggled academically during the first year of college. Reverse transfers accounted for the behavior of only about 10 percent of Adelman's sample of students (2006).

Students who complete a reverse transfer are less likely to earn a bachelor's degree than students who complete upward or horizontal transfers, a finding Adelman (2006) calls "outrightly redundant" (p. 64). Adelman's dismissal notwithstanding, the interaction between socioeconomic status (as measured by parental education), reverse transfer behavior, and decreased bachelor's degree attainment is worthy of consideration by higher education researchers and administrators (Goldrick-Rab & Pfeffer, 2009). Goldrick-Rab (2006) found that only 22 percent of students who completed a reverse transfer completed a bachelor's degree within eight years, even though 41 percent of reverse transfer students eventually returned to a four-year institution. Although it could well be that many reverse transfer students in this study took longer than eight years to complete a bachelor's degree, the finding raises concerns about the negative consequences of reverse transfer.

Distance and Online Enrollment The advent of distance and online education continues to challenge the assumption of traditional enrollment patterns in higher education. Students are demanding online courses to meet increasing expectations for flexibility in scheduling and access (Parsad & Lewis, 2008; Van Der Werf & Sabatier, 2009). Faculty members report that teaching online is an important way to meet students' demands for flexible access, but also a means to reach a group (or groups) of students who might otherwise not be able to pursue higher education (Allen & Seaman, 2008). By most forecasts, student demand will continue, and higher education institutions will expand their online offerings to meet that demand.

In 2007 over 9.8 million registrations were reported for online, undergraduate-level, credit-generating courses at two- and four-year institutions (Parsad & Lewis, 2008). The vast majority of these registrants were in online-only, as compared to hybrid or blended, courses. Hybrid course enrollments made up less than 10 percent of online undergraduate enrollments. Whereas Parsad and Lewis reported "registrations," a head count of students enrolled in online courses might be more comparable to other numbers reported in this and previous chapters, as "registrations" could include some double counting of individuals.

Allen and Seaman (2010) reported a head count of 4.6 million students enrolled in at least one online course in fall 2008, the latest semester for which data were available. This number represents a 17 percent increase over the 3.9 million students enrolled in an online course just a year prior. The 4.6 million students in online courses in 2008 represented about 25 percent of the total 18.2 million students enrolled in postsecondary education that fall. Allen and Seaman (2010) tracked the number and percentage of online students from 2002 to 2008, chronicling a rate of growth that outpaces the increases in overall enrollments in higher education. Although the total number of students matriculating in online-only degree programs remains a relatively small portion of the total student population, the proportion of all students taking online courses continues to grow.

The vast majority of online students are enrolled in undergraduate-level courses (Allen & Seaman, 2008, 2010). In fall 2008 over 80 percent of online students were enrolled in undergraduate-level courses, compared to 14 percent enrolled in graduate-level courses, with the remaining students enrolled in certificate-generating or other forms of courses. And, perhaps not surprisingly given that community college faculty have more readily accepted the legitimacy of online education (Allen & Seaman,

2010; Van Der Werf & Sabatier, 2009), over 50 percent of all online students were enrolled through a two-year, associate's-degree-granting institution (Allen & Seaman, 2008).

Emerging Enrollment Patterns

In 2004 Borden concluded that "traditional students are no longer the tradition" (p. 10). According to Adelman (1999), beginning as early as 1970 college students were increasingly likely to attend more than one institution during their higher education career and proceed through college at varying rates. Although Adelman recognized what might be considered classic transfer students (going from two-year to four-year institutions) in the 1970s, by the early 1990s terms like *swirling* and *double dipping* were being used to describe nontraditional, multi-institutional enrollment patterns (de los Santos & Wright, 1990). Some scholars have declared that higher education has become a "marketplace" (Goldrick-Rab, 2006, p. 61), with students treating higher education institutions like shopping malls or buffet lines from which they can pick and choose products to meet their specific needs. This smorgasbord approach reached a zenith in the concept of "DIY U" (Kamenetz, 2010), which represents a complete de-institutionalization of higher education in favor of learners' accessing the resources they need to achieve their educational and professional goals.

Less radically, having periods of interrupted enrollment, a practice some have called *stopping out* (Goldrick-Rab, 2006; Horn & Carroll, 1996), remains common (DesJardins & McCall, 2010; Horn & Carroll, 1998). Students enroll in an institution, take time away, return, and proceed through to a degree. Like swirling, stopping out has implications for student success. The likelihood of completing a degree decreases as the length of time and number of stopouts in a student's educational career increase (DesJardins & McCall, 2010; Pascarella & Terenzini, 2005).

Swirling and Double Dipping According to de los Santos and Wright (1990), the term *swirling*, or the *student swirl*, has been used to describe an increasingly common back-and-forth attendance pattern among college students. Swirling implies a serial enrollment pattern in which a student moves between two or more institutions, although often only enrolled in one institution at a time. These authors' other term, *double dipping*, implies concurrent enrollment in more than one institution. This type of enrollment may or may not include formal transfer (McCormick, 2003).

McCormick (2003) articulated eight possible enrollment patterns that differentiate between and among swirling and double dipping patterns:

- *Trial enrollment:* A student from one institution experiments with the possibility of transferring to another institution by enrolling in a limited number of courses at the latter institution.
- *Special program enrollment:* A student completing a course of study at one institution takes advantage of a program or one or more courses offered at a second institution. Enrolling in a study abroad program at a second institution is one example of special program enrollment.
- *Supplemental enrollment:* A student completing a program of study at one institution enrolls in one or more courses at a second institution to accelerate completion or supplement learning. This type of enrollment is most likely to occur between terms, during the summer. Another form of supplemental enrollment occurs when a student enrolls temporarily (for one or two terms, for example) in another institution to lower costs or improve or maintain a GPA.
- *Rebounding enrollment:* A student alternates enrollment at two or more institutions. A student may choose to do this for any number of reasons, although financial reasons (saving money by living at home or enrolling in a less expensive institution) are common.
- *Concurrent enrollment:* This pattern is what de los Santos and Wright (1990) called double dipping. A student enrolls in two or more institutions simultaneously.
- *Consolidated enrollment:* A student creates a program of study comprising a collection of courses taken at several institutions. This scenario is perhaps the most extreme example of the shopping mall effect, whereby a student picks and chooses to form a series of courses. Still, in this scenario a student is required to satisfy both the residency requirements and degree requirements of the degree-awarding institution.
- *Serial transfer:* A student transfers one or more times en route to a final institutional destination and outcome. According to McCormick, this may be considered a special case of consolidated enrollment in that students collect credits from multiple institutions to be applied toward a degree at one institution. Serial transfer, according to McCormick, results in a more linear route than one might expect from consolidated enrollment more broadly defined.
- *Independent enrollment:* A student enrolls in courses unrelated to a degree or certificate program, purely for personal or professional enrichment. This enrollment pattern does not necessitate the transfer

of credits between institutions because students are not pursuing a formal degree program.

Goldrick-Rab (2006) concluded that students' sociodemographic characteristics (for example, race, ethnicity, and socioeconomic status) are related to the likelihood that they will engage in swirling behaviors. Although she intentionally avoided the term *swirling*, favoring instead more descriptive labels, such as "fluid movement" and "interrupted movement" (p. 68), the relationship with the broader term, *swirling*, is clear. According to Goldrick-Rab's analysis, women are more likely than men to engage in fluid movement between institutions, the behavior most closely aligned with swirling. Men, black and Hispanic students, and students from lower-SES backgrounds are more likely to interrupt their education, a phenomenon we discuss in the next subsection. Students' socioeconomic background is the strongest predictor of whether they will engage in swirling or stopping out—with students from lower-SES backgrounds more likely to stop out.

Stopping Out Stopping out is, quite simply, interrupting college enrollment for a period of at least one term before reenrolling (Goldrick-Rab, 2006; Horn & Carroll, 1998). Reenrolling in higher education after interrupting initial enrollment distinguishes stopouts from dropouts; the presumption is that dropouts do not return to higher education following their initial departure. Researchers further delineate between those who restart their education at the same institution and those who transfer to a different institution following their interruption. This distinction has implications for student success, particularly student persistence to graduation (DesJardins & McCall, 2010; Goldrick-Rab, 2006; Horn & Carroll, 1998). We explore in greater detail the effects of stopping out on retention in Chapter Eight.

Both methodological and definitional issues make counting the number of stopouts difficult. Methodologically, stopouts can be counted retrospectively by asking currently enrolled students if they have ever stopped out of college. Stopouts can also be counted longitudinally, by tracking current students' enrollment patterns for a number of years. Both approaches have limitations; the former relies on self-reported data, and the latter requires complex data management and student tracking over an extended period of time. Both approaches also have the potential to undercount those former students who have not yet reenrolled, which leads to a definitional concern: How long can a student be out of higher education prior to returning and still be considered a stopout? No clear answer to this question exists.

Methodological and definitional concerns notwithstanding, existing research provides some understanding of the prevalence of stopping out. Horn and Carroll (1998) noted that about 16 percent of students who entered higher education in fall 1989 stopped out after their first year. In a study that followed students beyond the first year at a four-year institution, DesJardins and McCall (2010) found that one-third of students in their sample stopped out and returned to the same institution at least once. According to these authors, having an initial interruption increases the likelihood of subsequent interruptions: 70 percent of students who stopped out once had a second interruption, for example.

The more often a student interrupts enrollment, the less likely that student is to eventually graduate (DesJardins & McCall, 2010). This relationship makes sense, particularly because Horn and Carroll (1998) found that stopping out often is related to students' academic difficulties and low GPA, particularly at four-year institutions. Even after controlling for academic performance among students, DesJardins and McCall found a marked decrease in the likelihood of graduation with the initial stopout period, and each subsequent stopout period.

As mentioned in Chapter One, the number of returning student veterans has increased and will continue to do so (Rumann & Hamrick, 2010). These students deserve an extra mention during this discussion of stopping out. The enrollment patterns of military reservists (those in the National Guard and others who may be called to service while employed or in school) are likely to be similar to those of students who stop out, although the reasons for stopping out may be different for returning veterans. When a reservist is called for active duty, he or she leaves behind a life in progress, including work, family, and school commitments; deactivation may bring, but does not guarantee, a return to these commitments. Rumann and Hamrick (2009) offered several suggestions to ease the transition back to higher education that are specific to students who have been deployed to military zones. Returning student veterans, especially those who were deployed suddenly, may face administrative obstacles upon their return to higher education. Efforts to ease transcript issues, such as incomplete credits, or financial aid issues will assist these students as they reenter higher education. Returning veterans, according to Rumann and Hamrick (2009), also face obstacles in regard to identity, often struggling to find peers who can relate to their experiences while deployed. Higher education institutions should facilitate these connections through veteran services offices and student veteran organizations. If higher education leaders are to fulfill the sense of obligation many feel to these returning student veterans, they would do well to attend to veterans' specific reentry needs as well as any obstacles to success caused by interrupted enrollment patterns.

Broader Implications of Emerging Enrollment Patterns

Emerging enrollment patterns, including those offered by McCormick (2003), have implications for higher education institutions and students (Borden, 2004). On the one hand, from a student perspective, the mobility associated with the increase in nontraditional enrollment patterns can be seen to expand choice, increase institutional competition, and provide avenues to achievement for nontraditional college students. On the other hand, because differential outcomes are associated with the various attendance patterns, and because different types of students are more likely to engage in certain patterns, the prevalence of nontraditional attendance patterns has the potential to perpetuate disparities among student groups (Goldrick-Rab, 2006). As we noted in Chapter One, white students and students from higher-SES backgrounds are more likely than their peers to enter a four-year institution on a full-time basis immediately following high school.

From an institutional and higher education research perspective, the prevalence of nontraditional enrollment patterns challenges long-held assumptions and behaviors. Student swirling behavior has implications for how institutions classify and track student progress. Increased mobility of credits from other institutions necessarily challenges institutional administrators to reconsider curricular planning. Finally, increased movement of students between institutions may change the way that institutions work together. Transfer agreements, collaborative academic advising, and shared admissions counseling are among the potential areas of change.

Conclusion

Although a true grasp of the enrollment patterns of current college students is elusive, some estimates exist (Adelman, 1999, 2006; McCormick, 2003). As Borden's earlier quotation (2004) indicated, there is a growing sense that "nontraditional" is the new norm in higher education. Choy

(2002), for example, estimated that only one-quarter of undergraduate students in 2000 would have qualified as "traditional" students. Choy's description of nontraditional students encompassed such characteristics as parental status, age, or marital status—a much more inclusive definition than one concentrated solely on enrollment patterns. When we focus narrowly on enrollment patterns, however, the current student population looks much more traditional than one might expect.

In a sample of students who attended at least some postsecondary education, Goldrick-Rab (2006) noted that approximately 52 percent of her sample followed a traditional pattern of continuous enrollment in a single institution of higher education. Estimates from the National Center for Education Statistics (Aud, Hussar, Planty, et al., 2010) suggest that the growth in number and percentage of full-time undergraduate students will outpace that of part-time students through 2013. After 2013, the proportion of full-time to part-time undergraduate students in the United States is expected to stabilize at about 63 percent full-time and 37 percent part-time through 2020.

Although full-time enrollment continues to be the norm for the majority of college students, the number of students who engage in other, emerging enrollment patterns is not trivial. Approximately 37 percent of Goldrick-Rab's sample (2006) engaged in a pattern of continuous enrollment, but had enrolled in more than one institution. Adelman (2006) drew a sample of college students who had attended more than one institution, at least one of which was a four-year institution, estimating that 15.4 percent of students in the sample moved between two-year and four-year institutions, accumulating at least ten credits in both sectors; that is to say, 15.4 percent of his sample "swirled" between two-year and four-year institutions. By examining the transcript data from these students, Adelman was able to determine that 63 percent of these swirlers began in four-year institutions, whereas 37 percent began in two-year institutions. Interestingly, in Adelman's sample, about 42 percent of those students who swirled completed two or more cycles of swirling, meaning these students moved back and forth between the two institutional sectors at least two times.

The lower percentages of students who engage in these emerging enrollment patterns do not relieve higher education faculty and administrators of the responsibility to attend to these students' needs. In well-designed studies, purposefully transferring from a community college to a four-year institution or transferring between four-year institutions has been associated with a greater likelihood of degree completion. Students who exhibit "nomadic multi-institutional attendance behavior increasingly known as 'swirling'" (Adelman, 2006, p. xxi) are less likely to graduate. In Chapters

Eight and Nine we revisit and further develop the relationship between enrollment and outcomes.

Points of Discussion

Implications for Students

- How can higher education professionals educate students, prospective students, and families about the relationship between enrollment status and patterns and outcomes (especially retention)? Is there an obligation to discuss the potential effects, particularly the potential negative effects, of the emerging enrollment patterns on student success?
- How can higher education professionals help students balance their need to control their expenses through the use of various enrollment patterns with the understanding that doing so can, in some cases, decrease their chances of success?
- What information do students need to make informed choices about the right enrollment patterns for their specific situations? How might students gain access to this information?

Implications for Institutions

- How can institutions attend to the interaction between nontraditional enrollment patterns, their consequences, and the sociodemographic characteristics of the students who are likely to engage in these emerging patterns?
- What are the implications of the emerging enrollment patterns for academic advising at the institution level? How can institutions help part-time advisers, such as faculty advisers, understand and navigate the increasingly complex enrollment patterns and credit mobility issues associated with today's college students?
- What are the implications for college affordability and financial aid when students are engaged in nontraditional enrollment patterns? How can institutions of higher education keep higher education affordable for students who are swirling?

Implications for Policy and National Discourse

- Federal and state policymakers have focused on student mobility, articulation agreements, and credit transfer policies in recent years. How do federal- and state-level policies that encourage student mobility affect the emerging enrollment patterns discussed in this chapter?

- What are the implications for state-level funding formulas for public institutions when counting students becomes more complex?
- Is there a need for a national (or federal) system for student tracking? What are the implications of such a system for students, institutions, and the public?
- How does increased student mobility make a widely shared understanding of outcomes and competency assessment more important? How might efforts, like the one headed by Lumina Foundation for Education, to generate a generally accepted outcomes rubric for higher education be affected by increased student mobility?

Learning Activities

- Think about the enrollment pattern or patterns discussed in this chapter that most reflect how you navigated higher education up to this point. As you prepare to read the next chapter on transitions to higher education, think about how your enrollment pattern or patterns affected your transitions and success as a college student. What obstacles did you face? What support services did you use? What could have been done to assist you?
- Visit your institution's Web site or Institutional Research Office to determine the various enrollment patterns most represented at your institution. How do students' various enrollment patterns affect the learning environment on campus? How does the institution support students with different enrollment patterns? What policies are in place for such procedures as transferring credits or reenrolling after stopping out?

Resources Related to Student Enrollment

Community College Research Center (http://ccrc.tc.columbia.edu/)

The Community College Research Center (CCRC) is housed at Teachers College at Columbia University. The mission of CCRC is to "conduct research on the major issues affecting community colleges in the United States and to contribute to the development of practice and policy that expands access to higher education and promotes success for all students."

The CCRC Web site provides access to research publications related to students enrolled in community colleges. CCRC also provides evaluation research for Achieving the Dream, a national project dedicated to helping lower-income community college students succeed. Information about *Achieving the Dream* can be found on the CCRC Web site.

Integrated Postsecondary Education Data System (http://nces.ed.gov/ipeds/)

The National Center for Education Statistics annually publishes national data on enrollment patterns through their Integrated Postsecondary Education Data System (IPEDS). Data are accessible to researchers through the interactive IPEDS Data Center (http://nces.ed.gov/ipeds/datacenter/). Students and parents can access similar data through the College Navigator Web site (http://nces.ed.gov/collegenavigator/). The Data Center and the College Navigator sites are available through the IPEDS home page.

National Student Data Clearinghouse (www.studentclearinghouse.org)

The mission of the National Student Data Clearinghouse (or simply "the Clearinghouse") is to track and verify student enrollment across and between institutions. This mission serves primarily higher education institutions and financial aid providers, but the Clearinghouse does work with researchers and publication outlets to provide nationally representative enrollment information. A comprehensive listing of publications using Clearinghouse data is available from the "News" section of the Web site.

University of Southern California's Center for Enrollment Research, Policy, and Practice (www.usc.edu/programs/cerpp/)

The mission of the University of Southern California's Center for Enrollment Research, Policy, and Practice (CERPP) is to analyze "enrollment issues through the critical perspectives of social science researchers, policymakers, and college and university practitioners." CERPP uses traditional conference meetings along with webinars to bring together researchers and practitioners to discuss college enrollment issues and improve enrollment practices.

PART TWO

ENVIRONMENTS

CHAPTER FOUR

TRANSITION TO COLLEGE

The [new student] in college is a novice in an unfamiliar social organization, and is therefore confronted with the values, norms, and role structures of a new social system and various subsystems. Such an experience involves desocialization (pressures to unlearn certain past values, attitudes, and behavior patterns) as well as socialization (pressures to learn the new culture and participate in the new social structure).

FELDMAN & NEWCOMB, 1969, P. 89

When one searches existing research using such terms as *transition to college* or *college transition*, one locates a broad set of literature. In Chapter Two we covered to some degree much of this transition-to-college literature, especially that which focuses on readiness and academic preparation, two of its major components (Goldrick-Rab, Carter, & Winkle Wagner, 2007). Following more closely the I-E-O framework (Astin, 1985) for this book, in this chapter we focus primarily on what institutions of higher education can do to help students successfully transition *after* they have already matriculated. Rather than addressing the transition literature as it informs input characteristics (such as preparation, socioeconomic status, or aspirations), this chapter focuses on transition as an *experience*. It therefore draws on literature related to socialization to college academic and social life, experiences of newly matriculated college students, and those interventions within postsecondary education that are commonly referred to as the *first-year experience*. Finally, in this chapter, we briefly touch on issues related to transitions for transfer students, an important (and growing) but often forgotten population of students.

Although we address academic preparation in secondary education in an earlier chapter, we must acknowledge here that academic preparation in high school is a precursor to a successful transition to college. In fact, academic preparation, in terms of both quality of high school coursework and student performance in those courses, might be the most important predictor of student success in college (Adelman, 1999; Goldrick-Rab et al., 2007). High school preparation, particularly for students who receive positive messages about the quality of their work or who are "tracked" into college preparatory courses, often positively affects students' aspirations and academic self-efficacy, providing them with an added benefit.

Unfortunately, as much of the literature about the transition to college points out, high school preparation is inequitably distributed, with lower levels of preparation provided to students of color and lower-income students (Goldrick-Rab, 2006; Goldrick-Rab et al., 2007). These same students are likely to receive less information about higher education and financial aid resources (Cabrera & La Nasa, 2000b). These students are also less likely to have the social information necessary to facilitate the transition to college and positively influence important outcomes (Tierney, 1999). Programs and interventions designed to ease academic and social transitions to colleges may be particularly effective for these students, although we argue that all students can benefit from such transition assistance. After a brief discussion of the concept of socialization to college and identification of the most prevalent issues related to transitions to college, this chapter focuses on interventions during the first year of college designed to facilitate transitions.

The Concept of Socialization

Before turning to interventions meant to positively influence students' socialization to college, a clear understanding of the socialization process is necessary. Weidman (1989) defined socialization as the process by which undergraduate students acquire the knowledge, attitudes, and skills necessary to succeed in college. The concept of socialization underlies several theories of student change and development (see, for example, Chickering & Reisser, 1993; Tinto, 1987, 1993) and explains how forces within and outside the college environment exert normative control over student behaviors (Pascarella & Terenzini, 1991, 2005). Weidman (1989) highlighted the interaction among students' characteristics, their social support networks, and socializing forces at work on a college campus. Although this chapter focuses specifically on the important socialization of first-year students, Weidman contends that the process of socialization is ongoing throughout the undergraduate experience.

Socialization occurs through support networks, such as peers and family (Weidman, 1984, 1989). Of course, when students enter college—often moving away from a home community for the first time—social support networks from which they have previously drawn their knowledge, attitudes, and skills are significantly disrupted (Mattanah, Lopez, & Govern, 2011). Many interventions offered early in a college student's career are meant to connect the student to peers and institutional agents, including faculty members and student affairs professionals, to expand social and academic support networks. Orientations, residence hall meetings, and student involvement fairs are examples of such interventions. Smart, Feldman, and Ethington (2000) also highlighted the role academic departments and personnel play in socializing students to college, particularly in helping students build relationships with faculty members and academic support staff.

Socialization to college is not a value neutral process, as many researchers have pointed out, especially when critiquing Tinto's concept of integration (1993; see Chapter Eight for an in-depth discussion of Tinto's model). Tinto defined integration as a sense of congruence and adaptation that resulted from being socialized into the college environment. Tierney (1999) and Rendon, Jalomo, and Nora (2000) suggested that socialization to college could result in assimilation for students from underserved populations. Tierney contended that "Tinto's notion is that college initiates must undergo a form of cultural suicide, whereby they make a clean break from the communities and cultures in which they were raised and . . . assimilate into the dominant culture of the college they attend" (p. 82). Socialization for students from nondominant populations could result in full integration (assimilation) into the dominant academic culture and a loss of identity in regard to their home culture.

Rendon and her colleagues (2000) suggested adopting a form of academic biculturalism as a goal of socialization for students from nondominant cultures. This approach involves identifying and strengthening the shared characteristics of academic and home cultures. Such a stance would not require students from nondominant populations to separate from their home culture to fully integrate into the academic culture, but would allow students to be dually socialized into both cultures (de Anda, 1984; Museus & Quaye, 2009). This dual socialization, according to Rendon and her colleagues, should assist underrepresented students to modify (but not sever) existing relationships as they build supportive relationships within the new academic culture. Students from nondominant cultures, to navigate the delicate balance between dual socialization and assimilation, will need connections with peers and institutional agents that assist them in making meaning of both the overlap and disconnections between the two cultures (Museus & Quaye, 2009).

Transition Issues and Outcomes

Existing research on students' transitions to college provides some insight into how researchers conceptualize what constitutes a transition issue (and why transition issues arise during college) and the outcomes associated with successfully or unsuccessfully addressing transition issues. Much of the existing research (see Compton, Cox, & Santos-Laanan, 2006; Lester, 2006) related to adjustment to college uses Baker and Siryk's Student Adjustment to College Questionnaire (see http://portal.wpspublish.com). This measure positions the transition to college clearly as a psychological phenomenon, focusing on issues of stress, emotional adjustment, goal commitment, and a sense of institutional attachment.

The focus on the first year of college as a time during which students need support is based on the understanding that moving from high school to college can be personally and psychologically disruptive (Mattanah et al., 2010). Specifically, Mattanah and colleagues suggested that transitioning to college disrupts existing social support networks that are essential to buffering stressful life events. Social support networks also help alleviate loneliness and isolation during the transition to college (Mattanah et al., 2011). Pratt and colleagues (2000) linked interventions meant to increase social support in the first weeks of college to better adjustment to college.

In a meta-analysis of research articles, Mattanah and colleagues (2011) identified over 150 articles focused on parental attachment and adjustment to college. Because these authors were focused on parental attachment, the articles identified represent a subset of the empirical research on adjustment to college, but provide insight into how researchers defined transition and adjustment issues. It is clear from the research that the successful resolution of transition issues is connected to almost every important college student outcome, including academic outcomes (persistence, academic self-efficacy, and career development, for example) and developmental outcomes (such as a sense of personal identity, social competence, and relationship satisfaction).

First-Year Experience "Movement"

The attention currently paid to issues of transition to college for newly matriculated students can be understood as arising from what some would call the first-year experience (FYE) movement. The FYE movement had its origins in 1970 at the University of South Carolina, where a group of students persuaded the administration to institute a seminar to assist first-year students in making the transition to college (for a brief history of the FYE movement see www.sc.edu/fye/center/history.html). This action began University 101 in 1972 at the University of South Carolina. The emphasis on first-year seminars eventually expanded to an emphasis on and the study of the first year of college, which led to the establishment of the National Resource Center for the First-Year Experience (later renamed the National Resource Center for the First-Year Experience and Students in Transition). The inaugural annual Conference on the First-Year Experience occurred in 1981, and this conference celebrated its thirtieth anniversary in 2011.

More recently, conceptions of the first year of college have expanded to incorporate communication between higher education institutions and students at the moment of first contact (normally during a student's senior year in high school), through the matriculation of that student, and into the second year of college (Reason, Terenzini, & Domingo, 2006, 2007). Since 2003, the Foundations of Excellence in the First College Year (www.fyfoundations.org) initiative, under the leadership of John N. Gardner, has worked with hundreds of two- and four-year institutions to "guide measurement of institutional efforts and provide an aspirational model for the entirety of the beginning college experience (initial contact with students through admissions, orientation, and all curricular and co-curricular experiences)" ("Foundations of Excellence," n.d.).

Even before the Foundations of Excellence project challenged higher education administrators, faculty, and researchers to think more holistically about the first year of college, research into the importance of the first year was abundant. So, too, were institutional efforts to positively influence students' first-year outcomes, particularly retention to the second year and beyond. The National Survey of First Year Practices found in 2000 that 80 percent of all four-year and 62 percent of all two-year institutions had a first-year seminar (Barefoot, 2000). A 2006 survey found that 95 percent of four-year institutions had first-year seminars, with over 54 percent of all institutions *requiring* seminar participation for all incoming students (Reason, Cox, McIntosh, & Terenzini, 2011). We turn now to a discussion of some of the most common institutional initiatives, including the ubiquitous first-year seminar, and the research that explores the effectiveness of these efforts at improving student outcomes.

Specific Interventions Designed to Address Transition Issues

The following subsections highlight several common interventions designed to improve students' transitions to college. Each subsection includes a description of the type of programs that would fall under that intervention category, as well as an overview of the research related to the efficacy of each intervention. The interventions we discuss range from summer bridge programs implemented prior to students' arriving on campus to living-learning communities designed to span the entire first year of college. We limit our discussion to interventions that integrate both social and academic transition issues, a characteristic of effective interventions according to research on transition programs (Gardner, Upcraft, & Barefoot, 2005).

Orientation Programs

Barefoot (2005) found that approximately 96 percent of institutions responding to a 2000 national survey reported having some form of orientation program for new students. Although hosting a new student orientation (NSO) is common in higher education, how institutions enact NSOs varies considerably. The same survey showed that NSOs ranged from half-day programs to multiday programs; were offered in the spring, in the summer, or in the days immediately preceding the beginning of the fall semester; and assumed some balance of social and academic emphases—although Barefoot and others (Mullendore & Banahan, 2005) have noted a marked increase in the attention paid to academics among institutions in the 2000 survey compared to earlier surveys.

Orientation programs, regardless of the form they take, assume four common goals: to improve students' likelihood of academic success; to assist in students' social adjustment to college; to begin to facilitate connections between incoming students; and to provide information about the college experience to students, parents, and family members (Mullendore & Banahan, 2005). An early study by Pascarella, Terenzini, and Wolfe (1986) supported the conclusion that NSOs achieve these goals.

Pascarella and his colleagues found that participation in NSOs resulted in greater social and academic integration. Further, participation in NSOs influenced persistence into the second year of college directly and indirectly (through social integration, for example).

Although research informs some good practices for NSOs, Barefoot (2005) concluded that determining the most effective form of orientation was an institutional matter. Institutional context (for example, two-year, regional comprehensive, or open access institutions) and student characteristics (for example, well-prepared, second-generation, or first-generation students) should dictate the format of the NSO employed at a given institution. As with all of the interventions discussed here, the NSO must be viewed and evaluated as part of a larger emphasis on the first year of college within an institution.

Summer Bridge Programs

A summer bridge program is a form of orientation program that combines a strong curricular emphasis with social activities during the summer months prior to when a student begins college (Muraskin & Lee, 2004). Such an intervention is often targeted at lower-income or underprepared students and is meant to provide an opportunity for them to acclimate to college prior to the start of the academic year. Students in summer bridge programs often come to campus for several weeks, live in residential facilities, participate in college-level or developmental coursework, and engage intentionally with academic and career advisers on campus (Pascarella & Terenzini, 2005).

Research involving summer bridge programs points to many positive outcomes. Muraskin and Lee (2004) cited several studies indicating that participation in summer bridge programs increased students' likelihood of persisting into the second year of college, a conclusion supported by Pascarella and Terenzini's more extensive review (2005). It is important to note that summer bridge participants reported more active engagement in campus life, a greater sense of belonging to the campus community, and a stronger perception of adjustment to college (Muraskin & Lee).

Living-Learning Communities

Living on campus has long been connected to better academic performance, stronger social connections to the institution, and an increased likelihood of persistence in college (Pascarella & Terenzini, 1991, 2005).

As several researchers have pointed out, however, the positive effects of on-campus living are greatest when campus environments facilitate and support educationally purposeful activities (Kuh, Kinzie, Schuh, Whitt, & Associates, 2005; Terenzini & Reason, 2005). Living-learning communities are programmatic interventions meant to bring together the academic and residential components of a student's life (Laufgraben, 2005). Common models of living-learning communities may require students in the same residence area to share at least one common course, group students with common academic interests into the same residence area, or include collaborative programming by faculty and student affairs staff in the students' residential area. As Zeller (2005) pointed out, recent residence hall designs include spaces for studying, academic support offices, and even classrooms—structural components meant to facilitate the goals of living-learning communities.

Much of the most recent research linking living-learning environments to outcomes has come from Karen Inkelas and her leadership of the National Study of Living-Learning Programs (Inkelas, Daver, Vogt, & Leonard, 2007; Inkelas, Vogt, Longerbeam, Owen, & Johnson, 2006; Inkelas & Weisman, 2003). Of importance for this chapter, participating in a living-learning community was linked to first-generation college students' perceived ease with academic and social transitions to college (Inkelas et al., 2007). This relationship is of particular note because first-generation college students may experience some of the most difficult transition issues due to a lack of information about the college-going process (Davis, 2010). Further, it seems reasonable to assume that the benefits first-generation students gain from living-learning communities may be similar for other traditionally underrepresented and underserved groups of students—although this hypothesis is not yet fully demonstrated in the empirical research and must be tested.

Learning Communities

Living-learning communities are best understood as a subset of a larger set of interventions: learning communities. Learning communities share many of the goals and characteristics of living-learning communities, but the former do not include a residential component. We highlight nonresidential learning communities in this section because these interventions attempt to meet the transition needs of students who cannot engage in the more intensive living-learning communities, either because the institution does not offer residence halls or because the student cannot live on campus due to other commitments, such as a family. Nonresidential learning communities can be very effective in easing transitions for community college and commuter students (Bailey & Alfonso, 2005; Tinto, 1997).

Tinto (1997) found that learning communities facilitated the creation of supportive peer groups for students not living on campus, which in turn influenced greater integration and ultimately persistence for these students. Learning communities may be particularly effective for community college students and commuter students because these interventions engage students "in a more intensive way than normally occurs in the classroom" (Bailey & Alfonso, 2005, p. 17), which might be the only location on campus that groups of students gather. Brock and his colleagues (2007) found that community colleges were beginning to institute learning communities because of their demonstrable success in easing students' transitions and helping students achieve their educational goals.

MDRC, a nonprofit, nonpartisan policy institute founded as the Manpower Demonstration Research Corporation, has focused much attention on the effectiveness of learning communities for lower-income, community college, and commuter student populations (www.mdrc.org). The library of research projects under the MDRC appears to demonstrate that learning communities, like their residential counterparts, ease transitions, positively affect cognitive and noncognitive outcomes, and ultimately improve student persistence. These nonresidential interventions seem to be effective alternatives for students who would not be able to engage in residential living-learning communities.

First-Year Seminars

As we noted earlier in the chapter, first-year seminars (FYS) are ubiquitous in higher education, with over 95 percent of all institutions having some form of FYS (Reason et al., 2011). The National Resource Center for the First-Year Experience and Students in Transition (2002) at the University of South Carolina identified several types of first-year seminars: extended orientation models, academic seminars with consistent content, academic seminars with varying content, professional seminars, and basic study skills seminars. Although successful transition to college is a common goal among FYS, each type of seminar has different goals, strengths, and outcomes (Hunter & Linder, 2005; Pascarella & Terenzini, 2005). Extended orientation seminars, for example, with their emphasis on introducing students to resources on campus, are designed to increase a sense of community and connection with the institution. Basic skills courses, by contrast, focus on building study skills among underprepared students.

Although colleges and universities should provide the type or types of FYS that best meet the needs of their students, Barefoot and Fidler (1996) suggested several good practices for all seminars. These authors suggested that all seminars should be offered for academic credit, preferably three credits, to demonstrate their importance and legitimacy within the curriculum. Collaborations between faculty and student affairs professionals and an active assessment program—both assessment of student progress and assessment of seminar effectiveness—are other hallmarks of high-quality FYS.

FYS participation has been shown to increase a sense of community, improve the perception of the quality of academic advising, and increase the likelihood that students will have educationally beneficial experiences in the first year (Hendel, 2007)—all outcomes related to successful transition to college. Although the evidence is less clear, Pascarella and Terenzini (2005) found that FYS participation results in a greater likelihood of first-to-second-year persistence for students and increased first-year GPA. Further, and importantly for our consideration of transition and socialization to college, these authors concluded that much of the effect of FYS participation on these outcomes occurs through various aspects of academic and social integration. It appears from the abundance of evidence available that FYS participation positively affects transition to college.

Comprehensive Support Programs

In this subsection we offer short descriptions of programs designed to provide comprehensive support for college students. These programs focus on populations of students who might have a more difficult time transitioning to college and are thus at higher risk of not succeeding. These programs target services at lower-income, underprepared, and traditionally underrepresented and underserved racial and ethnic populations within higher education. These programs are also funded through foundations and state-level or federal appropriations, often with considerable financial investment from the participating institution as well. Although there are many such programs, in the paragraphs that follow we highlight the work of the Posse Foundation, Pennsylvania's Act 101 program, and the federal TRIO programs as examples. Research shows that these comprehensive approaches to student support result in positive outcomes for college students (Pascarella & Terenzini, 2005).

Although the programs we highlight here are meant to serve only as examples of contemporary, successful initiatives, each demonstrates characteristics that Yourke and Thomas (2003) and Perna (2002) have identified as critical components of comprehensive programs. Specifically, successful programs such as the ones highlighted recruit students early in high school, increasing their disposition to attend college; offer support and communication during the critical first year of college; emphasize social aspects of learning along with cognitive outcomes; and provide a personal means of contacting the institution, normally through a program director who is responsible for the success of participating students. The best of these programs support students from before they matriculate until they have reached their educational goals, hopefully through to graduation (Perna, 2002). Another way to think about them is that successful programs address participating students' academic preparation, academic integration, and social integration throughout their college career (Reason, Evensen, & Heller, 2009).

Posse Foundation In March 2010 President Barack Obama donated a portion of the monetary award from his Nobel Peace Prize to the Posse Foundation, drawing attention to a successful program that has been growing since its inception in 1989 (Posse Foundation, 2010). The Posse Foundation provides scholarships for talented students from urban high schools to attend participating colleges and universities. According to their most recent annual report, the Posse Foundation has provided scholarships for over 4,200 students at thirty-eight colleges and universities. The majority of these scholarship recipients are either African American (39 percent) or Latino (36.5 percent), with white, multiracial, and Asian American and Native American Pacific Islander students each constituting about 7 to 9 percent of all Posse Scholars.

The Posse Foundation partners with colleges and universities to support the success of Posse Scholars. Each campus must agree to admit a group of qualified Posse Scholars and assign a campus-based mentor. The mentor meets regularly with the group and individually with each Posse Scholar at least every two weeks. Programs are planned throughout each academic year to engage Posse Scholars with the larger student body, faculty members, and administrators. These activities, along with participation in the Posse Scholars group itself, are meant to provide Posse Scholars with the skills needed to succeed in college as well as opportunities for both academic and social integration into the college environment (Tinto, 1993). The Posse Scholars group provides a natural academic and social support system and is intended to develop the type of academic biculturalism called for by Rendon and her colleagues (2000).

Although the Posse Program has been around for over two decades, the research related to its success is primarily internal to the participating institutions or the Posse Foundation itself. Much of the published literature related to the Posse Program focuses on the innovative manner in which students are selected as Posse Scholars (Bial & Rodriguez, 2007), which includes a set of intensive group interviews designed to identify students likely to succeed in college in spite of low GPAs and standardized test scores. This intensive process may account for some of the reported success of the Posse Program intervention. More research into the effectiveness of this particular intervention, and similar types of cohort-based interventions, is needed.

Pennsylvania's Act 101 Program Pennsylvania's Act 101 program, officially called the Higher Education Equal Opportunity Program, is one example of a state-funded program meant to assist higher education institutions in easing transitions for students ("Act 101 Program," 2011). The Act 101 program provides a good example of a state-level policy initiative and demonstrates a comprehensive approach to supporting students' transitions.

Specifically, the Commonwealth of Pennsylvania allocates money to participating higher education institutions to provide academic, social, and cultural support programs for underprepared and lower-income students. Institutions of higher education design campus-based interventions that best meet the needs of their student populations. Although programs are institution-specific, quantitative and qualitative assessments of the Act 101 programs across Pennsylvania revealed components shared by several participating programs (Reason et al., 2009). These common components were connected to positive student outcomes as well. Specifically, institutions that provided extra tutoring for Act 101 students; included cultural programming opportunities (plays, ethnic art exhibits, musical performances); and created a sense of coherence within the Act 101 student groups had students who did well in terms of both GPA and persistence at the institution.

Findings from the Pennsylvania Act 101 evaluation (Reason et al., 2009) reinforce the importance of thinking holistically and systemically when designing support programs meant to assist students who might be underprepared to transition to college. As was found to be the case with the Posse Program, building a cohesive group identity that supports students' academic endeavors and success seems to be an essential component of comprehensive support programs. Similarly, finding a connection between these students and the institution, a campus-based mentor in the case of the Posse Program and a tutor in the case of Act 101 programs, provides a point of contact that increases the likelihood of student success.

Act 101 evaluation findings also reinforce the importance of the socialization process early in a student's college career (Reason et al., 2009). Engagement and recognition were identified as two key components of each successful Act 101 program. That is, programs found ways to engage students academically, socially, and culturally in the life of the college, and they rewarded students for their successes. Certainly, this approach raises concerns, such as those expressed by Tierney (1999) and Rendon et al. (2000), about assimilation to majority campus cultural norms and requires attention to which successes are being recognized. The inclusion of culturally specific events and an understanding of academic biculturalism are necessary to avoid this pitfall.

Federal TRIO Programs Federal TRIO programs are a cluster of several initiatives designed to provide services for lower-income or first-generation college students, or students with disabilities. Eight TRIO programs currently exist, but one—Student Support Services (SSS)—provides comprehensive support for current college students. For information on the other TRIO programs, see the program Web site (www2.ed.gov/about /offices/list/ope/trio/index.html). Like Pennsylvania's statewide initiative, SSS awards funding to higher education institutions to provide campus-based support to students. The program requires that all campus-based SSS projects include academic tutoring, academic counseling, and financial counseling. The program also encourages all campuses to include personal counseling, career counseling, mentoring, and opportunities for cultural enrichment.

Much of the recent research on the effectiveness of SSS programs is in the form of evaluations of programs at single institutions (Davis, 2008; Fike & Fike, 2008; Shipp Meeks, 2009), although multisite research does exist (Chaney, Muraskin, Cahalan, & Goodwin, 1998; Zhang & Chan, 2007). These local studies almost universally conclude that participation in SSS programs is beneficial for students, with much focus on improved retention and academic self-efficacy. In a large multisite study, Chaney and colleagues found that SSS participation did increase retention, especially into the second year of college. Although the authors could not prove a causal connection, they suggested that much of the effect of SSS program participation on retention was through students' increased sense of institutional loyalty and belonging.

Transfer Students

No discussion of college-related transitions would be complete without some attention paid to the transition issues faced by transfer students. We noted in Chapter Three that transferring between institutions, including student swirling, is becoming more common as students search for effective and efficient means to achieve their educational goals. Although it would easy to conflate transfer students (who presumably have completed some postsecondary education prior to transferring) with newly matriculated first-year students because both are new to a specific institution, such a conflation would be overly simplistic and potentially detrimental to transfer students. Although transfer students face some of the same issues as first-year students, transfer student issues are also distinct. In this section we briefly address these distinct transfer student issues and how institutions have attempted to improve student transfer success.

Throughout this chapter we have made the assumption that newly matriculated students under discussion are entering their first postsecondary institution. The interventions highlighted have been shown to be effective in easing the transitions to college for these students. We have made an effort to remind the reader that these students are not monolithic, and that transition issues must be understood and addressed within the culture of the institution and with individual students in mind. These caveats remind readers that not all newly matriculated students are the same; this reminder is even more important when discussing transfer students. Transfer students not only confront different issues from those facing the students we have been discussing but also tend to be more diverse than first-time, first-year students (Lester, 2006).

The most common form of transfer remains the vertical transfer, whereby a student moves from a two-year institution to a four-year institution. Students completing this type of transfer are likely to face many of the same concerns as first-time, first-year students, especially if the transfer to the four-year institution involves leaving a familiar community. Transfer students may be leaving established support networks for a new environment, but they are not new to postsecondary education. Transfer students bring with them some understanding of how higher education institutions operate and some skills related to navigating the various processes within higher education. Although these students need to learn the specific processes of their new institution, they do not need to start from the beginning.

Transfer students have some specific concerns that first-time, first-year students do not (Lester, 2006). Transfer students must determine how their existing course credits will transfer into their intended plan of study. Transfer students must also attend to issues of financial aid, not only applying for aid at a (presumably) more expensive institution but also attending to paperwork associated with existing loans to avoid interruptions in deferments and the consequent requirement to begin repaying loans.

High-quality academic advising is essential to a smooth transition between institutions (Lester, 2006). Transfer students must work with knowledgeable academic advisers to align previous coursework with courses into which they will transfer. Courses at each student's two institutions are likely to be named and sequenced differently, giving rise to concerns about academic preparation and readiness.

Finally, transfer students face social issues as they move into a new institution (Compton et al., 2006). Like other newly matriculated students, transfer students must identify a peer group with similar interests and goals for support throughout their education. Transfer students, like non-traditional-age students, are likely to have different life experiences from most students who enter higher education immediately after graduation from high school. These differences may make identifying a peer group more difficult. Similarly, older transfer students tend to be more acutely focused on academic coursework, with less interest than younger students in the social aspects of college, particularly the party and relationship scene.

Because transfer students confront some very different transition issues from those facing other newly matriculated students, institutions must provide services specific to their needs to smooth the transitions (Compton et al., 2006). Compton and his colleagues provided several suggestions for good practice in this area, including a proactive review of traditional orientation programs, an examination of coursework delivery systems with an eye to identifying methods to make delivery more friendly to adult students, and an intentional focus on integrating transfer students into the social fabric of the institution.

Administrators at colleges and universities that receive significant numbers of transfer students must understand that transfer students are not just like other newly matriculated students. Including transfer students in new student orientation programs without addressing the specific concerns of transfer students not only wastes the time of these students but also risks sending the message that transfer student concerns do not matter to the institution. Offering specific orientation programs for transfer students at the start of each academic term is good practice (see "Foundational Dimensions," 2010). Similarly, transfer students should be given opportunities to make social connections with other transfer students, who are more likely than other students to share similar concerns and experiences. Finally, institutions should review not only academic policies as Compton and his colleagues (2006) suggested but also nonacademic policies. An institution with a policy requiring all newly matriculated students to live in an on-campus residence hall, for example, ignores the specific life situations of many transfer students, particularly those who are older adults.

Conclusion

In this chapter we discussed students' transitions to college, specifically focusing on the foundational time immediately after matriculation and throughout the first college year. Successfully navigating this time period is crucial to student success because students are presented with myriad new challenges while simultaneously losing some existing social and family support. Since the 1970s, a movement emphasizing the need to support students during the first year has grown on U.S. college and university campuses. Many of the interventions reviewed in this chapter can be traced back to this broader first-year experience movement.

Existing research suggests that comprehensive initiatives designed to support students as they transition to college are generally successful. Campus-based initiatives are most effective when they address the specific needs of the students on a given campus. The format of a first-year seminar or a new student orientation program, for example, determines its emphasis and how well it meets certain goals. As Barefoot (2005) highlighted, these interventions must be designed with an understanding of the population they are meant to serve and with the most pressing needs of that population in mind.

State and federal policy initiatives have also demonstrated some success in easing students' transitions to college. Public policy interventions should allow institutional agents to design interventions targeted at the specific needs of campus populations rather than mandating general requirements for institutions. That said, existing research shows that some general characteristics of these initiatives are important. Public policy initiatives that support a comprehensive approach, encouraging campus-based programs that provide academic, social, and cultural support to students, are likely to be most successful.

Again, the transition-to-college literature is broad. It encompasses research related to high school preparation, family socioeconomic status, and the availability of college-related information—topics covered earlier in this book. The research literature also includes the study of interventions designed to support students immediately prior to and after matriculation to college, as well as when transferring between colleges. The breadth of the literature addressing transition issues indicates the complexity and importance of understanding and supporting students as they transition to a new college. It reinforces the need to assume a holistic perspective of transition issues, perhaps beginning well before a student applies to a postsecondary institution, and continuing well into a student's college career.

Points of Discussion

Implications for Students

- What are the specific transition needs of different groups of first-year or transfer students at a particular institution? How are these needs met?
- Where can students go to locate information on the transition to college? How accessible is that information? What questions are left unanswered, and where could a student go to find these answers?

Implications for Institutions

- What are the essential components of a comprehensive institutional program to support students as they transition to college?
- Because the students who are likely to need the most support during the transition to college are also the students least likely to have access to needed information, how can institutions make certain that these students are aware of—and make use of—the support services available to them?

Implications for Policy and National Discourse

- What are the essential characteristics of a public policy initiative designed to support students' transitions to college?
- How do legislators and government agencies balance the need to create policies at a general level with an understanding that student support initiatives must be designed to meet the needs of specific campus populations?
- What are the relative benefits of government-supported initiatives (such as Act 101 programs) and foundation-supported initiatives (such as the Posse Program)?

Learning Activities

- Visit the Foundations of Excellence Web site (www.fyfoundations.org) and identify the Foundational Dimensions for an institutional type (either a four-year or two-year institution) and a student group (either first-year or transfer students) that fit your interests. Thinking comprehensively about students' transitions to college, identify specific practices that would meet the standards presented by the Foundational Dimensions. If you were designing a comprehensive program to ease students' transitions to your institution, which practices would you include?
- Identify a group of students who are underrepresented on your current campus. This group could comprise students with learning disabilities; lesbian, gay, bisexual, and transgender students; or Asian American students, or it could be any group of students that makes sense for your institution. What does the research suggest are major obstacles to successful transitions to higher education (broadly) and your institution (specifically) for this group of students? Design an intervention that would assist students in this group to transition more easily to your institution. Articulate your rationale for designing this intervention and why you believe it will be effective.

Resources Related to Students' Transitions

John N. Gardner Institute for Excellence in Undergraduate Education (www.jngi.org)

The Gardner Institute serves as the umbrella organization for many initiatives designed to improve institutional practices related to facilitating students' transitions. Gardner Institute initiatives include Foundations of Excellence in the First College Year (www.fyfoundations.org) and Foundations of Excellence— Transfer Focus (www.fyfoundations.org/transfer.aspx).

MDRC (www.mdrc.org)

MDRC is a nonpartisan policy research group that uses research to inform a wide variety of policies related to social issues. MDRC maintains a focus on both K–12 and higher education, which allows for access to research related to the transition into higher education, particularly the transition to community colleges. MDRC focuses much of its analysis on the needs of students from lower-income backgrounds.

National Orientation Directors Association (http://noda.orgsync.com)

The National Orientation Directors Association exists "to provide education, leadership, and professional development in the fields of college student orientation, transition, and retention." The organization offers a professional home for many who work with college students around orientation and transition issues; its Web site offers a comprehensive schedule of professional development activities and a list of some of the most up-to-date publications related to students' transitions. A professional membership may be required for access to some pages on the Web site, but publications and other resources can be ordered by everyone.

National Resource Center for the First-Year Experience and Students in Transition (www.sc.edu/fye/)

The mission of the National Resource Center (NRC) is to support efforts to improve student learning and transitions. The NRC publishes monographs on issues related to students' transitions as well as the *Journal of the First-Year Experience and Students in Transition.* The NRC also supports research on transition issues and hosts conferences, including the annual Conference on the First-Year Experience.

CHAPTER FIVE

COLLEGE ENVIRONMENTS

An institution of higher education is more than a collection of students and faculty, buildings, and green spaces. Greater than the sum of its main parts, a college or university is at once a behavior setting that regulates the behavior of its members, a theater-in-the-round where the scripts of the past get played out in the process of seeking solutions to contemporary ills, a highly leveraged subsidiary that annually consumes an increasing amount of its parent company's resources, a social club with numerous cliques of faculty, students, and administrators, a cultural and recreational oasis where the number and variety of events and activities outstrip any one individual's capacity to partake of them all, a game of chance in which members of various groups are assigned to physical spaces not always compatible with their personal or academic preferences and aspirations, and an intellectual theme park where the only limits to what one can discover are imposed by the learner.

KUH, 2009, P. 77

In Astin's I-E-O model, the "E"—environment—is the element over which higher education leaders have the greatest influence. Higher education environments are diverse, multiplying, and changing in the twenty-first century. They include residential bricks-and-mortar liberal arts colleges of a few thousand students, urban and rural community colleges, comprehensive commuter institutions, elite research universities, and fully online institutions that may be nonprofit or for-profit. As we noted in Chapter Three, more and more students accumulate credits from multiple institutions on the way to a degree, and even when they stay at the same institution students may take courses in multiple formats (in-person, online, hybrid, study abroad). The idea that each student experiences only one college environment—and that the environment is experienced the same way by all students in it—no longer applies in U.S. higher education, if it ever really did. Is it possible, then, to describe "campus environments" in ways that are useful to administrators at different types of institutions? We believe it is.

In this chapter, we introduce an ecological framework for interpreting higher education environments, describe a number of the most common institutional types, give a brief history of postsecondary education in the United States, discuss how students experience those environments (campus climate), and make suggestions for supporting diversity on campus.

Campus Ecology as a Framework to Understand Higher Education Environments

When considering campus environments it is critical to take into account the human-built, organizational, and natural elements that make up the milieu in which student learning and development occur. Human ecology (see Bubolz & Sontag, 1993) laid the groundwork for campus ecology and developmental ecology in higher education. These three families of theories draw from biological notions of ecology in which organisms and their environments interact in processes of mutual adaptation. The underlying principles are that (1) individuals (students) encounter environmental stimuli that reinforce particular traits and behaviors or that require adaptation; (2) individuals may cause adaptations in the environment; and (3) outcomes (such as learning, development, and student success) are the product of interactions between the individual and the environment. In essence, these theories attempt to explain what is going on in the "E" segment of Astin's I-E-O model. What happens when student input characteristics interact with elements in the campus environment to produce particular outcomes? In Chapter Six, we describe developmental ecology in detail in relation to student developmental inputs and outcomes. Here we focus on principles of campus ecology and environments to lay a foundation for analyzing the varying institutional types and characteristics we describe later in the chapter.

James Banning and Leland Kaiser (Banning & Keiser, 1974) introduced campus ecology as a perspective for student affairs. Drawing from ecological psychology of the Stanford school (see Moos, 1973; Moos & Insel, 1974), campus ecology is "the study of the relationship between the student and the campus environment" (Banning, 1978, p. 4). It "incorporates the influence of environments on students and students on environments" (Banning, p. 4). Evans, Forney, Guido, Patton, and Renn (2010) summarized the theoretical foundations of campus ecology, which include person-environment theories related to behaviors (Barker, 1968; Stern, 1970); subcultures (Walsh, 1978); personality types (Holland, 1966); and interactions (Moos, 1973, 1979; Pervin, 1967, 1968). The campus ecology movement was prominent in the 1970s and 1980s, coinciding with campus expansion and with renovations to make aging buildings more fully accessible to individuals with disabilities.

Banning and C. Carney Strange (Strange & Banning, 2001) advanced the field of campus ecology by advocating for campus design that promoted four goals: inclusion, safety, involvement, and community building. Notably, the four goals highlight measurable perceptions of individuals (Do I feel included? Safe? Am I involved?) and interactions among groups (community building). The goals are relevant to students, faculty, and staff at any type of institution and can be achieved even during times of lean resources when a focus on building or renovation is not possible for administrators aiming to increase student success.

In addition to the four goals, Strange and Banning (2001) focused on the physical (natural and human-built), human aggregate, organizational, and constructed components of the campus environment. Here is where we consider the ways that human-built (architecture, sidewalks, parking lots, green space) and natural (geography, climate) physical elements shape and are shaped by student interactions in the environment (Strange, 2003; Strange & Banning, 2001). The human aggregate element accounts for people and their interactions with the environment (Strange, 2003). Organizational structures (for example, academic departments, administration, and governance) are the location for much decision making and planning related to accomplishing the four goals, and constructed components include environmental press (the enactment of institutional values, such as inclusion and academic excellence) and campus climate (Strange).

Strange and Banning's work (2001) forms a cornerstone for assessing campus environments in the twenty-first century. We describe a number of institutional types in the next section. Keeping in mind the four goals (safety, inclusion, involvement, community building) and the four components (physical, human aggregate, organizational, constructed), these types can be examined for their ability to promote success for diverse contemporary students. In addition, campus leaders at any type of institution can consider what adaptations to the environment are necessary to promote and increase success for students with a broad range of backgrounds and characteristics.

Diversity of Postsecondary Environments in the Twenty-First Century

Following the establishment of one colonial college (Harvard College) in 1636, postsecondary institutions expanded in number, size, and type to the over 4,400 degree-granting institutions now operating in the United States (National Center for Education Statistics [NCES], 2011b). A dizzying array of public, private, nonprofit, for-profit, online, bricks-and-mortar, large, and small institutions offer courses, certificates, degrees, and open access course content, in uncounted academic disciplines, professional fields, job-related skills, self-study, and enrichment programs. It is not necessary to describe every institutional type currently operating—or the new types that may emerge within a few years. Instead we present a set of institutional characteristics that are helpful in understanding institutional types and a brief history of institutional diversification in the United States. Within the brief history we provide an overview of common contemporary institutional types.

Institutional Characteristics

There are a number of key institutional characteristics that affect campus environments and student populations. Several typologies and categorization schemes have emerged over time, some based on empirical characteristics (for example, size and curriculum) and others on criteria as varied as athletic conference participation (Big Ten, Ivy League, Central Intercollegiate Athletic Association); history (Historically Black Colleges and Universities, the Seven Sisters); and research-related activities (as indicated by membership in, for example, the Association of American Universities). Perhaps the best known is the Carnegie Classification System, begun in 1970 by the Carnegie Foundation for the Advancement of Teaching "to support its program of research and policy analysis" (Carnegie Foundation for the Advancement of Teaching, n.d.). Our purpose here is to describe several key characteristics that are useful for understanding institutional differences and similarities.

Key characteristics include

- *Size.* Size is typically measured by the number of full-time students or full-time equivalents (FTEs), a number derived from dividing the total number of student credit hours at the time of measurement by the number of courses required for full-time student status. An "undupli-cated head count" measure counts the total number of students enrolled, regardless of full-time or part-time status. A "duplicated head count" results from measures that might count the same student more than once, for example in counting the number of undergraduate science majors and counting students with double majors (such as physics and mathematics) twice. Occasionally the number of faculty is considered, but generally it is the student body that counts when discussing the size of an institution.

- *Control.* Public institutions are typically chartered by states as account-able to government, usually state but sometimes county or municipal. Governing boards may be elected or appointed by a public official. Private institutions operate outside direct government control and have boards that are not public entities. Religious institutions may require denominational representatives on the board of trustees. For-profit institutions may operate without a governing board. Although many people consider "public" institutions to be those that receive state funding and "private" institutions to be those that do not, the reality of higher edu-cation finance is that public and private funds intermingle at nearly every institution, through government-backed student loans, federal grants, student tuition payments, and so forth. Indeed, some public universities draw less than 10 percent of their annual budget from state per-student funding. Private, for-profit institutions are required to operate at a ratio of at least 10 percent non-government-supported funds to 90 percent government-supported funds (Skinner, 2005). For example, up to 90 percent of income can come through government-related funding, such as students' Pell Grants, Federal Supplemental Educational Oppor-tunity Grants, and federally subsidized student loans. At least 10 percent of institutional income must be from non-federal sources, which may include private pay, nongovernment student funding, or unsubsidized loans.

- *Curriculum.* This category includes certificates and degrees offered (associate's, bachelor's, master's, doctoral) and academic programs (such as liberal arts, comprehensive, professional, and medical), as well as specialized curricula (for example, a pharmacy school, design institute, or music conservatory). Among doctoral-degree-granting institutions, the level of research activity may be considered as part of curriculum. The Carnegie Basic Classifications are based substantially on curriculum, as are several commercial college ranking schemes (including *U.S. News & World Report* and the *Princeton Review*). An important note is that curriculum cannot always be assumed from an institution's name; some "colleges" offer advanced degrees, and some "universities" offer only undergraduate degrees. In addition, many universities are organized internally into colleges or schools based on curriculum (for example, college of education, school of law). It is also important to recognize that the designations "two-year" and "four-year" institutions, though common, do not fully describe all curricular options. Some community colleges (historically considered two-year institutions) offer bachelor's (four-year) degrees, and some four-year institutions offer certificates and associate's degrees as well as noncredit courses.

- *Mode of instruction.* Some institutions offer no online courses, and some offer only online courses. An increasing number offer a mix of online and in-person courses, as well as courses that are themselves hybrid (partly in person, partly online). Other modes of distance education—simultaneous video at multiple locations, correspondence courses—persist in the digital age, facilitated by new technologies. The proportion of on-campus and distance learners and instructors affects the campus environment and the need for both bricks-and-mortar and technology solutions and programs.

- *Student residence.* For institutions that are primarily bricks and mortar, students' living arrangements affect the campus environment. Some institutions require all students to live on campus until they graduate, some require first-year students to live in residence halls and offer the option to upper-class students, and others offer no campus housing. Students at urban institutions may have more options for living in the community than do students at rural campuses. The facilities, services, and programs provided at an isolated residential college might be different from what is available at a downtown commuter institution. Administrative structures organized around support for students at these institutions would differ as well. Even in an online environment, student residence matters. For example, a faculty member might be able to participate in real-time chat with students within a few time zones, but a student in Australia or China might not be available at a time convenient for a professor in the United States. Collaborative projects may also be harder for students to undertake when they live in different corners of the world.

Our list of characteristics does not cover all of the diversity of U.S. higher education, but it provides five categories in which to consider the environment for student learning and success. To be clear, we believe that every institution, regardless of size, control, curriculum, mode of instruction, and student residence, has an obligation to provide conditions in which admitted students can reach their goals, whether those goals are completing enrichment courses at a community college or receiving a doctoral degree from a research university. Not every student's goals can be met at every institution, but given the diversity of institutions in the United States, students should be able to find a good match. In the next subsection we provide an overview of common institutional types and how they came to be.

Brief History of Postsecondary Education in the United States

There are several excellent histories of U.S. higher education, both book length (for example, Thelin, *A History of American Higher Education*, 2011) and chapter length (for example, Geiger, 2005), and we advise readers to avail themselves of these resources. Knowing something about the history of postsecondary institutions helps explain matters of contemporary finance, governance, student body, faculty, and administrative structures. For example, the lack of a centralized, federal-level authority, such as the Ministry of Education or Ministry of Higher Education in many other countries, has long-standing implications for how national policy priorities can be enacted through colleges and universities. In lieu of direct control over postsecondary education, an elaborate system of regulations, laws, policies, and nongovernment accreditation compels institutions to conform—or nudges them in the direction of conformity—with national priorities. One major lever in this system is the Higher Education Act of 1965 (HEA) and its subsequent reauthorizations. But the HEA came along comparatively late in the history of higher education in the United States.

The "master narrative" of U.S. postsecondary education begins in 1636 with the founding of Harvard College to educate white men to be religious and civic leaders for the colony, and continues over the nearly four centuries since then to become ever increasingly inclusive and diverse. Although this narrative is not untrue, it is incomplete. It fails to account for the full diversity of institutional types active in the twenty-first century, and it ignores long-standing tensions concerning the purposes of higher education and for whom higher education is available. It also masks the stop-and-start progress of opening access to women, students of color, recent immigrants, adult learners, and other populations not originally included in the missions of the colonial colleges.

From 1636 until after the American Revolution there was little change in the overall landscape of higher education. A handful of colonial colleges educated a tiny minority of the white population on the North American continent. The curriculum was modeled after that of Oxford and Cambridge. Colleges were to varying extents religiously oriented, with boards of trustees comprising denominational leaders (usually Baptist, Congregationalist, or Puritan). One or two efforts to include indigenous people—essentially a Christian mission to convert and "save" them—were unsuccessful, but were publicized in England as a way to raise funds for the fledgling colleges (Wright, 1988).

Following the American Revolution and with westward expansion of the newly founded United States, small denominational institutions spread north to south and from the Atlantic to the farthest-west reaches of white settlement. These institutions were generally accepting of students of different Christian backgrounds (Horowitz, 1988), but remained all male until Oberlin Collegiate Institute (now Oberlin College) opened its baccalaureate program to women in 1837. In the same year Mount Holyoke Female Seminary (now Mount Holyoke College) welcomed its first students, leading a trend toward separate institutions for women. De facto and de jure discrimination kept all but a few known black students out of the denominational colleges (Thelin, 2011). These colleges were subject to religious revivalist movements of the nineteenth century and to substantial debate about curriculum. Specifically, they argued over the tension between a prescribed classical curriculum and a more modern one that sometimes included electives. The colonial, denominational, and women's colleges formed the historical foundation for today's private liberal arts institutions, whether freestanding (for example, Oberlin and Mount Holyoke) or as undergraduate colleges within universities (for example, Harvard College as the undergraduate division of Harvard University).

At the same time, states recognized a need to educate at least a small proportion of citizens and began to open institutions that we now recognize primarily as public universities. There were three main types: institutions with a classical curriculum, land-grant institutions, and normal schools. Institutions offering a classical curriculum mirrored the denominational colleges in most ways except religious orientation. Land-grant institutions were established as a result of the 1862 Morrill Act, which provided resources to each state for advanced agricultural, mechanical, and military training. Some states (such as Michigan and Pennsylvania) had already chartered state-funded agricultural colleges, and they appended the land-grant philosophy and resources to them.

Women were excluded from many of these public institutions at their founding, but with time, effort, and advocacy they gained admission to degree programs or separate curricula, such as a "Ladies Course" (Solomon, 1985). In the North, there were no laws prohibiting enrollment of students of color, though few matriculated. In the Reconstruction South, black students were legally barred from the public institutions. A second Morrill Act in 1890 provided limited funds for separate public institutions for black students and established parallel public university systems that remain in place throughout the South. Together with denominational institutions for African Americans, these institutions are known as Historically Black Colleges and Universities (HBCUs) (for more information on HBCUs, see Brooks & Starks, 2011).

State normal schools were established to meet the need for teachers in a rapidly growing nation. They drew from all populations: men and women, white and black. Ogren (2003) decisively showed that the student populations at normal schools resembled what we now might call "nontraditional" students. They ranged in age. They attended for a few terms and then left to earn money teaching before coming back (that is, they stopped out). Most were from families of humble means. Normal schools rarely offered bachelor's degrees, but were sites of collegiate activities (debate, sports, student government) that mirrored those at other public and private institutions.

In the second half of the nineteenth century the influence of German universities reached the United States. Specifically, the idea that universities should be locations for research as well as teaching caught the attention of institutional leaders and legislatures eager to drive economic development through discovery and invention. The addition of the research mission to public and some private institutions was a crucial step in creating the flagship public universities, land-grant universities, and private research universities of today.

Over time, many normal schools expanded to grant bachelor's, master's, and sometimes doctoral degrees. These "state colleges" (most are now universities) have adopted to varying extents the research mission. Known to some higher education professionals as "directional" (for example, Western Connecticut State University and Southern Illinois University) or "regional" universities, they are part of a group of "comprehensive" institutions that offer wide curricula at the undergraduate and master's levels, with limited or no doctoral programs. State systems of higher education typically include these comprehensive state universities;

a land-grant university (possibly two, especially in the South); and one or more 'other public research universities.

A movement begun in the early twentieth century to create junior or community colleges emerged from both higher education advocates and from K–12 educators (Brint & Karabel, 1989). These colleges were designed to provide vocational training, general education in preparation for transfer to a bachelor's-degree-granting institution, or both. Over time, they also responded to local interests in community education, enrichment, workforce training and retraining, and adult education. Governance of community colleges varies by state, but typically includes a system approach of some kind, coordinated through a central agency. Institutions may have their own boards of trustees or may share one statewide. Many community colleges have articulation agreements with four-year institutions, designed to facilitate credit transfer and student progress toward a bachelor's degree. Some community colleges offer their own bachelor's degrees, though they remain the exception.

Alongside the nonprofit private and public institutions exists a long-standing tradition of for-profit higher education. In the twenty-first century some are fully online (for example, Walden University), but the tradition predates the Internet. For example, Herman DeVry opened a technical training institute in 1931, and it has since grown to offer accredited online and in-person undergraduate and graduate degrees in several academic and professional fields (see "About Us," n.d.). For-profit higher education is considered controversial by many people within the nonprofit sector (see Moodie, 2011), but its influence on the higher education landscape cannot be overstated. To be sure, there are institutions engaging in questionable (sometimes illegal) practices related to student recruitment and financial aid; it is a "buyer beware" market. Advocates of for-profits argue the same caution should be applied to many nonprofits. Regardless of one's opinion about the sector, for-profit higher education is well established and growing. There are hundreds of thousands of students voting with their feet and keyboards to attend for-profit institutions, often at a higher cost than local public options. It is unwise to ignore the learning, development, and outcomes of these students simply because they chose to attend for-profit colleges and universities.

It is worth noting that the amount of online teaching and learning—entire courses, hybrid courses, or in-person courses that use online courseware—is increasing at nearly every institution (Parker, Lenhart, & Moore, 2011). Even a residential liberal arts college will employ courseware, online resources, and digital media in some if not most courses, and students are expected to use online library and research resources. One can no longer think about higher education environments without including digital environments and the online interactions students have with one another, instructors, institutions, and the rest of the digital world. Outside of courses, students may be immersed in social media, online gaming, or just reading and watching the daily news. A campus ecology mind-set that fails to address the digital environment is one that cannot fully account for student interactions in the learning context.

Within the types of institutions just described, there are subsets that bear noting. Some institutions have highly specialized curricula, offering only, for example, art and design, music, pharmacy, or graduate psychology programs. Some institutions are designated "Minority-Serving Institutions" (MSIs), which include Historically Black Colleges and Universities, Tribal Colleges and Universities (TCUs), Hispanic-Serving Institutions (HSIs), and Asian American and Native American Pacific Islander–Serving Institutions (AANAPISIs; see Gasman, 2008). HBCUs emerged from the history of legal segregation and were established as a product of the Higher Education Act in 1965. TCUs are established and governed by American Indian tribes (American Indian Higher Education Consortium, n.d.). HSIs were recognized under Title III of the 1992 Higher Education Reauthorization Act. When student enrollment is 25 percent or more Hispanic, the institution can be considered an HSI. AANAPISIs are the most recent MSI category, designated in 2008 as institutions with at least 10 percent Asian American and Native American Pacific Islander enrollment. For AANAPISIs to qualify for additional federal support as MSIs, they must also illustrate that a substantial proportion (over half) of their students receive federal educational support. Any type of institution—community college, liberal arts college, comprehensive university, or research university—can be an MSI, though no new HBCUs can be established. Finally, a small number of U.S. institutions remain single-gender—fewer than fifty women's colleges and a handful of men's colleges. All are private, and most are liberal arts colleges, though a few offer graduate degrees.

After close to four hundred years, U.S. higher education now includes 4,400 institutions, educating 20.4 million students in 2009–2010 (NCES, 2011a). Public flagship and land-grant research universities educate approximately 17 percent of all students (National Association of State Universities and Land-Grant Colleges, 2008). Many former normal schools have morphed into public comprehensive institutions, a number of them offering master's degrees and some offering doctoral degrees. Public community colleges span the nation, enrolling 36.2 percent of all undergraduates in 2009–2010 (NCES, 2011a). A small number of states support public liberal arts colleges; with the 2,800 private liberal arts institutions, this sector educates 21 percent of U.S. students (NCES, 2011a). Other non-profit private institutions—including junior colleges, comprehensive universities, and research universities—educate 27 percent of all students. In 2009–2010 the for-profit sector, including online, hybrid, and bricks-and-mortar campuses, enrolled 9 percent of all students; the size and influence of this sector are increasing (NCES, 2011b).

Some scholars (Birnbaum, 1983; Huisman, 1995) have argued that the diversity of the U.S. "system" of higher education is one of its strengths, and the lack of direct government control maintains a market ecology that allows students to "vote with their feet" for the type of institution that they feel best meets their interests. Certainly competition for resources and students drives institutions to aim for better rankings and more (good) publicity. As we describe in the next section, students interact with institutional environments in different ways with divergent experiences and outcomes.

Student Interactions with Diverse Environments

Given the complexity of the postsecondary landscape, it is important to consider how students interact with and within different campus environments to produce the outcomes we address later in this volume. The campus ecology framework, as already discussed (Strange, 2003; Strange & Banning, 2001), points toward four goals (inclusion, safety, involvement, and community building) and four components (physical, human aggregate, organizational, and constructed) of campus environments to examine these interactions in diverse institutional types. But it should be recalled, as we pointed out in Chapter Three, that many students do not follow the so-called traditional route: graduate from high school, enter an institution the following fall, take courses only at that institution, and graduate four (or five or six) years later. Students swirl, transfer, dual enroll, stop out, double dip, and otherwise earn credits—sometimes continuously, sometimes with breaks in enrollment—toward degrees and, sometimes, no degree (Borden, 2004; Hoyt & Winn, 2004; McCormick, 2003). A single student, then, may interact with multiple campus environments simultaneously or in sequence.

It is also important to recall from Chapter Two that students from different socioeconomic and educational backgrounds access the diversity of higher education institutions differentially. That is, factors including socioeconomic status, immigration, race, and language influence students' predisposition to college and college choice. There are thousands of institutions and millions of students, but as we described in Chapter One, students are not distributed evenly by a number of characteristics across institutional types and locations.

Although the overall diversity of students is not evenly distributed across institutions, nearly all institutions have student populations that are diverse in some dimensions. Even a campus that appears homogeneous by race (for example, 95 percent of students from the same racial group) will have diversity by socioeconomic status and gender. A single-gender college will have students of different races, sexualities, and gender identities. But what to do with this diversity? Educating students to live and work in a multicultural society is a goal widely touted in institutional mission statements (Morphew & Hartley, 2006) and is a foundational philosophy of the student affairs profession (American College Personnel Association, n.d.; National Association of Student Personnel Administrators, n.d.). It is not enough, however, simply to bring together students who are different and hope for the best. Like the history of higher education itself, the history of diversity on campus is not without tensions. In this section, we outline the history of student diversity, discuss the concept of campus climate, and describe campus programs and services that support campus diversity.

History of Student Diversity in the United States

We have already established that with the exception of a few attempts to include American Indians in the colonial colleges, diversity in higher education prior to 1800 was restricted to variations in the social class backgrounds of the white men for whom higher education was deemed necessary. Women, students of color, immigrants, Jews, poor students, English language learners, and students with disabilities, among others, were excluded by law, policy, or practice (such as admissions quotas) for generations. Slow, unsteady progress from elite to mass higher education unfolded through a series of expansions and contractions of opportunity over time. The composition of the student body is an aspect of the campus environment, and diversification of the college student population has contributed significantly to changes in campus living and learning contexts.

Women in Higher Education The establishment of separate women's institutions and the slow opening of public universities to women occurred through the mid-1800s, although women remained a minority of enrolled students and a tiny fraction of all women were afforded this opportunity. The land-grant universities offered an opportunity in that the Morrill Act did not prohibit women's participation in the institutions it supported. Still, many land-grant and other public universities resisted women's enrollment (see Thorne, *Visible and Invisible Women in Land-Grant Colleges, 1890–1940*, 1985). As noted earlier, women were integral to the normal school movement, sustaining lively student cultures (Ogren, 2003), and they participated in junior and community colleges from their early years (Cohen & Brawer, 2008).

The story of women's enrollments can be told many ways, but with little variance it is one of consistently increasing absolute numbers; as higher education expanded, women's enrollments increased. In regard to the percentage of women enrolled in higher education, however, the story is not as linear. Women's enrollment reached 47 percent of all students in 1920, then declined in the 1930s (Solomon, 1985). With men away during World War II, it reached 44 percent, then declined to 30 percent when veterans returned and took up GI Bill benefits, including support for college expenses (Solomon). A simultaneous social press for women to make room in the workforce for veterans and to grow American democracy through homemaking and childrearing resulted in a period of stasis in women's enrollments as a portion of the whole (although they continued to increase in absolute numbers). The women's movement of the 1960s and 1970s, as well as key policies including affirmative action, equal employment opportunity, and Title IX, contributed to an increase in women going to college. As we noted in Chapter One, in 1979 women crossed over the 50 percent line, and they now constitute 57 percent of undergraduate enrollments (NCES, 2011c).

African American Students Although women's access to higher education in the nineteenth century was hard-won, undoing de jure and de facto racial segregation was an even harder fight and continues into the twenty-first century. In addition to the very few American Indians enrolled at the colonial colleges, a small number of students known to be of African descent graduated from these colleges before the Civil War. After the war, enrollment of black students remained scant in public and private institutions in the North and nonexistent in the South. Although located in the North, the Seven Sisters (a nickname given to a group of private women's colleges in the Northeast) excluded black women by policy and by practice (Perkins, 1997), even as they argued for equal access to higher education for both sexes.

Education for black Southerners was hotly debated, with industrialists, politicians, and Christian missionaries, among others, weighing in (Thelin, 2011). Two primary approaches emerged from the debate: an argument for "race uplift" through vocational training widely available (see Perkins, 1983, p. 18), and an argument for educating the "talented tenth" of the black citizenry who would become leaders in black society (DuBois, 1903). Associated, respectively, with Booker T. Washington and W.E.B. DuBois (a biracial Northerner educated at Harvard), these philosophies dominated discussion of black education from Reconstruction into the Progressive Era (Moore, 2003). While the debates were under way, the legislature passed the second Morrill Act in 1890, which provided funding for separate public universities for black students in the South. Together with private HBCUs, these public HBCUs enrolled 322,000 black students in fall 2009, approximately 11 percent of all black students enrolled in higher education (NCES, 2011f). Although HBCU enrollment accounts for a minority of all black students, HBCUs graduate a disproportionate number of black students and produce a disproportionate number of black graduate, medical, and law students (Freeman & Thomas, 2002).

Latino/a Students Latino/a students participated in small numbers in nineteenth-century higher education, primarily in the southwestern United States (MacDonald & García, 2003). Enrollments at public institutions in California, Texas, Colorado, Arizona, and New Mexico included small percentages (around 1 to 3 percent) of Spanish-surname students until after World War II (MacDonald & García). Catholic institutions appear to have educated more Latino/a students in the nineteenth century; bilingual and parallel Spanish and English courses opened doors for hundreds of Latinos/as (Kanellos, 1997; McKevitt, 1990–1991). MacDonald and García characterized the early and mid–twentieth century as a time of Latinos/as' "slipping through the college gates" (p. 24), with a strong political and education movement in the 1960s and 1970s leading to substantially increased Latino/a enrollments. Government policy and programs (such as affirmative action and TRIO programs) in the 1980s and 1990s provided this movement with further momentum, yet inequitable K–12 education led to a continued lag in Latino/a postsecondary enrollments compared to their increasing presence in the population. Latino/a students remain disproportionately overrepresented in community colleges. Reversal of affirmative action and bilingual education policies in the 2000s threaten the gains that Latinos/as have made in access to higher education.

One potential solution lies among the federally designated Hispanic-Serving Institutions. As we noted earlier in the chapter, the term *Hispanic-Serving Institution* was written into the 1992 Higher Education Reauthorization Act to designate accredited, degree-granting institutions in which Hispanic students make up at least 25 percent of the undergraduate student body. Unlike the designation HBCU, which comprises a fixed set of institutions, the HSI category is fluid. Institutions can become HSIs when undergraduate enrollments shift. Unlike the HBCUs, most HSIs were not established specifically to meet the needs of Latino/a students but are adapting to changes in the student population. HSIs enroll nearly 46 percent of all Latino/a students participating in higher education (Mercer & Stedman, 2008).

American Indian Students From the time when some of the colonial colleges botched their plans, largely arising from missionary impulses (Wright, 1988), to include American Indians among their students, American Indians have existed largely at the margins of U.S. higher education. American Indian students constitute 1 percent of enrollments at predominantly white institutions (PWIs) (NCES, 2011d), a number that has increased only slightly over the last half century. In 1968 the Navajo Nation founded Diné College, the first of the Tribal Colleges and Universities. A response to the civil rights movement and the desire to create institutions more culturally specific and responsive to American Indians, TCUs are accredited institutions with at least 51 percent American Indian students (Gasman, 2008). Twenty-eight are tribally controlled, and three are federally chartered (American Indian Higher Education Consortium, n.d.). Most are two-year institutions located on tribally controlled lands. They educate American Indians living in isolated regions and are designed to restore, preserve, and promote tribal cultures, traditions, and languages as well as enhance economic development (Pavel, Ingelbret, & Banks, 2001). TCUs enroll nearly twenty thousand students (both undergraduate and graduate), and that number represents approximately 10 percent of all American Indian students in higher education (NCES, 2011e).

Asian American and Native American Pacific Islander Students Until 1940, U.S. citizens of Asian descent made up less than 1 percent of the total population (Tamura, 2001); laws restricting immigration changed in 1965.

Asian Americans are still a relatively small percentage of the total U.S. population (only 4.2 percent of the total population in the 2010 Census; see Humes, Jones, & Ramirez, 2011), but students of Asian descent have been a fast-growing proportion of the student population since the mid-1970s (Nakanishi, 1995). Chang and Kiang (2002) presented convincing evidence of the diversity within the "Asian American" category and the complexity this diversity presents for accurately describing the educational experiences of groups that differ by ethnicity, nationality, immigration history, language, and socioeconomic status. The early history of Asian Americans and Native American Pacific Islanders in education is not well documented, but there are a number of more recent attempts to document diversity among Asian American participants in higher education. Asian American students as a group now represent nearly 7 percent of all students enrolled in higher education (NCES, 2011d).

Asian American and Native American Pacific Islander–Serving Institutions are accredited institutions that enroll at least 10 percent Asian American and Native American Pacific Islander students and in which 50 percent or more of all students receive federal aid (a proxy for estimating the overall socioeconomic status of undergraduate students). The 2008 Higher Education Reauthorization Act included this designation. The majority of AANAPISIs are urban community colleges, many located on the West Coast but also in Texas, Massachusetts, Illinois, New York, and Guam. The number of Asian American and Native American Pacific Islander students enrolled in these institutions is currently around sixty thousand (less than 5 percent of all such students enrolled nationwide), but this figure continues to rise: this newest category of MSI is expected to grow as student populations shift and more institutions apply for the designation (National Commission on Asian American and Pacific Islander Research in Education, 2010).

Working-Class and Poor Students Higher education in the United States has for centuries included wealthy students and those from humble means (Thelin, 2011). Poor students attended private colleges on scholarships, farm boys (and some girls) left the fields to attend land-grant institutions, and students at normal schools often took time off to earn money (sometimes through teaching) so that they could continue their studies (Ogren, 2003). Still, higher education remained largely the province of the wealthy and professional classes until the twentieth century, when a turn from elite to mass higher education took place (Geiger, 2005). Notable public initiatives that provided financial support for college attendance were the GI

Bill (in 1945) and the Higher Education Act of 1965 (Thelin, 2011). The former provided assistance with school and living expenses for returning veterans of World War II who enrolled in college. The latter established federal grants and loans for students meeting income eligibility guidelines. In the twenty-first century, extending higher education opportunities across the socioeconomic spectrum is a stated priority at the national and state levels, though rising costs and other public needs threaten this goal.

International Students International students form a critical component of campus diversity in the twenty-first century. Students have been leaving their respective home countries to join colleges and universities since ancient times (Bevis & Lucas, 2007). Given the strength of universities in other countries and the relative newness of those in the United States, it took some time for international students to become a noticeable part of U.S. higher education. By the mid-1800s, a trend had begun with early enrollments from China and Japan that would lead to an influx of 690,923 international students from around the world during the 2009–2010 academic year (Chow, 2010). Immigration policy, U.S. foreign policy, and economic factors played a role over time in the emergence of a sizable population of international students. The United States now finds itself in competition with Australia, the United Kingdom, and Canada, among others, for international undergraduate and graduate students.

The story of student diversity in higher education is, overall, a successful one. The national student body has grown more diverse by gender, race, socioeconomic status, religion, and other demographic categories over the years. Access has increased. A more nuanced examination of the story, however, reveals that student outcomes are not equal across categories, and that not all students benefit equally from higher education. We describe these differences in other chapters in this book. Research on campus climate—how students perceive higher education environments— helps explain some of these differences.

Campus Climate

Renn and Patton (2010) defined campus climate as "the overall ethos or atmosphere of a college campus mediated by the extent individuals feel a sense of safety, belonging, engagement within the environment, and value as members of a community" (p. 248). Campus climate is a product of the environment and individuals' interactions in and with it. As we will show, climate is typically measured from the perspective of the individual (students, faculty, staff), though some aspects of it can be measured using demographic and behavior-based data (such as reported harassment). It is fundamentally a "felt" concept; even if campus leaders and members of other groups claim that the climate is positive for X group (for example, women; students of color; lesbian, gay, bisexual, and transgender students; or international students), but members of X group report otherwise, the climate cannot be considered positive. The fact, then, that women are the majority of undergraduates on many campuses does not in and of itself mean that they experience a welcoming campus climate.

Two enduring concepts form the foundation for discussing campus climate. First, Roberta Hall and Bernice Sandler (Hall & Sandler, 1982, 1984) introduced the idea of the *chilly climate* to describe women's experiences. Second, Sylvia Hurtado, Jeffrey Milem, Alma Clayton-Pedersen, and Walter Allen (1998) introduced a four-dimensional model for understanding campus climate for students from underrepresented racial and ethnic groups. The four dimensions are (1) an institution's historical legacy of inclusion or exclusion of various racial and ethnic groups; (2) its structural diversity, or the numerical representation of various racial and ethnic groups; (3) the psychological climate of perceptions and attitudes between and among groups; and (4) the behavioral climate of campus intergroup relations. Two outside factors—historical context and government and policy context—also act to shape campus climate (Hurtado et al., 1998). Other scholars and social justice educators have extended the examination of chilly climate and the four dimensions to identities and experiences beyond gender and race, including sexual orientation and gender identity (Rankin, Weber, Blumenfeld, & Frazer, 2010); student veterans (Ackerman & DiRamio, 2009); students with disabilities (Junco & Salter, 2004), and students from minority religious backgrounds (Seggie & Sanford, 2010). Analyses of campus climate assessments (see Hart & Fellabaum, 2008; Hurtado, Griffin, Arellano, & Cuellar, 2008; Hurtado & Ponjuan, 2005) form a subset of literature on the topic.

Campus Gender Climate Campus gender climate historically has referred to women's experiences. The tendency to conflate "gender" with "women" (or "gender issues" with "women's issues"), however, masks experiences across the gender spectrum and ignores men's perceptions of the gender climate. The majority of research on campus gender climate does relate to the "chilly climate" for women (Hall & Sandler, 1982, 1984; Hart & Fellabaum, 2008; Pascarella et al., 1997). Hall and Sandler (1984) described such elements as sexist humor, sexual harassment, and lowered academic standards for women that fit into Hurtado and colleagues' description (2008) of behavioral climate.

Lest Hall and Sandler's work (1982, 1984) be seen as an irrelevant artifact of an earlier, more sexist era, it is important to note that in the thirty years since their landmark publications the chilly climate for women persists. Pascarella et al. (1997) found that women's perceptions of a chilly climate affected cognitive gains in the first year of college; Whitt, Nora, Edison, Terenzini, and Pascarella (1999) found that this effect continued past the second year. Sax (2001) reported that women are less likely to enter graduate school in science, technology, engineering, and mathematics (STEM) fields because of the chilly climate they perceive. Studies continue to show that women experience a chilly climate in nontraditional (for women) majors (Morris & Daniel, 2008; Sax, Bryant, & Harper, 2008). The problem of chilly climate extends beyond STEM fields. For example, in one study single mothers attending community college found the climate unwelcoming in the years after Clinton-era welfare reform (Duquaine-Watson, 2007).

Although the campus climate for women remains—at least in pockets—chilly, women do make up the majority of students nationwide. They also graduate at higher rates than do men. And when disaggregated by racial and ethnic groups, the gender disparity in college attendance and completion is stark: white women represent 55 percent of all white undergraduate students, and black women make up 63 percent of all black undergraduate students (NCES, 2011d). The disparity raises two questions that drive a recent trend in studying college men and masculinities: (1) If women are the majority and more successful in college, why is the climate still hostile to them? and (2) Is there something about the campus climate for men that contributes to their comparative lack of achievement? The answer to both questions lies partly in what Kimmel (2008) has described as a campus culture immersed in "Guyland"—an all-enveloping sociocultural milieu that promotes heteronormative masculinity at the expense of men's *and* women's ability to express themselves authentically. Guyland is pervasive and nearly inescapable, predicated on the idea that the goal for men is to be accepted as "one of the guys" and the goal for women is to be acceptable to "the guys." Guyland exists before, during, and after college, during the years of "emerging adulthood" (Arnett, 2000), and persists into the twenties.

In addition to the Guyland hypothesis, which is de facto situated primarily in majority (white) culture, complementary and competing explanations for the nature of the campus gender climate emerge from the ongoing work of several other researchers. Working from Critical Race Theory (see Yosso, Smith, Ceja, & Solórzano, 2009) and intersectional perspectives (see Crenshaw, 1991), scholars have teased out the ways that concepts specific to Latino/a identity and black identity operate in the experiences and campus cultures of men (Gloria, Castellanos, Scull, & Villegas, 2009; Harper, 2009; Morales, 2010; Patton, 2011a; Sáenz & Ponjuan, 2009; Saez, Castado, & Wade, 2009; Strayhorn, 2008, 2010). Harper, Wardell, and McGuire (2011) and Harris (2010) have provided frameworks for understanding the multiple, intersectional, contextual influences of college men's identities. Although these studies were not designed to measure campus gender climate per se, as a group they paint a portrait of campus experiences in which male students of color are actively engaged in the process of understanding themselves as college men, experiment with boundaries of masculine identity, and are aware of the ways that other people's perceptions restrict acceptable gender expression. The climate, then, can be described as one that offers male privilege but circumscribes gender identity.

Students who operate outside expected gender norms—women in STEM majors, men in nursing and education, transgender students anywhere—are subject to chillier environments than those who do not. We have already discussed women in nontraditional fields. Bell-Scriber (2008) found that men in nursing undergraduate programs faced hostility from some faculty. Every published study of transgender college students (see Beemyn, 2005; Bilodeau, 2005, 2009; Rankin et al., 2010) describes how negative campus gender climates are produced in ways that can be mapped onto the four dimensions (historical legacy of racism, structural diversity, psychological climate, behavioral climate) defined by Hurtado et al. (1998). Campus gender climate is dominated by a Guyland ethos and embedded in a system of genderism (Bilodeau, 2009) that mandates that everyone have a singular gender identity located at one of two binary poles (man, woman). Race and ethnicity intersect with gender in college to amplify these standards and expectations (Harper et al., 2011; Harris, 2010).

Campus Racial Climate Examinations of campus racial climate began in earnest in the 1990s and include landmark studies (for example, Feagin, Vera, & Imani, 1996; Hurtado, 1992) showing that students from racially underrepresented groups perceive a hostile racial climate at PWIs. Importantly, studies also repeatedly show that students of color perceive a more hostile campus climate for racial minorities than do white students (Ancis, Sedlacek, & Mohr, 2000; Cabrera, Nora, Terenzini, Pascarella, & Hagedorn, 1999; Rankin & Reason, 2005).

Because perceptions of campus racial climate affect the transition to college and student success (see Eimers & Pike, 1997; Hurtado & Carter, 1997; Hurtado et al., 2007; Locks, Hurtado, Bowman, & Oseguera, 2008), this difference in perception underscores the importance of attending to the felt effects of campus racial climate across diverse groups. A report that aggregates all student responses to a campus climate survey and claims that "a majority of respondents believe campus climate for students of color is positive" is not useful if there are measured differences across racial groups. As Bensimon (2004) pointed out in her work with the "Equity Scorecard" (http://cue.usc.edu/our_tools/the_equity_scorecard .html) the examination of data disaggregated by race and gender can lead to insights about campus equity.

A frequent first step in addressing campus racial climate is to improve structural diversity (Hurtado et al., 1998), which means increasing the number and percentage of students from different racial groups. But simply adding diversity to the student body does not do much (if anything) to improve the sense of belonging felt by underrepresented minority students. "Structural diversity is perceived as a catalyst for promoting a more hospitable campus racial climate; it is a necessary, but not sufficient, factor in creating a more comfortable and less hostile environment for all" (Hurtado et al., 2008, p. 207). Structural diversity enhances opportunities for students, especially white students, to interact with others who are from different racial backgrounds (Chang, Astin, & Kim, 2004; Chang, Denson, Sáenz, & Misa, 2006; Pike & Kuh, 2006; Sáenz, Ngai, & Hurtado, 2007). These interactions, in turn, have a positive influence on educational outcomes, such as cognitive skills and intellectual growth (see Pascarella & Terenzini, 2005).

Hurtado et al. (2008) pointed to two key sets of findings concerning the psychological dimension of campus racial and ethnic climate. The first is that students from different backgrounds experience the same campus in different ways. Perhaps unsurprisingly given the nature of race relations in the United States, most studies have found that students of color at PWIs report *experiencing* race-based discrimination and harassment more often than do white students (Hurtado & Ponjuan, 2005; Pewewardy & Frey, 2002; Suarez-Balcazar, Orellana-Damacela, Portillo, Rowan, & Andrews-Guillen, 2003). But when asked about *observing* the campus climate for students of color, white students still do not report the same level of discrimination and harassment that their peers of color observe and experience (Ancis et al., 2000; Rankin & Reason, 2005; Suarez-Balcazar et al., 2003).

The second key finding related to the psychological climate is that "perceptions of a hostile climate can negatively influence student outcomes, particularly for students of color" (Hurtado et al., 2008, p. 209). Perceptions of an unwelcoming or hostile campus climate have negative effects on academic, social, and personal outcomes, as well as on one's sense of belonging in or attachment to the institution (Cress & Ikeda, 2003; Cureton, 2003; Locks, Hurtado, Bowman, & Oseguera, 2008; Lopez, 2005). Effects may differ across racial and ethnic groups, but perceptions of a hostile racial climate influence students in *all* racial groups—majority and minority (Fischer, 2007; Pike & Kuh, 2006; Rankin & Reason, 2005; Sáenz et al., 2007). Students who perceive their campus as more discriminatory report lower academic and social integration. This effect is stronger for students of color than for white students, but cuts across all groups (Cabrera et al., 1999; Hurtado et al., 2007; Locks et al., 2008).

The behavioral dimension of campus racial climate includes formal and informal interactions among students from different racial groups, as well as participation in campus diversity activities and diversity-related courses (Hurtado et al., 2008). Early behavioral climate research measured the frequency of interaction among diverse peers (for example, Chang, 1999; Pascarella, Edison, Nora, Hagedorn, & Terenzini, 1996), with more recent work concerned with the quality of interactions and their influence on student outcomes (Antonio et al., 2004; Chang et al., 2004; Gurin et al., 2004; Hurtado, 2005; Pike & Kuh, 2006; Sáenz et al., 2007). There are differences in outcomes based on precollege experiences (see Sáenz, 2005) and specific cross-racial interaction patterns (Chang et al., 2004; Hurtado, Engberg, Ponjuan, & Landreman, 2002; Sáenz et al., 2007), but abundant evidence supports the conclusion that informal interaction with diverse peers benefits students from all racial groups.

Drawing conclusions about the effects of formal, campus-facilitated practices (such as courses and cocurricular programs designed to promote intergroup dialogue) is more complex, in part because just over 40 percent of surveys of campus racial climate collect information about student outcomes (Hurtado et al., 2008). Useful for understanding campus climate "in the moment," these surveys typically are not longitudinal. Some national data are available through the National Survey of Student Engagement, the Higher Education Research Institute (home of the Cooperative Institutional Research Program), and ACT student surveys. These data support the idea that institutional practices can have a positive influence on campus racial climate and student success (Chang, 1999; Chang et al., 2004; Chang, Cerna, Han, & Sáenz, 2008; Chang & Kiang, 2002; Mayhew & DeLuca Fernández, 2007). Putting the pieces together, structural diversity creates opportunities for informal and formal interactions (behavioral dimension) that may influence perceptions (psychological dimension) of the climate and lead to positive or negative student outcomes. In short: campus racial climate matters to all students, regardless of their heritage.

Campus Climate for Lesbian, Gay, and Bisexual Students The acronym "LGBT" (sometimes GLBT) conflates sexual orientation (lesbian, gay, bisexual [LGB]) with gender identity (transgender [T]), a distinction we discuss in Chapter Seven on student development. When discussing research literature we use LGB and LGBT in accordance with the original authors' usage. Our discussion here focuses primarily on campus climate for sexual orientation minorities.

Much early research (from the 1970s and early 1980s) on what were then called gay and lesbian (since expanded to include bisexual) students arose from a psychological paradigm that aimed to show that these students were "normal"—that is, they were like other students except in having a nonheterosexual orientation (Tierney & Dilley, 1998). Professionals and scholars also designed studies to increase the visibility of LGB people on campus (Tierney & Dilley). According to Tierney and Dilley normalcy and visibility were the foundational approaches for LGB campus climate reports and arguments to include sexual orientation in institutional nondiscrimination policies. Renn (2010) noted that these campus climate studies

> focus on three areas: 1) perceptions and experiences *of* LGBT people, 2) perceptions *about* LGBT people and their experiences, and 3) the status of policies and programs designed to improve the academic, living, and work experiences of LGBT people on campus. (p. 134).

In general, the climate on many campuses is not positive for LGB students (see Brown, Clark, Gortmaker, & Robinson-Keilig, 2004; Engberg, Hurtado, & Smith, 2007; Rankin & Reason, 2008; Silverschanz, Cortina, Konik, & Magley, 2007; Wolf-Wendel, Toma, & Morphew, 2001). A national college climate survey indicated that LGBT individuals are the least accepted group when compared with other underserved populations (Rankin et al.,

2010). Rankin and colleagues surveyed 5,149 students, staff members, faculty, and administrators representing the fifty U.S. states and all Carnegie Basic Classifications. Key findings of this national report were that among lesbian, gay, and bisexual student respondents:

- Sixty-eight percent reported being the target of derogatory remarks.
- Forty-five percent felt deliberately ignored or excluded.
- Thirty-two percent felt intimidated or bullied.
- Forty-one percent felt isolated or left out when working in groups.
- Seventeen percent feared for their physical safety.
- Forty-nine percent of those harassed indicated that harassment occurred in class.
- Fifty-five percent also experienced harassment in public or while walking on campus.
- Twenty-eight percent seriously considered leaving the institution (compared to 24 percent of heterosexual respondents).

We noted earlier that perceptions of campus climate vary among members of different groups. Rankin et al. (2010) reported that heterosexual respondents observed anti-LGB behaviors, but not at the same rate that LGB respondents observed them.

There is some good news, however. Some individual campuses have reported an improved campus climate over time (see Klymyshyn, Green, & Richardson, 2010; Pasque & Murphy, 2005). In addition, efforts to identify campuses with an especially positive climate for LGB people have brought increased visibility to the need to assess and improve campus climate. The nonprofit advocacy organization Campus Pride provides a Campus Climate Index (www.campusclimateindex.org/) that the organization also uses to compile an "honor roll" of LGBT-friendly campuses. Campus Pride sponsors college fairs so that institutional admissions officers can recruit LGBT applicants and so that these prospective students can ask frank questions about campus climate before they apply. Not without the kind of controversy that often surrounds college ranking schemes, the *Princeton Review* publishes a "Top 20 Gay Community Accepted" list of reportedly LGB-friendly institutions. One can quibble with the methodology, but the listing itself draws attention to the fact that LGB campus climate matters.

LGB campus climate studies remain central to understanding student experiences and promoting equitable policies (Renn, 2010; Sanlo, Rankin, & Schoenberg, 2002). They provide baseline data, justify improvements to campus climate, and signify the importance of LGB people as members of the campus community. Unfortunately, it can be difficult to assess campus climate for a group whose members are not easily identifiable. All institutions are required to report aggregated student gender and racial and ethnic data every year to the Integrated Postsecondary Education Data System (IPEDS). If one wants to assess campus gender climate or campus racial climate, one theoretically can survey members of different groups; compare findings; and report common measures of reliability, such as survey response rates. No such data exist for LGB students, who often are invited to surveys via student organization listservs, social media, and LGBT campus resource centers, where they exist (Renn, 2010). The Campus Pride National LGBT College Climate Survey provides some standardization of items and the ability to compare across institutions (Rankin et al., 2010).

Additional Research on Campus Climate Hart and Fellabaum (2008) conducted an analysis of institutional campus climate studies. Of 115 studies, 112 assessed campus climate for gender, 58 for race and ethnicity, 21 for sexual orientation, 8 for disability, 6 for religion, 4 for age, 3 for class or socioeconomic status, and 1 each for culture, indigenous status, marital status, parental status, region and geography, and reverse discrimination (the total exceeds 115 because many studies included multiple factors). Forty-five of the studies included students (70 did not), and faculty were the most frequently surveyed group. Hart and Fellabaum acknowledged limitations in their sample that preclude simple generalizations to the entire universe of higher education institutions, yet the spread of topical foci indicate that little is known about campus climate for substantial populations that may be of interest (for example, students with disabilities and members of different religious groups).

Empirical studies of campus climate indicate that higher education, like society, does not yet treat everyone equally. Groups that have historically been at the margins—for example, people with disabilities (Harbour & Madaus, 2011); immigrants (Erisman & Looney, 2007); students from poor or working-class families (Engle & Tinto, 2008); and students who practice a religion other than Christianity (Seifert, 2007)—remain at the margins on many campuses. Newly visible populations, such as mixed-race students, transgender students, students who are returning veterans from the wars in Iraq and Afghanistan, and students without U.S. citizenship documents, challenge higher education administrators to consider campus climate in new ways (see Ackerman & DiRamio, 2009; Bilodeau, 2009;

Gildersleeve, Rumann, & Mondragón, 2010; Renn & Shang, 2008). Campus climate may be improving—albeit slowly—for women, students of color, and LGB students, but it is not yet equally warm for all.

Policies, Programs, and Services to Support Campus Diversity

Given the complexities of campus ecology, institutional types, student diversity, and campus climate, colleges and universities have developed a range of policies, programs, and services that support diverse campus environments in at least two ways: (1) creating conditions for success for students from diverse backgrounds, and (2) creating conditions in which campus diversity itself becomes a vehicle for learning. We cannot provide a complete inventory of efforts in these areas, as thousands of institutional examples are available. We will address three key topics: access, support for specific populations, and support for learning from and with diversity.

Broadening access addresses Hurtado et al.'s call (1998) for improving the structural diversity of higher education. One means to this end is affirmative action, a policy typically employed in admissions and hiring. Although there have been legal challenges to the use of affirmative action in public institutions in some states, private institutions everywhere and most public institutions have the option to include race and gender in decisions about who is admitted or offered a job. The administration of affirmative action may look different in different admissions processes, but the main philosophy is the same: to take the common good derived from a diverse student and alumni/ae body into account in making decisions about individual candidates. Other efforts to broaden access include recruiting students from underrepresented backgrounds (which could mean a racial group entirely or women in STEM fields, for example); offering bridge programs to ensure that all entering students are ready for college courses; and providing financial aid packages that put higher education in reach of students from modest means. The history of student diversity shows that more students from diverse background are attending college than ever before, but this diversity is not spread evenly across all sectors and institutional types. Broadening access is a means of increasing structural diversity at individual campuses as well as in the aggregate.

Efforts to provide support for specific populations (such as women, students from different racial groups, students with disabilities, and LGBT students) exist at most postsecondary institutions in the United States. There are a number of models for this support, some of which focus on academic success, transition to college, cultural enrichment, career development, and mentoring. Federal TRIO programs that serve first-generation (a proxy for socioeconomic status) and underrepresented minority students are an example (see Chapter Four for more discussion). Culture centers, such as an omnibus Multicultural Center or separate centers for women, members of specific racial groups, and LGBT students, are another (see Patton, 2010). The National Science Foundation, through its institutional grants to promote gender and racial diversity in the scientific workforce, funds programs that address the educational and career pipeline from elementary school through senior faculty. Offices, programs, centers, staff and faculty liaisons, curricula, and student organizations to support diversity exist at all types of institutions, though not every institution offers every type of support.

In the 1980s and 1990s the predominant mode of thinking about population-specific programs was a "deficit model" that assumed that members of underrepresented groups did not have the necessary skills, knowledge, or cultural capital to succeed in higher education (Patton, 2011b). More recent thinking (see Howard-Hamilton, Hinton, & Hughes, 2010; Patton, 2011b; Renn, 2011; Yosso & Benavides Lopes, 2010) holds that culture centers—and presumably other student support services—are locations for strengths-based identity immersion and exploration, leadership development, and resistance to hostile campus climate. Abundant evidence supports the conclusion that population-specific programs and activities contribute to positive student outcomes (see Chang, 2002b; Harper & Quaye, 2007; Inkelas, 2004; Renn, 2007). With increased structural diversity and population-specific programs that interrupt the effects of negative campus climate, the learning environment for all students can be improved.

If one of the desired improvements in the learning environment is an increase for all students in intercultural competence, institutions can provide programs and support that promote this goal. Earlier in the chapter we described the positive outcomes that all students can gain from formal campus diversity activities and diversity-related courses (Hurtado et al., 2008). Examples of these initiatives include interfaith and cross-cultural dialogues, multicultural leadership development programs, and first-year seminars focused on diversity. Training student staff (for example, resident assistants, peer educators, and academic mentors) on how to facilitate intercultural competence is an opportunity to increase their skills and equip them to help their peers learn from and about the diverse student body. Purposeful reflection before, during, and after international experiences and service learning can increase participants' capacity for intercultural communication and empathy (Jones & Abes, 2004; Pagano & Roselle, 2009).

In addition to building intercultural capacity, institutions can take steps to reduce discriminatory and harassing behaviors. Dealing effectively with negative incidents is essential in discouraging behaviors that contribute to a hostile or chilly climate. Multicultural training and awareness-raising for staff and faculty are important elements, especially on campuses with a relatively stable employee population and a changing student body. Considering campus ecology, all individuals with whom students have contact or who make decisions that affect students have a role to play in improving the campus climate across categories of difference and commonality.

Conclusion

In this chapter we have described the foundational structures of campus environments, exploring the development of different institutional types, the emergence of increasingly diverse student populations, and the experience of campus climate. All of these factors feature in the "E" of the I-E-O model, as they form the context in which, ideally, students learn, grow, and develop. Yet it is also true that not all students thrive equally in all environments. As should be clear from our discussion of transition in the previous chapter, we place responsibility for designing environments and experiences for student success in the hands of educators and institutional leaders. To be sure, students must do their part to engage with the environment in ways that will lead to success, but environments clearly matter, as will be demonstrated in the chapters that follow.

Points of Discussion

Implications for Students

- How do students learn about institutional types and environments? To what extent do precollege interactions (in person, online, through other media) help students understand the type and culture of a campus? To what extent are students able to consider these factors before enrolling? What is the relationship among a good "fit" with the campus environment, persistence, and success?

- How do students understand the role of MSIs and single-sex institutions? Through what means do they learn about these institutions before applying to college, and to what extent do they consider attending one?
- Given the prevalence of swirling (as discussed in Chapter Three), how can students maximize the benefit of attending different institutional types?

Implications for Institutions

- How can an institution overcome a history of having an unwelcome campus climate for particular groups?
- Who at an institution is responsible for creating—or attempting to change—the campus climate?
- In the competitive marketplace of higher education in the United States, to what constituencies (for example, the public, students, families, or local communities) are different institutions most accountable? Where does accountability to students fit?
- How often is it realistic and reasonable to conduct campus climate studies? After what period of time or series of events should a campus climate study be repeated to assess change? At what level of an institution does the responsibility lie for conducting campus climate studies and implementing recommendations that emerge from them?
- What is the role of MSIs and single-sex institutions in the overall landscape of U.S. higher education? What would happen to the rest of higher education if these institutions radically changed their mission and moved away from MSI or single-sex status? What would be lost? What would be gained? Who would benefit? Who would be worse off?

Implications for Policy and National Discourse

- What historical and contemporary features of national and state sociopolitical contexts led to the development of the current highly decentralized "system" of postsecondary education in the United States?
- Higher education in the United States encompasses a very wide array of institutional types and environments. In the absence of a public system for accreditation, how do federal- and state-level education agencies hold diverse institutions accountable?

- What are the benefits and drawbacks of having such a diverse, loosely formed "system" of higher education in the United States?
- Given national efforts to increase college-going and degree completion rates among diverse populations, should there be federal- or state-level policies that create institutional accountability for campus climate? If so, what might they look like? If not, what role, if any, does campus climate have in affecting the national college completion agenda?

Learning Activity

- Reflect on your own institution and the overall environment for students. What key characteristics define the institution? How? Which students are central to the campus history and culture, and which are more marginal? Choose a marginalized student group and consider what might be revealed in a campus climate study about their experience. Review campus policies; your institution's online presence; newspapers; past and current events; as well as institutional faculty, staff, and student demographic breakdowns in your consideration. How might you use this hypothetical campus climate study to improve your institution's service to students?

Resources Related to Campus Environments

Campus Ecologist (www.campusecologist.org/)

The site includes resources, research, and a newsletter about campus ecology.

Carnegie Classification of Institutions of Higher Education (http://classifications.carnegiefoundation.org/)

Updated classification information for U.S. higher education institutions, searchable by name or IPEDS unit ID, is available at http://classifications .carnegiefoundation.org/lookup_listings/institution.php. The main site includes reports and publications about the Carnegie Classification System, including Carnegie's Community Engagement Classification.

Minority-Serving Institutions (www2.ed.gov/about/inits/list/index.html)

Specific information related to the following is available:

- White House Initiative on HBCUs (www2.ed.gov/about/inits/list /whhbcu/edlite-index.html)

- White House Initiative on TCUs (www2.ed.gov/about/inits/list/whtc /edlite-index.html)
- AANAPISI Program (www2.ed.gov/about/inits/list/asian-americans -initiative/aanapisi.html)
- HSI Program (www2.ed.gov/programs/idueshsi/index.html)

National Science Foundation Broadening Participation Initiatives (www.nsf.gov/od/broadeningparticipation/bp.jsp)

In addition to general program information, the site includes reports and publications about efforts to increase the participation of women and underrepresented groups in STEM fields (www.nsf.gov/od/broadening participation/bp_portfolio_dynamic.jsp).

Women's College Coalition (www.womenscolleges.org)

The site includes a list of women's colleges, research, and reports on women's colleges and alumnae outcomes.

CHAPTER SIX

APPROACHES TO COLLEGE STUDENT DEVELOPMENT

Student affairs educators are frequently faced with complex decisions in their daily practice. Consistent with the goals of student affairs, our roles often include overlapping responsibilities and obligations to promote student development, design campus environments that are educationally purposeful, and understand higher education as an organization (McEwen, 2003). Theories provide an important and necessary lens through which to engage our roles and responsibilities and make decisions. Theories do not inform us about what exactly to do, but they do provide us with ways to make decisions and to think about how to interpret individuals, environments, and organizations.

JONES & ABES, 2011, P. 161

The definition of *student development* has evolved with the maturation of the student affairs profession in higher education and its underlying empirical and theoretical foundations. Like Evans, Forney, Guido, Patton, and Renn (2010), we use Rodgers's definition (1990): "the ways that a student grows, progresses, or increases his or her developmental capabilities as a result of enrollment in an institution of higher education" (p. 127). We also rely on Sanford's definition (1967) of *development* as "the organization of increasing complexity" (p. 47). Student development involves an increased capacity for complexity that results from participation in higher education, not merely an increase that may be attributed to maturation. *Student development theory* is a body of theories—some derived specifically from research on college students, others adopted from psychology, sociology, human ecology, and other fields of study—that guides higher education practice related to promoting student learning and growth.

In 1978 Knefelkamp, Widick, and Parker identified five clusters of theories into which student development research could be sorted: psychosocial theories, theories of cognitive development, maturity models, typology models, and person-environment interaction models. Despite periodic attempts to merge these clusters under the umbrella of "student learning and development" (for example, the American College Personnel Association's *Student Learning Imperative*, 1994, and Keeling's *Learning Reconsidered*, 2004), they have remained largely distinct and durable. These categories, for example, form a rough outline of graduate courses and textbooks on student development theory (see Evans, Forney, Guido, Patton, & Renn, 2010).

In the last decade, Marcia Baxter Magolda (2009) and other scholars have pressed for a holistic approach to understanding student development, basing their arguments on empirical findings that development across these five constructs cannot be fully disentangled. What may, however, be overlooked in adhering to a fully integrated approach are variations in student development based on individual characteristics and differential environmental presses on students from different backgrounds. Therefore, we present holistic, integrated student development theories in this chapter and cognitive, moral, and psychosocial identity theories in Chapter Seven. This chapter provides a foundation for understanding the nature of student development theories and how they may be used in practice to promote student learning and success. These theories can be used to examine both process and product: a guide to achieving the end goals of institutional missions for student learning and a way to measure outcomes of participation in higher education.

General Concepts

Practitioners and scholars do not agree completely on what constitutes the body of student development theory, yet many would agree on a core set of theories that includes those we describe in this chapter and the next. They would also agree that the core theories display a number of characteristics in common. One such characteristic is that the theories describe or include a process that moves from less complex to more complex ways of being, knowing, or doing. Many theories that have emerged from psychology, for example, describe stages (also called, for example, levels, phases, or orders) through which an individual passes. Ecological theories do not typically include stages, but do rely on increasingly complex person-environment interactions to stimulate development.

Another common characteristic among theories is an emphasis on the role of individual experiences in the developmental context. Not every student will seek out or react to environmental stimuli in the same way. Not every institutional context provides similar levels of developmental stimuli. These differences among students and institutions account for substantial variation in learning and developmental outcomes, even among similar students at the same institution.

A third characteristic common among theories is a focus on the specific role of higher education institutions in promoting or inhibiting development. Many student development theories come from other fields, such as psychology, sociology, and social psychology, yet they persist among student development professionals because they are easily adapted for explaining what happens in higher education settings. For example, popularly taught racial identity development theories (Cross & Fhagen-Smith, 2001; Helms, 1990, 1995) were developed largely in the psychological tradition, but can be applied effectively to college students with the addition of context-specific details.

In addition to these three common characteristics, there are two key concepts that provide a foundation for understanding student development. Sanford (1967) introduced the notion of balancing challenge and support. That is, for students to develop they require an optimal balance of challenge (novel situations, demands, apparent contradictions) and support in the form of intellectual, social, and emotional buffers. A student who experiences too much challenge with too little or mismatched support will be overwhelmed, and a student experiencing insufficient challenge with too much support will not engage in activities that promote increasing complexity. The second key concept that undergirds student development theory is Astin's now well-supported claim (1984) that students learn and develop in accordance with their involvement in educationally meaningful activities. Basic tenets of "involvement theory" are that more involvement in increasingly complex activities yields greater outcomes and that students' time and energy are finite resources, implying that time and energy spent on one activity means less time and energy available for other pursuits. Taken together, the concepts of challenge and support as well as involvement provide insight into *how* and *where* student development might occur. They are at work behind the scenes even in those student development theories that do not refer to them explicitly.

Holistic, integrated approaches to college student development account for cognitive (intellectual and moral), interpersonal (social), and intrapersonal (psychosocial) aspects of individual growth. There is a substantial literature base in each of these areas, and in the next chapter we present several examples from it. The focus here is on the ways that these three areas of development intersect, overlap, influence, and reinforce one another. Understanding how they work holistically helps explain how they work as separate domains of development. Knowing, for example, that increasing cognitive complexity helps a student make sense of his or her social identities, such those related to race and gender (Abes, Jones, & McEwen, 2007; Pizzolato, Chaudhari, Murrell, Podobnik, & Schaeffer, 2008; Torres & Baxter Magolda, 2004; Torres & Hernandez, 2007), deepens an understanding of social identity development. Similarly, integrated approaches, such as the ecology models, can provide a background for understanding how development occurs in the college context. We present holistic approaches first to set the stage for theories related to the more specific aspects of development (moral, cognitive, and psychosocial identities) we discuss in the next chapter.

Development of Self-Authorship

Baxter Magolda's line of research has provided a central organizing construct for understanding how young adult college students develop and make meaning. For over twenty-five years, Baxter Magolda has followed the cognitive, interpersonal, and intrapersonal development of a group of young adults who began college in 1988 (Baxter Magolda, 1992, 2001b, 2008, 2009). This study is one of the longest-running qualitative longitudinal studies in the field and provides evidence for understanding development in and after college. A particularly important aspect of the study is that Baxter Magolda continues her examination from young—or emerging—adulthood through middle age, providing a wide sweep of development that yields insight into "traditional-age" students (those entering college immediately from high school) and "adult learners." Another appealing aspect of this line of research is that Baxter Magolda has offered periodic reflections on her own experience with the study, explaining how her thinking has evolved over time (see Baxter Magolda, 2004a). These reflections connect the theory and its evolution to the larger field of higher education and human development research.

Central to Baxter Magolda's findings is the development of self-authorship, a way of making meaning that incorporates cognitive, interpersonal, and intrapersonal elements. The term *self-authorship* comes from Robert Kegan's theory of self-evolution, introduced in his book *The Evolving Self* (1982) and elaborated in *In Over Our Heads: The Mental Demands of Modern Life* (1994). Two concepts underlie Kegan's theory. First, development is in part a process of resolving the tension between differentiated self and self immersed in surroundings (Kegan 1982, 1994). Second, development reflects the evolution of the ways people make meaning of life experiences. Thus there is a distinctly cognitive component to development; organization of self (psychosocial identity) and self-in-immersion (interpersonal relations) become more complex as cognition becomes more complex. Kegan varied his terminology over time, but settled on the term *orders of consciousness* to denote a series of stages. Kegan called the fourth order "the self-authoring mind" (2009, p. 16), in which individuals can balance the needs of self in relation to those of others. According to Baxter Magolda (2008), self-authorship is "the internal capacity to define one's beliefs, identity, and social relations" (p. 269). Throughout her writing, Baxter Magolda has focused on the development of self-authorship, or the self-authoring mind, as a critical outcome of young adult development, and has concentrated on the potential of higher education to help students move toward it.

Phases of Self-Authorship

Kegan (1994) identified the transition from the third order of consciousness to the fourth order, in which self-authorship occurs, as the principal transformation into adulthood. It marks "the capacity to stand outside of [one's] values and form a deeper internal set of convictions that form a context for and regulate behavior" (Love & Guthrie, 1999, p. 72). Although Kegan (1982, 1994) proposed that this order would be uncommon among young adults, and although few of the participants in Baxter Magolda's longitudinal study (2001b) reached self-authorship during college, evidence is emerging that self-authorship may be more prevalent among college students than once believed (Baxter Magolda, 2007; Meszaros, 2007; Pizzolato, 2003, 2004, 2005, 2010; Pizzolato et al., 2008; Pizzolato, Hicklen, Brown, & Chaudhari, 2009). An explanation for this discrepancy may lie in the homogeneous nature of Baxter Magolda's research sample, made up of individuals who are all white, began college directly from high school, and attended the same selective public institution. Pizzolato has pointed out that students without these privileges may engage in self-authoring behavior sooner, as a necessary precursor to getting to college at all. Baxter Magolda developed the learning partnerships model (Baxter Magolda, 1992, 2001b; Baxter Magolda & King, 2004) to guide educators in their efforts to create environments that best promote the transition to self-authorship. The learning partnerships model is based on four phases of the journey toward self-authorship, each of which incorporates cognitive, interpersonal, and intrapersonal dimensions.

Phase One: Following Formulas As the name of this phase implies, students at this point of development rely on external formulas to guide decisions about what to do and what to think about themselves and the world (Baxter Magolda, 2001b). Roughly equivalent to Kegan's third order of consciousness (1994), the Following Formulas phase focuses substantially on relationship building and the approval of important others. Young adults seek approval by following expectations set by society, parents, significant others, and mentors (Baxter Magolda, 2001b).

Development in this phase carries across contexts, from school to home to work. Formulas for career success might include parental expectations related to one's academic major (such as premedical studies or business), faculty and academic advisers' expressed preferences for out-of-class activities (summer internships instead of hourly work in food service or retail), and peer culture (other new employees' engaging in competition about working long hours and sacrificing other aspects of life). Formulas may be mutually reinforcing (for example, the accounting major with the summer internship in a tax firm, in which other interns compete for "face time" with the boss). Or they may conflict, as when a significant other offers a formula for a successful relationship (such as spending more time together) that cannot be followed while observing the all-work-all-the-time formulas of the previous example. Baxter Magolda (2001b) learned that many young adults found themselves unable to follow some or all expectations and, lacking a firm internal foundation from which to proceed, either sought other formulas or advanced to Phase Two, the Crossroads.

Phase Two: Crossroads When following formulas does not work, or does not work well, individuals arrive at the Crossroads phase: an opportunity to choose a more complex way of thinking, feeling, and being. Baxter Magolda (2001b) found that the crossroads occurred largely out of young adults' dissatisfaction with how they had allowed themselves to be defined by others. Seeking approval turned out not to be the path that led to fulfillment, whether in personal life or career. Developmentally, young adults had hit a spot where their old ways did not work, new ways were not evident, and they had to stay, unhappily, where they were or begin to figure out a new way of approaching life.

College environments can be designed to provoke or stimulate Crossroads experiences for students when they question formulas but do not yet have answers. Service learning (Jones & Abes, 2004) and study abroad (Pagano & Roselle, 2009) are examples of learning contexts in which students may find that familiar formulas do not work. Leadership of complex organizations or in complex situations, such as student activism, is another venue for exploring new ways of thinking and acting (see Komives, Longerbeam, Owen, Mainella, & Osteen, 2006). Whether the Crossroads phase takes months or years, it is characterized by a sense that what one is doing is not working and that the formulas are not the answer (Baxter Magolda, 2001b). What the answer is, however, is not yet clear. The answers begin to emerge in the third phase, Becoming the Author of One's Life.

Phase Three: Becoming the Author of One's Life Questioning formulas may lead to questions about the sources of those formulas (relationships with parents, bosses, mentors, and significant others, for example). These questions indicate the arrival of a critical capacity to distinguish self from and in relationships, to hold the relationship as "object," or "to stand outside a relationship and make judgments about its demands without feeling the relationship itself has thereby been fundamentally violated" (Love & Guthrie, 1999, p. 72). Freedom from the fear that in disagreeing with important others they will lose these relationships allows individuals to begin to author their own lives, choosing their own beliefs, even in the face of conflicting external messages (Baxter Magolda, 2001b).

This new way of relating to self and others may require a renegotiation of relationships, as the individual asserts his or her beliefs and values in personal, academic, social, and professional contexts. It does not, however, require that the individual sever relational ties. As Kegan (1994) wrote, "The self-authorizing capacity to 'decide for myself' does not also have to implicate the stylistic preference to 'decide by myself.' I can be self-authorizing in a relational way" (p. 219). Authoring one's life may be an independent development, but it is not necessarily a solitary one. In the college context, students may benefit from support from advisers and mentors as they negotiate new ways of being in relationships.

Phase Four: Internal Foundations The desired endpoint of Baxter Magolda's theory of self-authorship is the establishment of internal foundations. In the cognitive dimension, the Internal Foundations phase encompasses a self-determined belief system. In the intrapersonal dimension, it entails a solid sense of identity and values. Relationships that are truly mutual round out the interpersonal dimension. Individuals understand and account for external influences, but do not allow them to determine beliefs, values, or actions. Individuals also understand and can reflect on their own emotions, identities, and relationships. Internal foundations do not represent selfish impulses, but provide a source for meaning-making that accounts for responsibility to self as well as others. Baxter Magolda (2008) identified three elements of self-authorship at the level of Internal Foundations. Individuals *trust the internal voice, build an internal foundation,* and *secure internal commitments* (Baxter Magolda, 2008). Together, these three elements solidify a sense of self-authorship and the transition to adulthood. Not every student will achieve this transition, but for those who do, colleges and universities can offer curricular and cocurricular opportunities to explore and enact internal foundations across academic, professional, and social domains.

Integration Across Cognitive, Interpersonal, and Intrapersonal Dimensions

Drawing from Kegan, Baxter Magolda (2009) argued for the importance of a holistic perspective on student development that focused on "addressing tensions and intersections between existing theoretical frameworks and new ones generated from specific populations" (p. 622). Referring specifically to self-authorship, she proposed *meaning-making* as a context for understanding cognitive, interpersonal, and intrapersonal dimensions of individual development. In this subsection, we describe what this integrated perspective entails and offer examples from contemporary research.

As noted earlier, Kegan (1994) framed his theory of development in part on how individuals make meaning of life experiences. He advocated for an approach that did not pit emotion against reason and interpersonal against intrapersonal. He proposed that meaning-making offered a context in which to create "a sophisticated understanding of the relationship between the psychological and the social, between the past and the present, and between emotion and thought" (Kegan, 1982, p. 15). In other words, examining how individuals make meaning—and the more complicated ways in which they learn to make meaning—provides a prime location for understanding the integration of cognitive, intrapersonal, and interpersonal dimensions, without requiring resolution of the question of which dimension is preeminent.

Other scholars weighed in with descriptions of meaning-making among traditional-age college students. Parks (2000) wrote that meaning-making "includes (1) becoming critically aware of one's own composing of reality, (2) self-consciously participating in an ongoing dialogue toward truth, and (3) cultivating a capacity to respond—to act—in ways that are satisfying and just" (p. 6). Basing their definition on Kegan's (1994), Abes, Jones, and McEwen (2007) called meaning-making "sets of assumptions that determine how an individual perceives and organizes one's life" (p. 4). It is on this simplified definition that we rely for the purposes of discussing integrated, holistic student development.

Baxter Magolda (1992, 2001b, 2008, 2009) led the way in considering the codevelopment of the three dimensions of self-authored forms of meaning-making, as described in the four phases discussed earlier. Baxter Magolda did not originally design her longitudinal study with the three dimensions in mind, but they emerged as central to the ongoing research design and analysis. Baxter Magolda (2001a, 2002, 2009) demonstrated over time how the cognitive, interpersonal, and intrapersonal dimensions intersect as young adults mature from age eighteen to age forty. Other scholars have examined meaning-making for specific populations of students or in specific contexts. For example, Torres (2003; Torres & Baxter Magolda, 2004; Torres & Hernandez, 2007) is conducting a longitudinal study of Latino/a students, and Abes (2009; Abes & Jones, 2004; Abes & Kasch, 2007) has studied lesbian students' meaning-making using integrated and queer theory. Pizzolato (2003, 2004, 2005, 2010; Pizzolato et al., 2008; Pizzolato et al., 2009) examined self-authorship of diverse students in multiple educational contexts. The meaning-making of liberal arts college students is one outcome studied in the Wabash National Study of Liberal Arts Education (see King, Baxter Magolda, Barber, Kendall Brown, & Lindsay, 2009; King, Kendall Brown, Lindsay, & VanHecke, 2007). In all of these cases, it is evident that the development of complexity along each dimension (cognitive, interpersonal, and intrapersonal) involves a process integrated across them.

The empirical evidence from these and other studies supports a call for the integration of student development theories across the clusters of theories identified by Knefelkamp et al. (1978). Clustering theories does have some utility, as we will describe in Chapter Seven, but after several decades of research on college student learning and development, it seems clear that cognitive, interpersonal, and intrapersonal development cannot be considered wholly apart from one another. We began this chapter with the holistic perspective as a way of providing a theoretical foundation for understanding this integration before discussing in the next chapter the various theories that are used within each dimension. Before we turn to these theories, however, we describe another holistic approach—developmental ecology—as a foundation for understanding how and where student development occurs.

Developmental Ecology

Developmental ecology models take a different approach from self-authorship theories in depicting holistic, integrated student development. Where self-authorship theories focus on *what* is being developed (cognitive, interpersonal, and intrapersonal complexity), ecology models focus on *how* and *where* development occurs. They explain how increasingly complex interactions between individuals and environments, supported with adequate buffers, foster development.

There are two prevailing approaches to ecology models in research and practice with college students: a developmental ecology model adapted from the work of Urie Bronfenbrenner (1974, 1979, 1993, 2005) and the campus ecology model introduced by James Banning and Leland Kaiser (1974) and elaborated by, among others, Carney Strange and Banning (2001). We concentrate here on developmental ecology because it is more central to understanding processes of student development, whereas campus ecology, outlined in Chapter Five, is more central to understanding campus environments.

Bronfenbrenner's Theory

Bronfenbrenner (1979, 1993, 2005) proposed an interactive developmental model of four components: process, person, context, and time, or PPCT. Interactions among the components influence the development of the individual in the environments of family, school, and work. Like other person-environment theories (Banning & Kaiser, 1974; Holland, 1966; Moos, 1979; Tinto, 1987, 1993; Weidman, 1989), Bronfenbrenner's ecology of human development illuminates the ways that relationships among individual inputs (such as personal characteristics or preferred ways of interacting with surroundings and the environment) may result in observed outcomes, including learning, identity development, and behavior. The model is useful in understanding how an individual's characteristics (person) mutually shape relationships (process) with people and objects in the environment (context) over time to promote or inhibit various developmental outcomes.

We use the fictional student Ana to illustrate how the pieces fit together. Ana is a junior business major at a comprehensive university. Her parents support her tuition, and she works off campus to pay for her living expenses. She lives off campus and is an active member of a women's business student association, a local faith community, and an intramural soccer team. She volunteered to help with a research project that her favorite professor was conducting, and that professor is now an academic and professional mentor.

Process The *process* component is at the heart of how development occurs. It "encompasses particular forms of interaction between organism and environment, called *proximal processes*, that operate over time and are posited as the primary mechanisms producing human development" (Bronfenbrenner & Morris, 2006, p. 795). Just as self-authorship theory requires demands from the environment for increasingly complex ways of making meaning for development to occur, the ecology model calls for proximal processes of increasing complexity. Increased complexity may be required, for example, from proximal processes with larger or more diverse groups that the individual encounters or from competing messages from significant others of equal importance to the developing individual (Renn & Arnold, 2003). For Ana and other college students, proximal processes may occur in formal learning settings (classrooms, laboratories, online instruction); cocurricular settings (athletics, student organizations); work (full-time, part-time, on or off campus); family (parents, partners, children); and peer groups (on or off campus, in person or digitally). It is important to note that process interactions are two-way: the person and environment influence one another.

Person The individual is typically the object of interest in student development theory and practice, and is represented in Bronfenbrenner's developmental ecology model as the *person*. The person component of the PPCT model encompasses background and demographic characteristics, abilities, and preferred ways of interacting with the environment. To describe these preferences, Bronfenbrenner (1993) proposed four types of *developmentally instigative characteristics*. These characteristics are "the attributes of the person most likely to shape the course of development, for better or for worse" because they "induce or inhibit dynamic dispositions toward the environment" (p. 11). The first are those that act to inhibit or invite varying responses from the environment. Characteristics of selective responsivity, or ways that individuals explore and react to the environment, are second. Third are structuring proclivities, related to how individuals engage in or deflect increasingly complex activities. Last are directive beliefs, which describe how individuals understand their agency in relation to environments.

Renn and Arnold (2003) demonstrated how these developmentally instigative characteristics might operate for college students, pointing to the ways that different students attract mentors more or less easily (inhibiting or inviting varying responses), interact with faculty and peers (selective responsivity), avoid or persist in complex intellectual or social activities (structuring proclivities), and attribute success or failure to themselves or to their environment (directive beliefs). Over the course of a student's college career, from application to career planning and graduation, there are myriad opportunities for these characteristics to influence decisions and actions in ways that result in vastly different developmental and learning outcomes, even across groups of students who may appear similar in background. Ana demonstrated these characteristics through her willingness to get involved in a voluntary research project; as a result, she has attracted a faculty mentor who supports her increased involvement as an officer in the women's business student association.

Developmentally instigative characteristics combine with other personal qualities to fit or unfit students to their postsecondary contexts. A student who seeks close connections with faculty might find them easily at a liberal arts or community college, but might have to draw on an ability to negotiate more complex systems and relationships to locate opportunities for such connections at a large research or comprehensive university. Conversely, a student who thrives in the complexity and diversity of a research university environment might not feel adequately challenged at a small, homogeneous institution. According to Bronfenbrenner (1993),

> Developmentally instigative characteristics do not *determine* the course
> of development; rather, they may be thought of as "putting a spin" on a
> body in motion. The effect of that spin depends on other forces, and
> resources, in the total ecological system. (p. 14)

These forces and resources modulate the influence of developmentally instigative characteristics, creating niches that favor certain ways of being and disadvantage others. This central principle of the ecology model ties Sanford's challenge and support postulation (1966) together with individual characteristics of the developing person.

Context When considering an ecological perspective, the first element that comes to mind may be the context: the natural, intellectual, relational, and human-built environments in which students live, learn, and work. In Bronfenbrenner's ecology model (1979, 1993, 2005), the context comprises multiple levels, or systems, in which developmental encounters take place between the individual and his or her environment. Throughout his career, Bronfenbrenner labeled these *microsystems, mesosystems, exosystems,* and *macrosystems.* Renn and Arnold (2003) created an example of the context of college student development, depicting these systems as nested layers (see Figure 6.1).

Microsystem. Microsystems are the location of direct interactions between the individual and the environment. According to Bronfenbrenner (1993), a microsystem is a

> pattern of activities, roles, and interpersonal relations experienced by the developing persons in a given face-to-face setting with particular physical, social, and symbolic features that invite, permit, or inhibit engagement in sustained, progressively more complex interaction with, and activity in, the immediate environment. (p. 15)

We believe that in the twenty-first century "face-to-face" relationships as conceived by Bronfenbrenner may also include digitally mediated interactions, as they represent a substantial number of interactions that students have with peers, family, and others (see Martínez Alemán & Wartman, 2008). Microsystems for college students might include roommates, family, classes, homework groups, athletic teams, on- or off-campus workplaces, laboratory teams, and peer groups from high school as well as college. They are the closest—or most proximal—contexts in which development occurs. For Ana, they are her classes, the student organization, the soccer team, her apartment-mates, and her workplace.

Mesosystem. Mesosystems are created by the coexistence and connections of microsystems, whereby they form "an interactive development field in which an individual is embedded" (Renn, 2004, p. 37). A mesosystem

FIGURE 6.1 BRONFENBRENNER'S ECOLOGY MODEL APPLIED TO COLLEGE STUDENTS

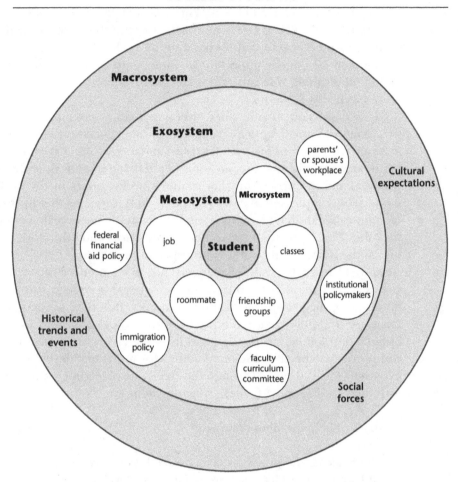

Source: Renn & Arnold, 2003, p. 268. Reconceptualizing research on college student peer culture. *Journal of Higher Education, 74.* Copyright The Ohio State University. Reprinted by permission.

"comprises linkages and processes taking place between two or more settings containing the developing person. Special attention is focused on the synergistic effects created by the interaction of developmentally instigative or inhibitory features and processes present in each setting" (Bronfenbrenner, 1993, p. 22). Mesosystems of peer culture (Renn & Arnold, 2003) have been shown repeatedly to be among the greatest influences on college students, their learning, and their development (see, for example, Astin, 1968, 1977, 1984, 1993a; Clark & Trow, 1966; Feldman & Newcomb, 1969; Kuh, Hu, & Vesper, 2000; Pascarella & Terenzini, 1991, 2005; Tinto, 1993; Weidman, 1989). Other mesosystems, such as those formed by interactions of family and school settings, or work and school, may be equally important to students from diverse backgrounds, including student veterans, first-generation students, and underrepresented minority students.

It is important to note that mesosystems may contain microsystems that reinforce and amplify certain values or expectations (for example, parental expectations for school success and a rigorous curriculum); competing or contradictory microsystems (a job that demands thirty-five hours per week and a curriculum that requires twelve hours in the lab); or a mixture of complementary and competing microsystems that forms a web of supportive and challenging elements. None is necessarily better than the others. Each creates developmental instigators and inhibitors, depending on the nature of the values and expectations that are being amplified, contested, supported, and challenged. Just as we pointed out in previous chapters that there is no one "right" way to be a college student or to undertake college enrollment, there is no one best developmental system for every student. What is required for an ecological system to promote optimal development is the demand from the environment for increasing complexity balanced by adequate buffers for individual development. Ana experiences this balance through the challenge of leading a student group with increased support from her faculty mentor.

Exosystem. The exosystem comprises

> the linkages and processes taking place between two or more settings, at least one of which does not contain the developing person, but in which events occur that indirectly influence processes within the immediate setting in which the developing person lives. (Bronfenbrenner, 1993, p. 24)

As counterintuitive as it may first seem to consider contexts that do not contain the student, there are myriad settings in which decisions are made that affect a student's education that do not contain that—or any—student. For example, federal and state financial aid policies affect the resources available, which in turn may determine how many hours a student will have to work while in college. For dependent students, parental workplace changes, such as layoffs, promotions, or transfers, may influence students' lives. Moreover, the learning and developmental opportunities of students who are themselves parents may be affected by changes in children's day care or school. Federal immigration policy, curriculum decisions, NCAA rules, public transportation schedules—all of these are outside the student's immediate setting but interact with his or her more proximal developmental contexts to create the totality of the ecosystem. Ana's college experience is affected by her parents' careers as well as national accreditation standards for business curricula, among other components of the exosystem.

Macrosystem. Beyond the exosystem lies the macrosystem, an all-encompassing sociohistorical context that contains historical trends, social forces, and cultural expectations that shape the developmental possibilities for individuals and groups of students. Bronfenbrenner (1993) defined the macrosystem as

> the overarching pattern of micro-, meso-, and exosystem characteristics of a given culture, subculture, or other extended social structure, with particular reference to the developmentally instigative belief systems, resources, hazards, lifestyles, opportunity structures, life course options and patterns of social interchange that are embedded in such overarching systems. (p. 25)

The macrosystem, perceived as far from or distal to the individual, contains the sociocultural building blocks that become visible in the proximal processes of student development. Gender, social class, race, ability, and veteran status, among others, are dealt with in the macrosystem differently across time and cultures, creating and denying opportunities for individuals in accordance with larger principals and beliefs related to capitalist and neoliberal ideologies, meritocracy, and contemporary culture. The fact that women, people of color, and working-class people can go into and excel in higher education in the twenty-first century is in part due to changes over time in the macrosystem. Renn and Arnold (2003) proposed that "who attends college and on what terms might seem to be an individual or at least family-based decision, but the conditions that govern college-choice making are located in the macrosystem and only made manifest locally" (p. 273). Ana's decision to attend college, her ability to do so, and her choice of a business major are in part made possible by macrosystem factors.

Time In developmental ecology, time has at least three meanings: the times in which one lives, the timing of an event in an individual's life, and changes in the person and context over time. In some of his writing, Bronfenbrenner called time the *chronosystem* and described its influences thus:

> The individual's own developmental life course is seen as embedded in and powerfully shaped by conditions and events occurring during the historical period through which the person lives . . . A major factor influencing the course and outcome of human development is the timing of biological and social transitions as they relate to the culturally defined age, role expectations, and opportunities occurring throughout the life course. (Bronfenbrenner, 1995, p. 641)

For college students, the era in which they live matters for their educational options, as noted in the earlier discussion of the macrosystem. The time in life in which an individual begins postsecondary education, stops out, and reenters may affect his or her odds of completing a degree, as we described in Chapter Three. The timing of such events as a parental divorce, undertaking military service, partnering, and parenting may all have an influence on the development of the individual student. At the family microsystem level, the same event—the birth of a sibling or death of a parent—may even have different influences on the development of siblings, given their varying ages at the time of the event. The timing of macro-level events, such as the terrorist attacks on the United States on September 11, 2011, may have common effects across an age cohort as well as diverse effects on individuals within that cohort, depending on students' developmentally instigative characteristics and trajectories.

Taken together with their constituent parts, the four components of Bronfenbrenner's developmental ecology model provide a useful framework for understanding *how* development occurs, if not *what* the outcomes of that development will be. Indeed, the framework suggests that development is a highly individual process. Considering the near-infinite possible variations of PPCT factors, it is moderately surprising that anything at all can be said about common developmental trajectories or outcomes. It is important to note that Bronfenbrenner proposed the PPCT model for young children, and that it only recently has been adopted for use in higher education settings (see Guardia & Evans, 2008; King, 2011; Renn, 2003, 2004; Taylor, 2008). It seems, though, to offer a useful perspective for understanding development in context. We turn in the next chapter to the content of student development: *what* is being developed within the PPCT framework.

Conclusion

Holistic and ecological approaches to explaining college student development provide frameworks for understanding diverse students in U.S. higher education. The holistic approach represented in Baxter Magolda's work on self-authorship takes into account interacting aspects of development in cognitive, interpersonal, and intrapersonal domains. The movement toward self-authorship—the ability to think and act from one's internal foundations—is one that many higher education institutions attempt to cultivate in students.

Ecological approaches to understanding student development do not indicate particular desired outcomes; instead they attempt to describe the processes and contexts in which student learning and development occur. They are useful in diverse institutional settings and with students in diverse circumstances (for example, residential students, commuters, online and distance learners, and students who are parents) because they do not prescribe one "best" way to participate in higher education. Taken together with the concept of holistic development toward self-authorship, ecology models provide a way to understand how students in different circumstances might develop in cognitive, interpersonal, and intrapersonal domains.

Points of Discussion

Implications for Students

- To what extent, if at all, is it necessary for students to understand institutional goals for their learning and development? Should institutions be explicit in describing cognitive, interpersonal, and intrapersonal development that they seek to foster in students?
- In what ways are students responsible for nonacademic learning and development? If institutions are to meet students "partway," how can students understand their responsibility to do their part?
- What is the difference, if any, between *learning* and *development*?
- What are the developmental ecologies of students in an array of learning contexts, such as residential campuses, online courses, and part-time programs? What role can or should the institution play in bridging the out-of-college microsystems with the college microsystems?

- What is the role of college choice and transition to college (as discussed in previous chapters) in student development? What opportunities and obstacles lie in those processes that may facilitate or inhibit development toward self-authorship?

Implications for Institutions

- In what ways do differences in type and mission have a bearing on the degree to which institutions consider student development a central purpose?
- To what extent should self-authorship be an explicit goal of higher education institutions?
- Thinking of a specific institution, what features and factors lie in students' exosystems, mesosystems, and microsystems?
- If administrators, like students, operate in ecological systems, what do these systems look like? What factors lie in the various levels of the ecological context that affect decisions and actions?
- Given the emphasis in self-authorship theories and in ecology models on creating contexts for increasingly complex interactions, how can a curriculum and cocurriculum be designed to maximize the likelihood that students will encounter these developmentally meaningful situations?

Implications for Policy and National Discourse

- To what extent should national policy related to college completion goals consider student development as a potential outcome of higher education? For example, when allocating funding, should the federal government take into account the likelihood that certain developmental goals might be achieved at a particular institution?
- How do various federal regulations (such as Title IX, the Cleary Act, FERPA, and those pertaining to student visas) help create an exosystem that affects the contexts for student development? To what extent do federal regulations actually shape developmental contexts?

Learning Activities

- By definition, holistic, integrated development theories require consideration of the overall student experience and multiple factors that affect student success. Considering interactions in your own institution, in what ways are students' holistic, integrated development needs being served? What programs, services, and policies are in place that promote or inhibit students' holistic development? In what ways do students engage in their own development in these areas, and how do they avoid or delay engagement?

- Draw a blank version of the Bronfenbrenner ecology model. Put yourself in the center as the student. Fill in the microsystems, mesosystem, exosystem, and macrosystem in which you participated at a given point in time as an undergraduate student. What developmentally instigative characteristics led you to interact in particular ways in these contexts? What contexts influenced your development, whether or not you were aware of them at the time?

- Consider the differences between self-authorship theories and ecology models of development. Does one or another approach do a better job of explaining why students succeed (or do not succeed) on your campus? For instance, if students at your institution are having difficulty integrating into your campus's system and culture, how would self-authorship theories help make sense of their obstacles? What about ecology models? Are there elements of these two approaches that can be integrated to explain what you see happening on campus for students and their development?

Resource Related to Holistic Student Development

Wabash National Study of Liberal Arts Education: Self-Authorship (http://sitemaker.umich.edu/liberalartstudy/self-authorship)

The site includes self-authorship resources and publications from the Wabash National Study of Liberal Arts Education.

CHAPTER SEVEN

COLLEGE STUDENT DEVELOPMENT THEORIES

Cognitive, Moral, and Psychosocial Identities

One of the basic purposes of higher education is the preservation, transmission, and enrichment of the important elements of culture: the product of scholarship, research, creative imagination, and human experience. It is the task of colleges and universities to vitalize this and other educational purposes as to assist the student in developing to the limits of his potentialities and in making his contribution to the betterment of society.

This philosophy imposes upon educational institutions the obligation to consider the student as a whole—his intellectual capacity and achievement, his emotional make up, his physical condition, his social relationships, his vocational aptitudes and skills, his moral and religious values, his economic resources, and his aesthetic appreciations. It puts emphasis, in brief, upon the development of the student as a person rather than upon his intellectual training alone.

AMERICAN COUNCIL ON EDUCATION, 1937, P. 3

In addition to the holistic and ecological models presented in the previous chapter, there are a number of theories specific to particular aspects of college student development. These theories help explain how students develop cognitively and morally over time, as well as how they develop psychosocial identities including those related to race, ethnicity, gender, and sexual orientation. Research on college students in the 1960s tended toward homogeneous samples; at that time, college campuses were much less diverse than they are in the twenty-first century. Groundbreaking models for understanding cognitive and moral (or ethical) and psychosocial development in college students (Chickering, 1969; Perry,

1970) emerged from this period. In the 1970s and 1980s, as the student population became increasingly diverse, scholars and practitioners seeking theoretical models related to race and gender looked outside the student affairs literature to psychology and sociology. In the 1990s more scholars began examining psychosocial identities among college students in particular. This trend continued into the 2000s, leading to a fairly robust body of literature on college student identity development. At the same time, scholars became interested in understanding how identities, cognition, and interpersonal relationships influence one another, and a parallel trend toward intersectional research is emerging. In this chapter, we describe commonly used models of cognitive, moral, and psychosocial development.

Although we began our discussion in the previous chapter with integrated models of student development that considered cognitive, interpersonal, and intrapersonal domains, we divide these domains into families in this chapter for ease of comprehending individual theories and their intellectual history. As we noted in Chapter Six, the tradition of studying college students has divided development into clusters (Knefelkamp et al., 1978). We believe that student development as a whole is best understood in an integrated fashion, but the specificities of cognitive, moral, and psychosocial developmental outcomes are best understood with the assistance of theories addressing individual domains. The underlying principles of challenge and support (Sanford, 1967); involvement (Astin, 1984); and increasingly complex demands (Bronfenbrenner, 1979, 1993; Kegan, 1982, 1994) remain across areas of development. The ways that cognitive, interpersonal, and intrapersonal development interact were addressed earlier and should be kept in mind while considering theories that address only one component of this complex system at a time.

Cognitive and Moral Development

Theories of cognitive and moral development in college students share common intellectual roots. Patricia King (2009), in defining the topic of cognitive and moral development, stated,

> Cognitive development encompasses a great many theories, constructs, and approaches, including intelligence, scientific problem-solving, metacognition, motivation to learn, learning styles, brain research, and many kinds of cognitive activities. Similarly, the study of morality is also

a broad domain, including character development, empathy, altruism, and spirituality, among others. (p. 598)

We concur with King's description of the topic as it relates to college students, and present here some well-tested and commonly used theories of development in student affairs.

Patrick Love and Victoria Guthrie (1999) provided an excellent summary and analysis of theories of cognitive development, and we recommend it to readers seeking more detail on this topic. They examined a number of cognitive development theories and determined that they shared key concepts. King (2009) noted that the similarities are not a coincidence, as these theories, including the Reflective Judgment Model (RJM) (King & Kitchener, 1994, 2002, 2004) and Women's Ways of Knowing (Belenky, Clinchy, Goldberger, & Tarule, 1986), have common intellectual roots in William Perry's work (1970, 1981).

The cognitive development theories are predominantly stage based. Each traces individual development from a point at which knowledge is absolute, true, and founded on information from authorities. Love and Guthrie (1999) called this *Unequivocal Knowing*. They identified the next common stage as *Radical Subjectivism*, in which truth is subjective, all views and opinions are equally valid, and intuition and personal experience are valued.

A substantial developmental milestone occurs as a *Great Accommodation*—"moving from viewing the world as predominantly known, certain, and knowable to viewing the world as predominantly ambiguous, complex, and not completely knowable" (Love & Guthrie, 1999, p. 79). At this shift, the self as knower emerges, with the ability to construct knowledge and make judgments about the validity of claims and evidence. *Generative Knowing* is the term Love and Guthrie used for the stages after the Great Accommodation, when theories describe in divergent ways individuals' meaning-making, ethical development, and judgment.

Although theorists have used different terminology and come to their conclusions through different means, Love and Guthrie's outline (1999) accurately describes the general trend of all of the theories from a simple, dualistic cognitive and ethical viewpoint to one that is complex enough to account for the messy realities of modern life and work. Perry's work in this area forms a solid foundation for understanding how college students come to think more complexly, and for that reason we highlight it here. For more detail on cognitive development theories we do not address in this chapter, including the RJM and Women's Ways of Knowing, see the original sources or the Love and Guthrie (1999) summary.

Perry's Scheme of Intellectual and Ethical Development

Perry (1970, 1981) based his model for understanding students' intellectual and ethical development on his work in the 1950s and 1960s in the Harvard University Bureau of Study Counsel (a center that combined aspects of contemporary academic advising, counseling, and teaching and learning assistance). He conducted year-end interviews with Harvard men and Radcliffe women, though the group from these elite institutions cannot be considered to represent all college students of the time or the diversity of students in the twenty-first century. Still, the model he developed has held up well as a general description of students' cognitive development and forms a reasonable foundation to guide practice and additional research, whether confirmatory or counter-confirmatory.

Instead of stages, Perry (1981) called the "resting points" (p. 78) in his model *positions.* The positions themselves are static, with development happening in the processes between, not unlike a stair tread (the position) and the stair riser (the developmental process). It is important to note, however, that Perry believed that the positions could vary in duration and that individuals could be in dynamic relationship to the positions, between or across resting points. There are nine positions in the Perry Scheme, divided into four major levels that are adequate to understand the model and to use it effectively (Evans, Forney, Guido, Patton, & Renn, 2010). The first three levels (positions 1 to 5) are cognitive, and the fourth level (positions 6 to 9) involves a shift to ethical development (see King, 1978).

The first level is *Dualism,* which fits into Love and Guthrie's Unequivocal Knowing category (1999). Students who are dualists see the world as black and white, ethical issues as right and wrong, and knowledge as true or false. Authorities, such as faculty, have the correct and true knowledge and judgments.

Second is *Multiplicity,* which evolves as dualistic meaning-making structures cannot accommodate the individual's observations and experiences. Learning that authorities disagree on a complex topic, or meeting peers with different worldviews, could set a student into a multiplistic perspective, which allows for multiple acceptable responses to an unresolved topic for which the "correct" answer is not yet known. In Multiplicity, everyone's opinions could be valid.

The awareness that opinions need evidence to be considered true, and that some "opinions" have reliable evidence to support them whereas others do not, prompts movement into the third level, *Relativism.* As an individual recognizes that some knowledge is more valid than other knowledge, he or she also begins the process of understanding the role of self in the construction and validation of knowledge. In other words, he or she has an active role as a knower.

The fourth level evolves the self-as-knower idea further, to *Commitment in Relativism*. In this level the individual makes ethical choices and commitments based on a relativist standpoint within which he or she must assess knowledge and goodness claims. Negotiating peer relationships, student leadership, or career development might prompt a student to reach this level. This final position in Perry's scheme moves from cognitive into ethical development and connects to theories of moral development in college students, the subject of the next subsection.

Moral Development

Based in psychology and moral philosophy, Lawrence Kohlberg's theory of moral development has dominated the field for several decades. James Rest extended this work, and Carol Gilligan's studies of women's moral development serve as landmarks in understanding the complexity of moral development in diverse populations. All are stage-based models and focus on self in relation to others, with competing or balancing interests of individualism and universalism. Like the cognitive and ethical development theories, these theories progress from less complex, received ways of understanding to more complex, constructed ways. In this case, the object of that understanding is moral decision making as opposed to knowledge and the nature of knowledge.

Kohlberg's Theory of Moral Development Kohlberg (1969) extended Jean Piaget's work (1932, 1977) with young children to address the moral development of adolescents and, later, college students. He revised Piaget's definitions of three early stages of moral development and added three more for adolescents and adults. The theory is based on three criteria: (1) *structure*, which states that an individual will be consistent in his or her stage across contexts and situations; (2) *sequence*, which states that the stages are invariant in their sequence, regardless of experience; and (3) *hierarchy*, which holds that each stage is more complex and highly developed than those before it because previous stages are incorporated into the present stage. Kohlberg further posited that moral development depends on cognitive structures and the ability to put oneself in the place of another. Development is prompted by two factors: exposure to higher-stage thinking and disequilibrium (a challenge to one's existing stage in which the individual experiences conflicts or internal contradictions). This claim reinforces the challenge-support approach to student development (Sanford, 1967), with challenges to the student's current way of reasoning as well as support provided by others who reason at the next-highest level.

Kohlberg (1976) proposed three levels of moral reasoning, which he divided into six stages. The levels are

- *Level One: Preconventional.* Individuals do not yet understand societal rules. They are individually focused, in an effort to avoid punishment and please authorities. Rules are followed if they benefit the individual.
- *Level Two: Conventional.* Individuals seek to meet expectations and rules, especially those held by authorities. Concern is focused outwardly on being seen as a good person, gaining approval, and supporting the system of rules.
- *Level Three: Postconventional or Principled.* Individuals base decisions on overarching moral principles, such as human rights. They evaluate social systems and laws according to their consideration of these moral principles. Participation in the social system is seen as voluntary and requires mutual commitment and trust.

Kohlberg's theory resonates with many scholars and educators. Student affairs professionals working in residence halls or judicial affairs can give abundant examples of students who make decisions at these levels, particularly the first two. Academic integrity and ethics education are other areas in which students' levels in the Kohlberg theory become evident, as students attempt to justify cheating on an exam ("I thought I wouldn't get caught"—Preconventional) or work through professional ethical dilemmas ("My internship supervisor is asking me to do something that I know isn't right"—Conventional).

Rest's Moral Development Stages Working directly from Kohlberg's stages, Rest developed a line of research on moral development, including the Defining Issues Test (DIT), which is widely used with college students. The DIT asks test takers to reason through moral dilemmas that have no clear solutions and that require them to balance individual and social good. Rest viewed moral development more broadly than did Kohlberg, and his theory reflects questions about Kohlberg's three criteria (structure, sequence, and hierarchy). Key among these differences is Rest's assertion that an individual may show evidence of reasoning from more than one stage at a time and that development is not a rigid, stepwise progression, but shifts in regard to the distribution of an individual's reasoning.

Rest (Rest, Narvaez, Thoma, & Bebeau, 2000) offered three schemas that align with Kohlberg's levels and can be tested using the DIT:

1. *Personal Interest Schema*, a childhood schema that focuses on the individual with limited attention to others or the good of the whole
2. *Maintaining Norms Schema*, which focuses on a desire for norms to govern, a belief that rules apply equally, a sense of duty to the whole, and a respect for authority as representative of society's good
3. *Postconventional Schema*, parallel to Kohlberg's Level Three, which focuses on shared ideals and reciprocity

The balance between self and other that is a hallmark of the Rest approach is also seen in Kohlberg's theory, but here it is in the context of a more flexible framework of development. Factors that may prompt an individual to advance across the schema are education, exposure to the world and different worldviews, and exposure to individuals at higher levels of development. The validation and widespread use of Rest's DIT with college students (see King & Mayhew, 2002) makes Rest's theory particularly appealing for research on postsecondary outcomes and practical application in university settings. In Chapter Nine we provide evidence that college students do, in fact, show growth in the complexity of their moral reasoning.

Gilligan's Theory of Women's Moral Development Kohlberg conducted his early research with all-male samples; when he eventually included women, he found that they typically did not reach the higher stages of his theory, which is based on an orientation toward autonomy, justice, and universalizable principles. Gilligan (1982, 1993) took a different approach and found that women's moral development was more likely to be grounded in care and responsibility for others. Moral development for women was a process of balancing self and others, but not in the more instrumental way that Kohlberg and then Rest reflected. Gilligan (1977) examined "progressive differentiation" in how women resolve "conflicts between self and other" (p. 482), moving from less to more complex.

Gilligan's theory includes three levels and two transitions between:

- *Level One: Orientation to Individual Survival*, in which the individual is focused on self and survival, unable to see moral questions that reach beyond herself. Desires and needs are not considered distinct, and self-preservation is the chief motivation.

- *First Transition: From Selfishness to Responsibility,* in which the individual shifts from a focus on self to a focus on others and relationships. Desires and needs are understood differently, and the individual is able to make decisions for reasons other than survival.
- *Level Two: Goodness as Self-Sacrifice,* in which survival is framed as social acceptance, to the point where an individual may resolve moral dilemmas in ways that are seen as most acceptable, even if these go against personal judgment.
- *Second Transition: From Goodness to Truth,* in which individuals question the balance of care for self with care for others, akin to the self-authorship process of locating internal foundations while also considering the interests and needs of others.
- *Level Three: Morality of Nonviolence,* in which the moral mandate not to hurt self or others becomes central. By recognizing that she has a right to include her own needs and desires in decisions affecting others, the individual creates more options for resolving moral dilemmas while not losing herself in the process.

Considering Gilligan's model next to Kohlberg's, it is easy to see how this ethic of care for self and others is not a factor in the latter. Comparison of the two models is usually framed in terms of an ethic of care or an ethic of justice, with women presumed more likely to reason from care and men presumed more likely to reason from justice. In the decades since Gilligan first presented her theory, much research has shown that men and women in college do reason in ways predicted by their gender (see Gump, Baker, & Roll, 2000; Lyons, 1983; Stiller & Forrest, 1990), but some has found small or no differences (Ford & Lowery, 1986). Gilligan herself (1982, 1993) has argued for considering justice and care not as binary but interdependent, and one can imagine individuals being high in both, low in both, or higher in one than in the other.

However moral development is considered, it is linked with cognitive development and the ability to see the world in abstractions that include self, others, justice, care, and social systems. The ability to see a moral dilemma or question is in and of itself a matter of cognitive development, as a dualistic worldview creates little space for understanding that one has a moral choice to make. Similarly, identity development relies in part on the development of cognitive complexity and the ability to see categories of social identities.

Psychosocial Development

Identity development in the higher education literature typically includes general psychosocial identity, such as that described by Erik Erikson (1959/1980, 1963); college student identity, such as that described by Arthur Chickering and Lori Reisser (1993); and more specific socially constructed identities, such as those related to race, ethnicity, gender, and sexual orientation. The study of college students' identities has a tradition in psychology, sociology, and social psychology, among others (see Torres, Jones, & Renn, 2009). The predominance of psychological foundations is due in part to the origins of many student affairs functions (such as career development) in the field of counseling. In this section, we address Erikson's concept of identity and James Marcia's elaboration of it, Chickering and Reisser's theory of identity development, the development of socially constructed identities, and theories related to multiple dimensions of identity and intersectionality.

General Psychosocial Identity Development

General theories of psychosocial identity development provide a foundation for understanding college student experiences and outcomes. The three we present here (originally introduced by Erikson, Marcia, and Chickering) also provide theoretical foundations for several of the theories on specific domains of identity (for example, race, ethnicity, sexual orientation, and gender) we describe later in the chapter.

Erikson's Identity Development Theory Building on the work of Sigmund Freud concerning childhood development, Erikson proposed a lifespan theory (1959/1980, 1963). He based his theory on the *epigenetic principle*, which locates particular developmental crises in the individual's life stage. Although not keyed exclusively to biological age, the crises are prompted by biological development and linked to social and historical constructs related to family, schooling, intimate partnerships, work, parenting, and so forth. In that sense, this principle considers the ecology of the developing person. Erikson proposed eight specific stages. Each stage is marked by a psychosocial crisis, which the individual resolves by balancing internal and external forces (similar to the tension between self and others that appears in Kegan's model). In each case, a healthy resolution forms the foundation for a subsequent stage (see Table 7.1).

TABLE 7.1 SUMMARY OF ERIKSON'S DEVELOPMENTAL STAGES

Stage	Time of Life	Crisis and Resolution
One: Basic Trust Versus Mistrust	First year	A crisis occurs when changes in caregiving require the infant to adapt, learning to trust and reciprocate even in the face of unpredictably.
Two: Autonomy Versus Shame and Doubt	Early childhood	A crisis occurs in the course of the child's developing autonomy through walking, talking, and toilet training. Encouragement and patience provide the child with a foundation for self-determination and confidence; a lack of encouragement—or shaming—results in a sense of shame and doubt.
Three: Initiative Versus Guilt	Preschool	A crisis arises out of conflicts between the child's developing conscience and his or her actions, thoughts, and fantasies. Initiative results from the child's imagination, interactions with others, and imitation of others. The development of moral awareness prompts this crisis.
Four: Industry Versus Inferiority	School age	A crisis occurs as children interact with multiple adults and youth, learning skills that are valued by others. A sense of inferiority may result from inadequate encouragement or recognition of a child's ability to contribute. Industry results from a sense of being appreciated.
Five: Identity Versus Identity Confusion/ Diffusion	Adolescence	A centerpiece of Erikson's theory, the identity crisis marks the transition from childhood to adulthood. Inadequate resolution may result from a lack of sense of self or purpose. Identity resolution occurs as individuals establish a durable internal sense of self that is congruent with external recognition from the earlier stages.
Six: Intimacy Versus Isolation	Young adulthood	A crisis arises out of decisions about fusing with others or remaining detached. Healthy resolution leads to intimate relationships and adult friendships. A lack of a strong sense of identity from the previous stage may result in difficulty establishing relationships and isolation.
Seven: Generativity Versus Stagnation	Midlife	A crisis surrounds the desire to contribute to society and future generations through work, parenting, or community involvement. Healthy resolution leads to an individual's satisfaction in regard to his or her purpose and accomplishments. A lack of direction or sense of purpose results in stagnation.
Eight: Integrity Versus Despair	Late adulthood	A crisis occurs as adults face the realities of changing physical and mental abilities and the awareness that death is inevitable. Integrity results from a feeling that one has accomplished something in one's life. Despair and regret arise from feeling that one has not taken advantage of life's opportunities.

Erikson's Stage Five, Identity Versus Identity Confusion/Diffusion, has been of primary interest to student development researchers because it occurs between childhood and adulthood, when traditional-age students are in college. As college students become more diverse in age and experience, and as the concept of *emerging adulthood* (Arnett, 2000) enters research on college students, increased attention to the developmental challenges of subsequent stages may be important. For example, balancing one's needs and interests as an adult learner may create challenges within intimate relationships (Erikson's Stage Six) or affect one's contributions to one's work, family, or community (Stage Seven). In addition, there may be differences in definitions and in the consideration of identity, self, and community for students from diverse cultural and national backgrounds.

Marcia's Ego Identity Statuses   Erickson's theory extended developmental studies to the lifespan but remained difficult to test empirically. Marcia (1966, 1975, 1980) provided empirical evidence on the identity development of adolescents and young adults. He focused on Erikson's Stage Five, Identity Versus Identity Confusion/Diffusion, and created a four-frame description of the exploration and resolution of adolescent identity crises. The four frames are based on a matrix of two key concepts: *exploration* and *commitment* (see Table 7.2). Exploration, also called crisis (Marcia, 1980), refers to the process of questioning values and goals, and considering alternatives. Marcia's concept of commitment refers to the decisions and actions that individuals take related to values and goals. Commitment can occur without exploration, and exploration does not always lead to commitment. Marcia identified four possible *ego identity statuses*.

TABLE 7.2 MARCIA'S EGO IDENTITY STATUSES

	No Exploration (No Crisis)	Exploration (Crisis)
Commitment	*Foreclosure*—accepts values and goals given by authorities	*Identity Achievement*—Resolves the crisis through considering alternatives and arriving at values and goals consistent with one's internal foundations
No Commitment	*Diffusion*—does not question values and goals given by authorities, but also is willing to accept other values and goals	*Moratorium*—actively questions values and goals given by authorities, without coming to a resolution

Foreclosure (Commitment Without Exploration). Individuals in foreclosure have not explored values and goals but are committed to those received from authorities (such as parents, teachers, and faith leaders). Unless or until they encounter a situation or crisis that cannot be resolved with existing values and goals, students in foreclosure may have little reason to question the status quo. A student may have accepted and committed to a particular career path laid out by family expectations (for example, a student who has always been told she will be a nurse) until something happens that interrupts that path. For example, she may have a transformative encounter that leads her to consider a career as a physician or, on a less happy note, she may struggle to meet grade point requirements for the major and need to adjust her career goals. Foreclosure is the most common identity status among college students (Marcia, 1994).

Diffusion (No Commitment, No Exploration). An individual in this status does not actively question values and goals given by authorities but is also not firmly committed to these values and goals. A "go with the flow" (Evans et al., 2010, p. 54) student who is susceptible to conformity and manipulation (Marcia, 1994), he or she reflects a state of unexamined noncommitment. Unsure what he or she truly believes and not particularly disturbed by this uncertainty, such a student might have trouble making or following through with decisions about his or her academic major, career, or intimate relationships.

Moratorium (Exploration Without Commitment). This status represents individuals who are actively questioning values and goals but have not yet reached a commitment. They may be working through anxiety related to resisting or conforming to authority, or trying out values and goals before fully committing to them (Marcia, 1994). Baxter Magolda (2001b) referred to a similar process as the Crossroads, when external formulas come into question and internal foundations must be constructed. A student considering a change in major and career might talk to friends, attend campus programs, consult with academic advisers and faculty, or explore online resources related to the new career. When he felt confident enough, he would proceed with his commitment, signaling his transition to Identity Achievement.

Identity Achievement (Exploration Followed by Commitment). According to Marcia (1980), Identity Achievement is the healthiest status and typically follows a period of crisis and exploration in Moratorium. The individual has explored values and goals, determined the personal best course, and acted (or begun to act) on a commitment to a particular direction. Although it sounds like a steady state of lifelong identity certainty, in fact this status is often a foundation for further explorations and commitments (Marcia, 1994). A student in this status is likely to have clear commitments to academic, career, and personal goals and to be able to explain those commitments in ways that are congruent with his or her values. He or she may yet change direction, but such a change would occur after another period of identity exploration and recommitment.

College Student Identity: Chickering's Seven Vectors In his 1969 book *Education and Identity*, Chickering proposed one of the most widely recognized student development theories. His theory expands Erikson's identity stages and Marcia's ego identity statuses into seven related but distinct "vectors" with "direction and magnitude" (Chickering, 1969, p. 8). Based on extensive data collection at small colleges in the early 1960s (see Thomas & Chickering, 1984), the first iteration of the theory (Chickering, 1969) was soon adopted by educators and counselors. Extensive testing of the theory through the Student Developmental Task and Lifestyle Assessment (Winston, Miller, & Cooper, 1999a, 1999b) and the Iowa Student Development Inventory (Hood, 1986, 1997) revealed that it is generally robust. The homogeneous nature of the original sample on which it was based and changing student demographics, however, called for a revision of the seven vectors, which Chickering accomplished with Reisser. Together they published a second edition of *Education and Identity* (Chickering & Reisser, 1993), in which they reordered some of the vectors and expanded the definitions of most.

Several important concepts form the foundation for the theory. First, progression through the vectors is not linear. This model is not stage based. Students may move through the vectors at different rates, be in more than one vector at a time, and circle back through vectors as circumstances change (Chickering & Reisser, 1993). Second, although the vectors are not linear, earlier vectors do form a foundation for growth along later vectors. Third, as with the other theories discussed in this chapter, a key to progress along the vectors is the development of a greater ability to manage complexity (Chickering & Reisser). Finally, there is evidence that the seven vectors are applicable to traditional-age students and adult learners (see Chickering & Reisser).

Testing of the theory shows that there are ways in which it does not fully describe the identity development experiences of diverse populations (see Pope, Reynolds, & Mueller, 2004; Torres, Howard-Hamilton, & Cooper, 2003). Reisser (1995) pointed out that more research was needed on issues related to age, sexual orientation, race, and culture in relation to identity development theories that claim to be inclusive. That said, the seven vectors remain a solid starting place for exploring identity development specific to college students. Educators and scholars can use the underlying concepts of the vectors to design culturally sensitive programs, curricula, and research that may contribute to student learning and development. We discuss the seven vectors and how they work in the college environment in the following subsections.

Developing Competence. Intellectual competence, physical and manual skills, and interpersonal competence make up the "three-tined pitchfork" (Chickering & Reisser, 1993, p. 38) of this vector. Intellectual competence—a primary goal of higher education generally—is made up of academic skills and knowledge specific to one's major and across general education areas. Physical and manual skills may relate to participation in sports, performing and visual arts, wellness activities, or even video gaming. Interpersonal competence encompasses the skills of relationship building and leadership, whether in person or using various communication media. These three tines are supported by the pitchfork's handle, which is the feeling of "confidence that one can cope with what comes and achieve goals successfully" (Chickering & Reisser, p. 53). Faculty, academic advisers, coaches, student leaders, and peers may reinforce this sense of confidence as students achieve competence across the three areas.

Managing Emotions. Recognizing, accepting, expressing, controlling, and acting on emotions appropriately are the focus of this vector (Chickering & Reisser, 1993). College students experience the full range of human emotions, yet may not have learned how to manage them. In this vector, students learn to accept emotions and find responsible outlets for expressing them (Chickering & Reisser). Student affairs professionals in a variety of contexts (academic and career advising, residence life, judicial affairs, counseling) have opportunities to help students recognize emotions and channel them into appropriate expressions. When things go wrong with excessive celebration, angry outbursts, or violence, campus safety officers may also be involved in helping students develop emotional management skills.

Moving Through Autonomy Toward Interdependence. Interdependence is marked by a sense of personal independence with an awareness of interconnectedness with other people. Students who are moving toward self-authorship (see Baxter Magolda, 2001b) and those who have more complex views of student leadership (see Komives, Casper, Longerbeam, Mainella, & Osteen, 2005; Komives, Longerbeam, Owen, Mainella, & Osteen, 2006) demonstrate the hallmarks of this vector. Advisers, mentors, and counselors may be able to help students understand themselves as both independent and interdependent.

Developing Mature Interpersonal Relationships. Growth in this vector involves developing intercultural competence, an appreciation of differences, and an understanding of mutuality in the establishment of intimate relationships with partners and friends (Chickering & Reisser, 1993). In-person and online college settings offer opportunities for students to learn about others from different backgrounds and to establish mature, mutual relationships with them.

Establishing Identity. Not surprisingly, given that Chickering's theory is about *identity,* this vector is a centerpiece. It builds on the four vectors before it and provides a foundation for the two that come after. In the second iteration of the theory (Chickering & Reisser, 1993), this vector includes explicit attention to gender, race and ethnicity, and sexual orientation. Understanding and being comfortable with who one is—one's body and appearance, heritage, self-concept, roles, and lifestyle—are critical tasks of this vector. Given the diversity of students it is impossible to pin down all of the elements that go into a healthy sense of identity, but the key concepts of acceptance of and comfort with self cut across variations of experience, demographics, social roles, and educational goals. Colleges and universities are locations for the exploration of various facets of self through academic, social, political, and peer contexts. Faculty, student affairs professionals, and peers play a role in providing exposure to cultural and intellectual expressions of identity. Viewed through the lens of Marcia's concepts (1966, 1980) of exploration and commitment, this vector represents a milestone of Identity Achievement.

Developing Purpose. Following the establishment of identity, this vector focuses on developing goals for one's vocation, personal interests, and activities in the context of interpersonal commitments. *Vocation* refers to paid or unpaid work that contributes to a more or less coherent sense of "career" (which does not have to be a traditional one-job-for-a-lifetime endeavor). Important others, such as partners, family, or close friends, influence the development of purpose, as do values and goals. Advisers and counselors may assist students in developing purpose by helping them connect academic activities to larger goals; faculty may be able to leverage students' developing sense of purpose to motivate and encourage them to persist with increasingly challenging academic activities that will further those goals.

Developing Integrity. Chickering and Reisser (1993) divided this vector into three components that are "sequential but overlapping" (p. 51): humanizing values, personalizing values, and developing congruence. Students progress from a rigid system of values to one that is more humanized, balancing others' needs with their own. Then they personalize their system of values by affirming their own core values while acknowledging the values of others. Finally, they develop congruence as values and actions align in a balance of self-interest and sense of social responsibility. This overall integrity permeates across the vectors to bring competence, emotions, relationships, identity, and purpose together in a coherent way. Providing opportunities for students to make these elements "object" (Kegan, 1982, 1994); examine them for coherence; and begin to work to align their values and commitments is one way that institutions can contribute to students' growth along this vector. Pointing out examples of individuals who embody this integrity is another. Many students may not be ready to pull their entire development into congruence, but by pointing out that this is possible—or by pointing out when students' speech and actions lack integral congruence—educators lay a foundation for potential future growth.

Putting the Vectors Together in the Environment. Chickering and Reisser (1993) proposed seven key factors in higher education environments that contribute to students' development along the vectors. They are (1) institutional objectives, (2) institutional size, (3) student-faculty relationships, (4) curriculum, (5) teaching, (6) friendships and student communities, and (7) student development programs and services. Taken in the ecological perspective we described in Chapter Six, these factors can be seen as influences on the exosystem, mesosystem, and microsystems of each student. These key factors represent critical components of how and in what context growth occurs along the vectors. Bronfenbrenner (1979, 1993) would point out that the student's developmentally instigative characteristics play an important role in how each of these key factors interacts with him or her as learning and development occur.

College students in the twenty-first century operate in a landscape different from those of students in the 1960s through 1980s, when the vectors were developed and revised. Connections to parents have extended into the period of emerging adulthood (Tanner, Arnett, & Leis, 2008), and commitment to life partners happens later in the life course than it did in previous generations (Kreider & Ellis, 2011). Digital media and social networking have altered communication patterns, and notions of privacy and intimacy have changed as well (Martínez Alemán & Wartman, 2008). Yet promoting student development along the lines of the seven vectors remains among the goals of student affairs professionals and other educators (Evans et al., 2010).

Racial and Ethnic Identity Development

In the early twenty-first century, race and ethnicity are highly salient central organizing categories and form the basis of identities in U.S. society and on college campuses (Patton, 2010). Most social scientists and educators agree that race is a social construction based on the meanings that individuals and groups give to observable physical features (such as skin color or facial features); ancestry; nationality; and culture (see Ladson-Billings, 1998; Omi & Winant, 2004; Smedley & Smedley, 2005). Ethnicity, also socially constructed, derives from meanings given to cultural and social practices and beliefs, such as language, traditions, and religion (Phinney, 1990). It is important to note that although race and ethnicity may be considered social constructions, these categories are also clearly defined by the federal government (Office of Management and Budget, 1997); affect public policy (including school desegregation, affirmative action, and immigration); and have real consequences in the lives of individuals. Throughout this book, we present evidence that people from different racial and ethnic groups experience education, including higher education, in different ways and with different outcomes.

We are concerned in this chapter with *racial identity* and *ethnic identity* as part of overall student development in the college environment. Although there is general agreement that race and ethnicity are socially constructed at macro and micro levels of society, there is less agreement about how racial and ethnic identities develop at the individual level. We present two general types of models, those that portray a more or less sequential progression along a set of stages, statuses, or "sectors" (Cross & Fhagen-Smith, 2001), and those that avoid a sequential portrayal of identity.

We start from three key assumptions. First, race and ethnicity are core components of overall psychosocial identity and development (Evans et al., 2010; Torres et al., 2009). Second, racial and ethnic identity development processes cannot be understood outside the context of racialized social, political, and economic systems that privilege whiteness (Kodama, McEwen, Liang, & Lee, 2001, 2002; Solórzano, Ceja, & Yosso, 2000; Torres, 2003; Torres & Hernandez, 2007). Racial and ethnic identities develop in, outside, and in relation to groups of which one sees oneself as a member and groups to which one does not belong. These groups are valued differently in society and by one another. Third, opportunities to develop a sense of identity and group membership vary according to factors in the individual's developmental ecology (Guardia & Evans, 2008; King, 2011; Renn, 2003, 2004; Taylor, 2008; Wijeyesinghe, 2001). In reference to college students, campuses—whether bricks and mortar or virtual—offer different micro- and mesosystems in relation to racial and ethnic groups and identities (see King, 2011; Renn, 2000, 2004). These three assumptions underlie the theories we present and processes we discuss.

Models of Progression to Black, Asian American, and White Identities Beginning in the 1970s, researchers, primarily from the psychological tradition, began examining the development of black and other minority identities (Atkinson, Morten, & Sue, 1979; Cross, 1971; Jackson, 1976). They found a recurring pattern of development that has held up in revised iterations and with different populations (see Cross & Fhagen-Smith, 2001; Kim, 2001; Sue & Sue, 2003). A version of this pattern was found to fit white identity development as well (Helms, 1990, 1995). In rough outline, the pattern follows a trajectory from a lack of awareness of race through an event or period of dissonance, to immersion in one's own race, to an integration of racial identity (see Sue & Sue, 2003). For traditional-age students, college may offer a number of opportunities for dissonance and immersion. We present three examples of these models and suggest deeper reading in other sources, for example Jackson and Wijeyesinghe's edited volume *New Perspectives on Racial Identity Development, Second Edition* (2012).

Black Identity Development. In 1971 William Cross introduced an enduring model for black identity development, with an updated model published in 2001 with Peony Fhagen-Smith. The model changed over time from four or five more or less linear stages to a lifespan approach. The 2001 iteration (Cross & Fhagen-Smith, 2001) includes six sectors that account for influences across the lifespan.

Sector One (Infancy and Childhood in Early Black Identity Development) occurs before the child is aware of racism or racial identity and includes family-related factors, such as income and social capital, and social networks through the school and neighborhood. *Sector Two (Preadolescence)* emerges from parental and other influences on the young person that result in three potential identity types: low race salience, high race salience, or internalized racism. Low race salience children receive few messages about the social and cultural importance of their race. High race salience children are taught to view black culture as valuable and important in their self-concept. Internalized racism results from observing patterns of negativity about black culture and identity.

Cross and Fhagen-Smith (2001) used Marcia's identity statuses (1980) to describe *Sector Three (Adolescence)*. Black youth enter adolescence with a foreclosed racial identity (not explored but committed); enter Moratorium as they begin to explore their racial identity and its meaning; then reach Identity Achievement when they realize that their racial identity is of their own choosing, not given to them by others (a self-authored identity). This identity may be of low or high race salience, or internalized racism.

Black teens then enter *Sector Four (Early Adulthood)* with one of three types of racial identity (foreclosed, moratorium, or achieved) and one of three saliences (low race salience, high race salience, or internalized racism). If they have high race salience and an Achieved Identity status, they are considered by Cross and Fhagen-Smith (2001) to have achieved *Nigrescence Pattern A*. Individuals with low race salience or internalized racism are most likely to undergo *nigrescence*, or "the process of becoming Black" (Cross, 1991, p. 147), in the next sector.

Sector Five (Adult Nigrescence) is Cross's original four-stage model of nigrescence (1991). The first stage is *preencounter*, which entails a lack of awareness of racial identity. *Encounter* occurs when an unexpected situation or series of events brings the individual's attention to racial identity. *Immersion-emersion* involves two processes: *immersion* entails disengagement from white culture and full engagement in black culture, with a pro-black perspective, then *emersion* begins a transition out of that dichotomous worldview into the fourth stage of nigrescence, *internalization/commitment*. Internalization/commitment may entail a black nationalist, a bicultural, or a multicultural perspective. Individuals who undergo this four-stage process are said to represent *Nigrescence Pattern B* (Cross & Fhagen-Smith, 2001).

Sector Six (Nigrescence Recycling), also considered *Nigrescence Pattern C* (Cross & Fhagen-Smith, 2001), occurs when a preexisting black identity is called into question. Cross and Fhagen-Smith (2001) theorized that this recycling occurs throughout adulthood. Recycling may lead to the development of *wisdom*, a complex and multidimensional meaning-making system related to black identity.

Strengths of the Cross and Fhagen-Smith (2001) model are its lifespan approach and (implicit) ecological orientation—individual development occurs across time, situated in home, school, work, and family contexts. For college student development, the model points to a number of situations in which racial identity could be enacted and development could be supported (or hindered). For example, the availability of curricular, cocurricular, and social programs and services related to black culture, history, and identity could prompt exploration, increase race salience, or counter internalized racism.

Asian American Identity Development. Based on her 1981 dissertation research, Jean Kim (2001) offered a model of "five conceptually distinct, sequential, and progressive stages" (p. 67) of Asian American identity development. The stages and the processes occurring in them are similar to elements of the Cross and Fhagen-Smith (2001) model for black identity development. They share an orientation toward examining the role of racism in the development of identity. Kim blurred distinctions between "race" and "ethnicity" in some of the language of her model, and it is important to note that "Asian American" is a federally designated racial category made up of diverse language, cultural, ethnic, and national groups that have immigrated to the United States.

The first stage is *Ethnic Awareness.* Before school, families are the primary source of identification for children in this stage, which focuses on the discovery of ethnic heritage (Kim, 2001). Stage two is *White Identification.* School-age children may have learned Asian American cultural norms, which Kim (2001) described in part as having a collective group orientation and avoiding sticking out in groups. When other children point to the differences between Asian Americans and other groups, these cultural norms may lead Asian American children to attempt to fit in and become high performers, potentially rejecting Asian identity and internalizing what they perceive as whiteness. Some students are likely to enter college in this stage. The third stage is *Awakening to Political Consciousness,* a time of externalizing responsibility for being treated differently and recognizing that one is embedded in a racist society. Individuals in this stage reject the superiority of whiteness. This awareness may lead to involvement in social and political action, such as that offered by some college student organizations. *Redirection to Asian American Consciousness* is the fourth stage. This stage entails pride in one's racial identity and conscious identification with other Asian Americans (Kim, 2001). Actors in the micro- and mesosystems (parents, siblings, friends, classmates, and faculty) can be important in this process of becoming part of a group and exploring cultural heritage. The fifth stage is *Incorporation*. Confidence in one's Asian American identity and positive self-concept are hallmarks of this stage (Kim, 2001). Emerging from the immersion-like aspects of the previous stage, individuals in Incorporation interact comfortably across racial groups. They also can focus on other identity dimensions, such as gender, sexual orientation, or ability, without threatening or abandoning their Asian American identity.

This progression—from the dawning of ethnic awareness through incorporation of a positive racial identity into the fullness of other identities and communities—is not unique to Asian Americans, but Kim's model (2001) accounts for some of the experiences specific to growing up Asian American in a predominantly white society. Social values of collective group orientation and shame avoidance, combined with pervasive expectations conveyed through the "Model Minority Myth" (see Museus & Kiang, 2009), create a developmental ecology that presses on individuals to express Asian American identity, regardless of ethnic and national heritage, in particular ways—not too loud or proud, but always high performing. Not coincidentally, these behaviors (conformity, academic excellence) are valued in higher education, where they may be further reinforced.

White Identity Development. Like Cross and Kim, Janet Helms (1992, 1995) recognized that racial identities in the United States are formed in and shaped by a social system of racial inequality. Although most attention went to creating models of so-called minority identity development (see the models discussed in this chapter, as well as Atkinson, Morten, & Sue, 1979; Sue & Sue, 2003), Helms turned her attention to the development of white racial identity. Drawing on the psychological intellectual tradition of which she is part, Helms (1992, 1995) proposed that white identity develops in two phases: *Abandonment of Racism* and *Evolution of a Nonracist Identity*.

Helms included six stages, which she called statuses, in a 1995 iteration of her White Racial Identity Model (Helms, 1995). The first three fall into the Abandonment of Racism phase. *Contact* is a "color-blind" status in which the individual is aware that race exists, but fails to understand the salience of race and racial identities. *Disintegration* occurs when the individual encounters an experience or knowledge that demonstrates the privileges of being white; guilt and shame are common reactions to this transition. If these negative emotions are overwhelming, the individual may move into the *Reintegration* status, in which he or she adopts a "blame the victim" attitude that white people are superior to members of other groups, who would not experience racism if they worked harder, behaved better, and so forth.

Overcoming these racist feelings leads an individual into *Pseudo-Independence*, the first status of the Evolution of a Nonracist Identity phase. Individuals in Pseudo-Independence look to people of color, not white people, to confront and remedy racism. In Pseudo-Independence, the white person still cannot hold "white" and "nonracist" in the same identity and thus puts his or her own "white" identity to the side, seeking validation of his or her nonracist self through the affirmation of people of color. In *Immersion/Emersion*, people attempt to make genuine connection to their white identity and to nonracism, sometimes working to educate other white people about racism. *Autonomy* represents the final status of the Evolution of a Nonracist Identity phase, in which the individual has a clear and positive sense of white identity as well as a commitment to pursuing nonracist and antiracist social justice.

A fully developed white identity, then, is one that accommodates the complexities of living with—and being aware of—privilege while also undertaking the work of changing the very system that perpetuates that privilege. It is this kind of complexity that illustrates the interconnectedness of cognitive, interpersonal, and intrapersonal (or psychosocial) development we discussed earlier in the chapter; an individual lacking the cognitive complexity to understand racial identity in context will struggle to reach the Autonomy stage, and an individual lacking well-developed interpersonal skills will be unable to muster the multicultural competence (see King & Baxter Magolda, 2005) to enact an antiracist social agenda.

Nonlinear Approaches to Latino/a, American Indian, and Mixed-Race Identities Finding that the more or less linear models did not represent the experiences and identities of some populations, researchers proposed other approaches to understanding the racial identity development of Latino/a (Ferdman & Gallegos, 2001); American Indian (Horse, 2001);

and mixed-race individuals (Renn, 2004). Rather than posit specific, ordered developmental milestones, these researchers described identity orientations, consciousness, or patterns exhibited by members of these respective groups. How individuals come to these identities is specific to the ways in which race, ethnicity, and color play a role for each group within U.S. society.

Latino/a Identity. Although the U.S. government defines Latino/a as an *ethnic* category,[1] there is plentiful evidence that in the lived experience of Latino/a people it is considered a *racial* category (Brown, Hitlin, & Elder, 2006; Harris & Sim, 2002). Whatever the category is called, there are a number of sociocultural factors that influence the identities of Latino/as in the U.S. that are distinct from those affecting other racial groups. A history of European colonization of the Americas, importation of African slaves, and enslavement of indigenous peoples resulted in a Latino/a population that includes multiple heritages, skin colors, and attitudes about racial categorization (see Ferdman & Gallegos, 2001). Contemporary immigration trends and backlash also play a role in Latino/a identification and identity development.

Bernardo Ferdman and Plácida Gallegos (2001) considered these factors and the racial system in the United States when they offered a framework for understanding Latino/a identity. They did not propose a stage-based model, but offered six "orientations" to Latino/a identity. The orientations are based on five factors: "one's 'lens' toward identity, how individuals prefer to identify themselves, how Latinos/as as a group are seen, how whites are seen, and how 'race' fits into the equation" (Ferdman & Gallegos, 2001, p. 49). Although not explicitly pointed out by Ferdman and Gallegos, these factors illuminate aspects of one's ecology (for example, person-environment interactions within an ecosystem) and of one's ability to self-author (following racial formulas or establishing internal foundations).

The six orientations are

- *Latino-integrated,* a holistic self-concept that integrates Latino identity with other aspects of identity (similar to the final stages of linear

---

[1]Specifically, the federal categories for ethnicity are "Hispanic or Latino" and "Not Hispanic or Latino" (Office of Management and Budget, 1997).

models). This orientation involves the ability to see racial constructs in the United States, to challenge racism, and to see self in relation to multicultural society.

- *Latino-identified*, a pan-Latino identification in which race is fluid and U.S. racial constructs are rejected. All Latinos are considered one racial group, and whites may be seen as supportive or not (similar to immersion-emersion in linear models).
- *Subgroup-identified*, a strong identification with one's subgroup of origin (for example Dominican, Mexican, or Puerto Rican), not aligned with the larger pan-Latino group. Race not as significant as culture or ethnicity, which define one's subgroup.
- *Latino as other*, a mixed identification and generic affiliation with people of color. Individuals with this orientation do not place themselves in a rigid racial category or identify with a specific racial group.
- *Undifferentiated/Denial*, a color-blind approach and belief that race is unimportant. Individuals with this orientation do not connect with other Latinos, they live according to the dominant culture, and they do not see racism as systemic. This orientation represents a somewhat passive approach to not identifying as Latino, similar to the White Identification stage in Asian American identity.
- *White-identified*, whereby an individual holds a white racial identity and lives his or her life as a white person. Individuals with this orientation see other racial groups, including Latinos, as inferior. This orientation constitutes an active approach to white identification.

The identities of Latino/a college students are of particular interest for the ways in which they involve complex understandings of the role of color, language, ethnicity, and culture on and off campus (see Guardia & Evans, 2008; Torres, 1999, 2003). In an elaboration of her study (Torres, 1999) of bicultural (Hispanic and Anglo) orientation among Latino students, Vasti Torres (2003) proposed a conceptual model of Latino ethnic identity. In a longitudinal study, she found three major influences on ethnic identity in the first year of college: the environment in which the student grew up, family influence and generational status, and the student's self-perception and status in society. Students underwent two processes in ethnic identity change: cultural dissonance and changes in relationships. Although not explicitly grounded in ecological theory, Torres's model (1999, 2003) reflects key tenets of the person, process, and context elements of the ecology model (Bronfenbrenner, 1979, 1993) described in Chapter Six.

Torres (Torres & Baxter Magolda, 2004; Torres & Hernandez, 2007) explicitly linked her longitudinal study to the holistic development model advanced by Baxter Magolda (2001b). Torres and colleagues showed that increased complexity in ethnic identity (intrapersonal) coincided with increased cognitive complexity. Students moved from external formulas, such as stereotypes, to internal foundations of Latino identity.

American Indian Identity. Very little research has addressed the issue of American Indian identity in college students. Given the diversity of tribal cultures, languages, histories, and contemporary circumstances, it is difficult to imagine one developmental model that can describe American Indian racial and ethnic identities (see Choney, Berryhill-Paapke, & Robbins, 1995; Horse, 2001). In addition, the category "American Indian" or "Native American" constitutes both a race and a political entity that has legal and contractual rights vis-à-vis the U.S. government (see Brayboy, 2005), so American Indian identity is potentially racial, tribal/national, or both. White colonization and ongoing resolutions of disputes between tribal nations and the U.S. government play a role in individual identification as well.

In light of these factors, Perry Horse (2001) proposed five elements of American Indian group and individual "consciousness" (p. 100):

- *Knowledge of native language and culture.* Language facilitates individual identity development and is a key means of transmission of culture, values, and behaviors. Knowledge of tribal culture and history includes what it means to be Indian.
- *Validity of Indian genealogical heritage.* Genealogical heritage is a matter of upbringing as well as tribal law.
- *Respect for Indian traditions and philosophical views.* This respect involves maintaining one's traditional culture and perspectives.
- *Self-identification as Indian.* Self-identification is rooted in the individual's commitment to his or her Indian identity.
- *Tribal membership status.* This element refers to one's legal status within an officially recognized tribe.

These five elements describe aspects of the person and the context (Bronfenbrenner, 1993) that contribute to identity development. Depending on the institution and its representation of American Indian students, faculty, and staff, individuals may find college a time for exploration of and commitment to their American Indian identity or a time of isolation from their family, heritage, and traditions. As we discussed in Chapter Five, Tribal Colleges and Universities have explicit missions to preserve and transmit tribal languages, traditions, and cultures (Guillory & Ward, 2008), though they are not the only places where students might encounter these opportunities.

Mixed-Race Identity. Beginning in the 1990s, researchers acknowledged that the identity development of people with parents from two or more racial groups (called biracial, multiracial, multiple heritage, or mixed-race individuals) did not follow the linear models of identity development that were in place for monoracial (that is, having parents from the same race) individuals. Walker S. Carlos Poston (1990) proposed a stage-based model that did not involve complete rejection of the majority culture (as "immersion-emersion" implies). Poston's pioneering work was followed by a number of studies specific to college students and young adults (Kilson, 2001; Renn, 2004; Rockquemore & Brunsma, 2002; Root, 2003a, 2003b; Wallace, 2001) that called for an alternative to a linear model.

Kristen Renn (2003, 2004) described five patterns of mixed-race identity in college students and the ecological factors that led to them. The five patterns are

- *Monoracial Identity,* or identifying with one racial heritage. "I'm black" or "I'm Asian American."
- *Multiple Monoracial Identity,* or identifying with more than one racial heritage—but only one at a time. "I am Latino and white."
- *Multiracial Identity,* or identifying with a new, multiracial category, outside the monoracial paradigm. "I'm *hapa*" or "I'm mixed."
- *Extra-Racial Identity,* or opting out of a racial identification system, deconstructing racial categories. "I don't check any box."
- *Situational Identity,* or shifting identification depending on environmental factors. "When I'm with my fraternity, I identify as white. When I'm with my Asian friends, I identify as Korean."

Variations on these patterns are seen across studies of mixed-race and bi- or multiracial identity (Kilson, 2001; Rockquemore & Brunsma, 2002; Root, 2003a, 2003b; Wallace, 2001), with Situational Identity being the most common (Renn, 2004).

Renn (2004) described a number of ecological factors involved in mixed-race identity, including family, peers, physical appearance, and cultural knowledge. Charmaine Wijeyesinghe (2001) proposed a Factor Model of Multiracial Identity, which included eight factors: (1) early experience and socialization, (2) cultural attachment, (3) racial ancestry, (4) physical appearance, (5) social and historical context, (6) other social identities, (7) spirituality, and (8) political awareness and orientation. Other scholars (Kilson, 2001; Rockquemore & Brunsma, 2002; Root, 2003a, 2003b; Wallace, 2001) have identified similar factors, with physical appearance, racial ancestry, cultural attachment and knowledge, and sociohistorical context key among them.

Sexual Orientation and Gender Identity Development

As noted in Chapter Five, although it has become commonplace to group sexual orientation and gender identity in the acronym LGBT (for lesbian, gay, bisexual, and transgender), the concepts are distinct but related. Gender identity is one's sense of self as male, female, or outside or in between these categories (Bilodeau & Renn, 2005; Lev, 2004). If gender identity matches biological sex, one is considered *cisgender*; if it differs, one is considered *transgender* (Bilodeau, 2009). Sexual orientation refers to one's gender identity and the gender or genders of those to whom one is attracted. A lesbian is a woman attracted to women, a gay man is attracted to other men, a bisexual man or woman is attracted to both men and women, and a heterosexual is a man (or woman) attracted to a woman (or man). Sexual orientation identity refers to one's sense of self as lesbian, gay, bisexual, or heterosexual (Levine & Evans, 1991).

Lesbian, Gay, and Bisexual Identity Development As with the racial identity development models, early work on sexual orientation identity followed stage-based patterns progressing from a lack of awareness, to identity exploration and immersion (or pride), to positive identity integration (see Cass, 1979, 1984; Savin-Williams, 1988, 1990; Troiden, 1979, 1988). The focus of these models was largely on resolution of internal feelings with the external presentation of self through a process of *coming out* to self and others (Bilodeau & Renn, 2005). Applying an ecological lens to these models shows that interactions with others in the immediate microsystems, as well as mesosystem influences, exosystem structures, and macrosystem cultures, influence whether and how an individual moves through the stages.

Ruth Fassinger and colleagues (Fassinger, 1998; Fassinger & Miller, 1997; McCarn & Fassinger, 1996; Mohr & Fassinger, 2000) proposed a model of lesbian identity development that addressed what they saw as the limitations of theories based on a linear progression of coming out to self, then others. They proposed parallel processes of identity development that relate to concepts of self-identity and reference group orientation (Cross, 1991). Within each strand there are four phases: awareness, exploration, deepening/commitment, and internalization/synthesis (Fassinger, 1998). By separating the processes, Fassinger and colleagues provided a model for understanding how an individual might be deeply committed to a personal identity without participating heavily in an LGB(T) community.

Anthony D'Augelli (1994) also split the processes of personal identification from group identification and participation in his lifespan model of LGB identity development. He proposed six nonsequential "identity processes" (p. 319) of LGB identity development:

- *Exiting heterosexual identity*—acknowledging to self (and possibly others) that one is not heterosexual
- *Developing a personal LGB identity status*—making meaning for oneself of LGB identity and challenging internalized stereotypes
- *Developing an LGB social identity*—creating a network of people who know and accept one's LGB identity
- *Becoming an LGB offspring*—telling one's parents and family about one's LGB identity and dealing with positive and negative outcomes
- *Developing an LGB intimacy status*—establishing intimate emotional and physical relationships according to one's sexual orientation
- *Entering an LGB community*—committing to various levels of involvement with social and political groups of LGB people

Higher education offers a number of opportunities for students to develop LGB identity. On many campuses, students can explore LGB identity through courses on film, history, literature, or biology, and can participate in campus groups. Around two hundred institutions (mainly four-year, public and private) staff an LGBT campus resource office (see www.lgbtcampus.org) that provides programs, education, networking, and other student services. With increasing numbers of students coming to higher education already identified as LGB and having participated in high school gay-straight alliances (see Russell, Muraco, Subramaniam, & Laub, 2009), these programs and services may need to adapt to meet changing needs.

Heterosexual Identity Development There are few published accounts of heterosexual identity development in college. Mueller and Cole (2009) examined "heterosexual consciousness" among college students to determine how they made meaning of their sexual orientation, finding among other themes that it meant "not being homosexual" (p. 326). Heterosexual identity for the fourteen participants in this study was established early in life and presumed by them to be the norm until they were faced with counterevidence. Mueller and Cole reported that few participants had "considered, questioned, or explored their sexuality" (p. 326).

Roger Worthington and colleagues (Worthington, Savoy, Dillon, & Vernaglia, 2002) proposed a Multidimensional Model of Heterosexual Identity Development that incorporates several ecological factors. Worthington et al. (2002) identified six "biopsychosocial" (p. 501) influences on heterosexual identity development: (1) biology; (2) culture; (3) religious orientation; (4) gender norms and socialization; (5) microsocial context; and (6) systemic homonegativity, sexual prejudice, and privilege. They specified two domains in which heterosexual identity development occurs, the Individual Identity and the Social Identity. Finally, they used Marcia's ego identity statuses (1966), based on exploration and commitment, to describe heterosexual identity development, pointing to a societal norm of "unexplored commitment" to heterosexual identity. Studies (Worthington, Dillon, & Becker-Schutte, 2005; Worthington, Navarro, Savoy, & Hampton, 2008) have begun to provide empirical support for the Multidimensional Model of Heterosexual Identity Development, which remains the most descriptive framework available for considering heterosexual college students' sexual orientation identity development.

Gender Identity Development It is generally thought that gender identity is established well before college (see Bem, 1983; Davis, 2002; Harris & Harper, 2008), though for transgender students college may provide opportunities to explore gender identity in ways that were not available in prior educational and social contexts (Beemyn, Curtis, Davis, & Tubbs, 2005; Bilodeau, 2009). Even for cisgender men and women, higher education may offer opportunities to reconsider their self-understanding in relation to gendered expectations for academics, social life, and career. The small number of theories about gender identity development in college reflect these opportunities.

Transgender Identity Development. There are no empirically tested models of transgender identity development. Brent Bilodeau (2005) proposed an adaptation of the D'Augelli (1994) interactive processes based on a case study of two transgender students, and the model has been adopted by other higher education scholars and practitioners as a reasonable description of what may be happening as transgender individuals come to understand and express their gender identities. The processes Bilodeau (2005) proposed parallel D'Augelli's (1994) six interactive processes (exiting cisgender identity, developing a personal transgender status, and so forth). Evidence from Bilodeau's case study (2005) and his larger study (2009) supports this model. It also points to the ways that transgender identity may be more difficult to express than LGB identities. Lack of a visible community is a key factor; social and medical stigma is another; and an overarching system of genderism (Bilodeau, 2009) that compels everyone to express gender identity within a binary (male-female) of expected behaviors is a third factor in the complexity of transgender identity development in college.

Cisgender Identity Development. Cisgender (nontransgender) identity is so universally assumed to be the norm that the process of developing a cisgender identity is rarely discussed as such in the literature. Sandra Bem (1981a, 1981b, 1983) introduced "gender schema theory" to explain individual sense-making and person-environment interactions that shape one's identification as masculine, feminine, both, or neither. In a sense, her theory is both ecological and holistic in that it connects the person with the environment through the interpersonal, intrapersonal, and cognitive dimensions of development.

Bem (1983) noted, "Like schema theories generally, gender schema theory thus construes perception as a constructive process in which the interaction between incoming information and an individual's pre-existing schema determines what is perceived" (p. 604). This statement underscores three key factors that form a foundation for gender schema theory. First, from a very young age, children learn and internalize society's expectations and cultural definitions of maleness (and masculinity) and femaleness (and femininity). Second, in the constructivist aspect of the theory, children sort incoming information according to what they already know about gendered expectations (for example, that rough play and loudness are associated with masculinity, boys, and men, and gentle, nurturing play and artistic expression are associated with femininity, girls, and women). Third, individuals construct their self-concept in accordance with these gender-based schemas, making decisions that reinforce membership in the "appropriate" gender category. Self-concept is based in part on how well one conforms to gender schemas one has developed. For cisgender students, these gender schemas match biological sex.

To be clear, there is substantial overlap across masculine and feminine categories, as well as change across time and cultures in what traits belong in which category. Higher education provides abundant examples of gender schemas enacted and in transition. For example, some academic majors and careers remain highly gendered (engineering is predominantly male, nursing is predominantly female), but some have undergone radical transitions (such as veterinary studies, which has shifted from mostly men to mostly women), and others have reached something of a gender balance (life sciences and business). Since the enactment of Title IX, women's athletics have become an acceptable—even admirable— pursuit on campus, even though the concept of women engaging in serious competition went against gender norms for most of the history of higher education. Women have made some gains in the previously male realms of university faculty and administrators, yet they remain somewhat segregated in lower-paid caretaking roles (such as student affairs staff) and such academic disciplines as education, social work, nursing, and humanities.

Cisgender students come to college with clearly established gender schemas that may then be challenged or reinforced. Researchers have shown that gender role attitudes may liberalize during college (Bryant, 2003; Pascarella & Terenzini, 1991, 2005), yet a persistent peer culture that values (white) men at the expense of women (and men of color) sends a message about the masculine qualities that are most valued in society (see Kimmel, 2008, for an analysis of the culture of "Guyland" that we described in Chapter Five; see also Edwards & Jones, 2009; Harris & Edwards, 2010). Shaun Harper and colleagues' line of research on men of color reveals insights into the construction and maintenance of masculinity in college that are applicable for all students (Harris & Harper, 2008; Harper, Harris, & Mmeje, 2005). Frank Harris (2010) has extended this work to determine that college men equate masculinity with being respected, being confident and self-assured, assuming responsibility, and embodying physical prowess. Harris also identified contextual factors that influenced men's meaning-making in regard to masculinity: pre-college gender socialization, campus involvement, and male peer-group interactions. The college environment does exert influences on students' gender schemas, but the larger societal norms have a firm hold on how students understand gender and their gender identities.

Multiple Dimensions of Identity and Intersectionality

Several student development researchers recognized that such psychosocial identity dimensions as race, gender, and sexual orientation do not stand alone, but work in interactive ways to form a whole identity. The model that is most used in student affairs derives from a line of research by Susan Jones and colleagues (Abes & Jones, 2004; Abes, Jones, & McEwen, 2007; Jones & McEwen, 2000). Jones and Marylu McEwen presented a "fluid and dynamic" (p. 408), three-dimensional Model of Multiple Dimensions of Identity (MMDI) consisting of three main components: (1) a central core sense of self (personal identity, including personal attributes, characteristics, and factors important to the individual) embedded in (2) the context within which identity occurs (one's family, sociocultural milieu, experiences, and career and life planning) and orbited by (3) intersecting circles representing significant identity dimensions (including race, culture, gender, family, education, sexual orientation, social class, and religion). Jones and McEwen represented the salience of each identity dimension with a solid dot, closer to or further from the core depending on its importance to the individual.

Reconceptualized Model of Multiple Dimensions of Identity Elisa Abes joined Jones and McEwen (Abes et al., 2007) to reconceputalize the Jones and McEwen (2000) MMDI, incorporating concepts from self-authorship theory. Specifically, they added a "meaning-making filter" (cognitive) and separated contextual influences (interpersonal) from self-perceptions of multiple identity dimensions (intrapersonal). This model is depicted in Figure 7.1, which incorporates the core and identity dimensions from the original MMDI in an approximation of an atom. The model illustrates the process by which messages from the context pass through (or are rejected

FIGURE 7.1 RECONCEPTUALIZED MODEL OF MULTIPLE DIMENSIONS OF IDENTITY

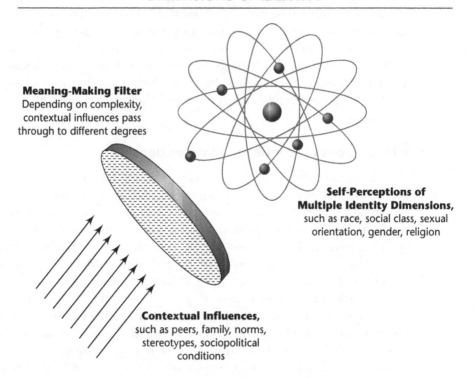

Meaning-Making Filter
Depending on complexity, contextual influences pass through to different degrees

Self-Perceptions of Multiple Identity Dimensions, such as race, social class, sexual orientation, gender, religion

Contextual Influences, such as peers, family, norms, stereotypes, sociopolitical conditions

Source: From Abes, E. S., Jones, S. R., & McEwen, M. K. (2007). Reconceptualizing the model of multiple dimensions of identity: The role of meaning-making capacity in the construction of multiple identities. *Journal of College Student Development, 48* (1), 7.

by) the meaning-making filter on the way to self-perception. For example, messages from peers and family about what it means to be a member of a certain race or religion are filtered through a cognitive lens in which the individual accepts or rejects tenets of those messages. As the individual comes to think in a more complex manner about race or religion, he or she has a more fine-grained filter and is thus less likely to accept unquestioned "truths" about these identities. A more simplistic meaning-making filter would lead one to accept more external formulas, as there would be fewer internal foundations to guide one's perception of these aspects of identity.

In the reconceptualized MMDI (Abes et al., 2007), the meaning-making filter is thus dynamic. Cognitive growth leads to a more refined understanding of self and others. In this sense, it is a driver of identity development, rather than aspects of identity prompting increased cognitive complexity. Although some theorists have found a similar role for cognitive complexity as leading identity development (see Torres, 2003; Torres & Baxter Magolda, 2004; Torres & Hernandez, 2007), the question remains unresolved, other theorists (Pizzolato, Chaudhari, Murrell, Podobnik, & Schaeffer, 2008) having found a parallel or leading role for interpersonal and intrapersonal components. In any case, there is evidence that messages from the environment about multiple dimensions of identity influence individual meaning-making about what it means to be, for example, a black Christian woman, a working-class Asian American lesbian, a heterosexual American Indian man, or a white man with a disability.

Intersectionality Deriving from critical legal studies (Crenshaw, 1991) and scholarship of women of color (for example, Collins, 2000), intersectionality has been brought into the study of college students as a perspective for understanding and conducting research on identities (see Torres et al., 2009). Intersectionality focuses on the connections of socially constructed identities. Dill and Zambrana (2009) pointed out four characteristics of intersectional approaches, which

1. Develop theory from the starting point of the lived experiences of people of color and other marginalized groups,
2. Explore complexities of individual and group identities, acknowledging within-group differences (such as experiences of African American women and men or experiences of women from different racial and ethnic groups),
3. Point out interconnected "domains of power" (p. 5) that sustain systems of oppression, and
4. Promote social justice through praxis.

Intersectionality is *not* a theory of development. It is a perspective on theory that may be useful in examining student development theories, who benefits from the application of those theories, and who is (further) marginalized by how theories are constructed and used. For example, the use of stage-based theories privileges individuals who reach the highest levels and may stigmatize individuals who do not "fully develop." An intersectional analysis would point out the ways that members of some subgroups (for example, men in general or students from wealthy backgrounds) have more opportunities than some others (for example, women or working-class students) to achieve the highest level of, for example, a stage-based racial identity development model. We include intersectionality in this chapter, even though it is not a theory of development, to highlight its utility as a critical perspective on student development theories in research and in practice.

Conclusion

In this chapter we have departed from the holistic approach of the previous chapter and considered aspects of student development in separate categories. As noted in the final part of the chapter, it is important to remember that development in one area (such as the cognitive domain) interacts with development in another area (such as racial identity). Students make meaning of lived experiences on and off campus through cognitive, interpersonal, and intrapersonal lenses (Abes, Jones, & McEwen, 2007; Pizzolato et al., 2008; Torres & Baxter Magolda, 2004; Torres & Hernandez, 2007). Although theoretical advances in these areas have transformed student development theory since Chickering's first iteration of the seven vectors in 1969, foundational ideas about the developmental tasks of college students endure. Developing competence, managing emotions, establishing identity, and moving beyond dualistic thinking and judgment are central developmental tasks that can be accomplished in higher education (in Chapter Nine we discuss college student outcomes and assessment of these tasks).

Points of Discussion

Implications for Students

- What responsibility do students have for their own development?
- If a student is interested in certain aspects of identity development that are not already addressed on campus, how might he or she go about this development?

- How feasible is psychosocial identity development in different institutional contexts, such as Historically Black Colleges and Universities, predominantly white institutions, or online institutions?
- How does a student's age affect development in the domains described in this chapter? Do adult students have the same needs as eighteen- to twenty-two-year-old students?

Implications for Institutions

- To what extent, if at all, is it the responsibility of the institution to promote students' cognitive, moral, and psychosocial development?
- If it is the responsibility of the institution to promote this development, what resources are available to do so? Whose job is it? How can an institution know if it is accomplishing this goal?
- How can student affairs professionals work with diverse student populations whose identity development may put them into conflict with other groups?
- What is the role, if any, of faculty in providing opportunities for student development in the domains described in this chapter?

Implications for Policy and National Discourse

- To what extent should institutional accreditors be concerned with cognitive, moral, and psychosocial outcomes for students?
- To what extent should federal goals related to college completion consider such nonacademic issues as student development in the domains described in this chapter?

Learning Activities

- Choose an area of administrative or educational responsibility in higher education (for example, residence life, academic advising, or financial aid). Consider the functions, programs, and policies of that area through the lens of either Perry's scheme of intellectual and ethical development or Chickering's seven vectors. In what ways do those functions, programs, and policies promote or inhibit cognitive and ethical development (Perry) or identity development (Chickering)? How do they balance the challenge and support students need for optimal development?

- Considering the cognitive, moral, and psychosocial development theories presented in this chapter, to what extent do you believe it is the institution's responsibility to facilitate student development in each category? Do different types of institutions have different responsibilities in these categories? Are there some categories that apply to all institutions? Are there some that are "optional" for some types of institutions, or for some students at all or some institutions?

Resources Related to Cognitive, Moral, and Psychosocial Identity Development

Institute for the Study and Promotion of Race and Culture (www.bc.edu/content/bc/schools/lsoe/isprc.html)

The Institute for the Study and Promotion of Race and Culture is directed by Janet Helms. The Web site includes research and resources on race, culture, and social justice.

King and Kitchener's Reflective Judgment Model (www.umich.edu/~refjudg/index.html)

This site, maintained by Patricia King, includes information on the model, how to assess Reflective Judgment, the Reasoning About Current Issues Test (an online measurement of Reflective Judgment), research on Reflective Judgment, and implications for education.

Society for the Study of Emerging Adulthood (www.ssea.org/index.htm)

This site includes information on conferences and publications related to emerging adulthood, the period between ages eighteen and twenty.

PART THREE

OUTCOMES

CHAPTER EIGHT

RETENTION AND PERSISTENCE

[We] have to ensure that we're educating and preparing our people for the new jobs of the 21st century. We've got to prepare our people with the skills they need to compete in this global economy. Time and again, when we placed our bet for the future on education, we have prospered as a result—by tapping the incredible innovative and generative potential of a skilled American workforce . . . And that's why, at the start of my administration I set a goal for America: By 2020, this nation will once again have the highest proportion of college graduates in the world. We used to have that. We're going to have it again.

PRESIDENT BARACK OBAMA (2009A), ANNOUNCING HIS GOAL TO INCREASE THE PROPORTION OF UNITED STATES CITIZENS WITH COLLEGE DEGREES

Student retention arguably has been *the* primary goal for higher education institutions for several decades and the focus of much research effort among higher education scholars. Certainly, President Barack Obama's goal to lead the world with the proportion of U.S. citizens with a college degree reinforces the importance of studying and improving college student retention. Lumina Foundation for Education, a major source for research and development funding in higher education, has set a similar goal: 60 percent of U.S. citizens will have a college degree by 2025. It appears retention-to-graduation will remain the primary goal for higher education institutions for some time to come.

By most accounts, six-year retention rates in U.S. higher education have remained around 50 percent for several decades (Berkner, He, & Cataldi, 2002). This stability in retention rates could lead to the conclusion that efforts to improve student retention have been ineffective, with attrition rates remaining relatively stable despite years of research and policy attention (ACT, Inc., 2004; Braxton, Brier, & Steele, 2007; Terenzini, Cabrera, & Bernal, 2001). Stagnant retention rates, however, also can be understood in the context of the increasing diversity of the student body;

as discussed in Chapter One, more students from traditionally underrepresented and underserved populations are gaining access to college. One could argue that the increase in first-generation and lower-SES students should have resulted in a decrease in retention rates. Through this lens, stagnant retention rates could be seen as a victory—albeit a minor one.

Based on research related to the differential life experiences of college graduates and non-college-graduates, the cost of student attrition is high. Individuals with college degrees enjoy generally more positive lives than individuals without college degrees. In summarizing the research related to quality of life after college, Pascarella and Terenzini (2005) concluded that individuals with more years of education had a longer life expectancy with fewer health problems, and that they smoked less, drank less alcohol, and had healthier diets. Estimates of the real economic cost of attrition are staggering. Schneider and Yin (2011) recently estimated that students who entered postsecondary education in 2002 but failed to graduate within six years lost a total of $3.8 billion a year in income and cost federal and state governments $566 million and $164 million, respectively, per year in lost income taxes. The cumulative loss in income for these students over the course of their work lives was estimated at $158 billion. Certainly, increasing student persistence-to-graduation is a laudable goal for policymakers and institutional leaders.

This chapter explores theories and research related to college student retention and persistence. We begin by building shared definitions of important terms, a surprisingly complex task. Next we address two theoretical perspectives often used to study student retention and persistence—Vincent Tinto's sociological perspective (1987, 1993) and John Bean and Shevawn Eaton's psychological perspective (2000)—as well as several research models that inform retention studies. Finally, we end the chapter with a discussion of what higher education researchers currently understand about factors that influence student retention and persistence.

Definition of Relevant Terms

To open Chapter Three, we used an anecdote that introduced the reader to a senior colleague's staff assistant, who was enrolled in four postsecondary institutions in one year. We originally introduced the staff assistant's experience to highlight the concept of swirling, one of many nontraditional enrollment patterns discussed in that chapter. As indicated in Chapter Three, the staff assistant eventually attained her degree at a local four-year university, but would have been assumed to be a dropout at three other institutions. A narrow understanding of student retention certainly minimizes the success of this hardworking student; it also complicates a complete assessment of institutional effectiveness and calls into question public policy initiatives meant to improve higher education in the United States. We begin this chapter, therefore, with a brief discussion of the various terms associated with the study of student retention and persistence.

Researchers and policymakers often use the terms *retention* and *persistence* interchangeably when discussing patterns of student enrollment, dropping out, and graduation. This practice not only is incorrect but also introduces some confusion around this topic. As Reason (2009) indicated, "Retention is an organizational phenomenon—colleges and universities *retain* students . . . Persistence, on the other hand, is an individual phenomenon—students *persist* to a goal" (p. 660). When students enter higher education with a goal other than graduation with a degree, the distinction between these two terms becomes important. Students may successfully persist to their goals without being retained to graduation.

A more complete discussion of the multiple terms used to describe student retention and persistence, and the nuances between the various definitions of these terms, can be found in Hagedorn's chapter titled "How to Define Retention" (2005). The list that follows offers only a brief summary of terms used, but provides some insight into the definitional problem that plagues research into student persistence behaviors (Braxton & Lee, 2005; Hagedorn, 2005; Reason, 2009). Common terms associated with this topic include *attrition, educational attainment, non-completion* (or *non-completer*), *dropout, stopout,* and *involuntary departure.*

For the purposes of this chapter, we primarily use the term *persistence.* Doing so focuses attention on individual-level student goal attainment rather than the institution-level goal of keeping students. Because the vast majority of higher education research assumes graduation as the goal to which a student is striving, we also assume that persistence-to-graduation is a positive *outcome* of college attendance. Others (see Reason, 2009) have discussed retention as an *experience* variable, but this view is not widely held in higher education or policy-related research. For these reasons, we present this chapter in Part Three of this text—Outcomes.

Recalling the discussion that introduced this chapter and Chapter Three, it is easy to note one of the implications of the difficulty around imprecise language. Assuming a focus on retention, the staff assistant in the anecdote is counted as a "failure" at three institutions. She was, after all, only retained to graduation at one institution. If, however, we assume a persistence or goal achievement perspective, she was certainly a success. She persisted to meet her goal of earning a bachelor's degree, although she did so through "nontraditional" means. Although recognizing the success of this staff assistant is important, the distinctions among the various perspectives related to retention or persistence have national, state, and institutional policy ramifications that move beyond any one individual student.

As legislatures move to hold institutions of higher education account- able for student success, legislators and policymakers tend to focus on retention-to-graduation as the main definition of success. Some states are adopting policies that connect funding to retention (Indiana Commission for Higher Education, 2008; Midwestern Higher Education Compact, 2009). Although these policies may make some intuitive sense, this measure of success misses the mark for open access institutions or institutions that serve as entry ports to higher education (Fain, 2011; Nelson, 2011). Com- munity college administrators have long argued, based on the proportion of students who enter these institutions with no intent to graduate, that retention-to-graduation is an inappropriate goal for their institutions. These administrators argue instead that a focus on improving skills for current or future work positions or transferring to a four-year institution is more appropriate for their students. Success for these institutions would be more fairly assessed based on students' goal attainment rather than the institutional perspective of retention-to-graduation (Committee on Mea- sures of Student Success, 2011).

Unfortunately, at the state and national policy levels, and to some degree even at the institutional policy level, assessing individual students' goal attainment is prohibitively difficult. First, it requires that institutions track each student's educational intent. Although this task could reason- ably be done as part of institutional data collection at the beginning of the academic term—perhaps at registration—because students' intentions change during the course of their academic career, an institution would need to reassess each student periodically. Further, a reasonable argument could be made that students have incentives to indicate a higher goal than they actually have, as financial aid and scholarship eligibility can be tied to enrollment in degree-granting programs. At the very least, the belief (now enshrined in national goals, such as those cited in the opening of this chapter) that college degrees are everyone's primary goal would provide some pressure for students to indicate graduation as their goal— even when an objective assessment of the student's occupational, aca- demic, or financial obligations would suggest a different goal (such as receiving a two-year degree or certificate, or advanced professional development).

A foundational understanding of the various terms used while studying student persistence, as well as some understanding of the policy-related implications of retention and persistence, allow for a more thorough examination of the models used to study persistence in higher education research. Building on the discussion in this section, the following section presents several models used to study persistence.

Overview of Important Persistence Models

Several models exist to explain student persistence in higher education, but none reaches the "paradigmatic" status of Tinto's Theory of Student Departure (Braxton & Lien, 2000, p. 11). Tinto's model (1993) serves as a foundation for studying student persistence and introduces the concepts of social integration and academic integration. Certainly, these concepts drive an understanding of retention, but Terenzini and Reason (2005, 2007) have suggested that these concepts also inform the recent attention placed on student engagement (for example, Kuh, 2008; Kuh, Kinzie, Schuh, Whitt, & Associates, 2005). Given the lasting influence of Tinto's model, no discussion of student persistence is complete without an examination of Tinto's ideas.

Yet Tinto is not the only scholar to offer explanations of student persistence. Whereas Tinto assumed a sociological lens to explore the issues of student departure, Bean and Eaton (Bean, 1982; Bean & Eaton, 2000; Eaton & Bean, 1995) examined student departure through a psychological lens. Understanding both disciplinary approaches to this vexing problem provides higher education administrators with multiple ways to examine and address issues of attrition. Finally, a group of "college-impact models" (Pascarella & Terenzini, 2005, p. 52), primarily used to study student outcomes, have been adapted to the issues of student persistence. Astin (1991), Weidman (1989), and more recently Terenzini and Reason (2005) have offered such models. Assuming as we do for this chapter that persistence is an *outcome* of college, exploring how these models inform the understanding of student persistence is appropriate.

Tinto's Theory of Student Departure

Like many researchers who study college student outcomes, Tinto (1987, 1993) assumed that students enter college with personal characteristics, aspirations and intentions, and goals (inputs in the I-E-O model). This initial assumption requires retention researchers and institutional agents to assume that, at some level, the persistence process is different for students based on these precollege characteristics. Tinto assumed that students' precollege characteristics directly affect their likelihood of persisting, as well as indirectly through their initial goal and institutional commitments (Braxton, Shaw Sullivan, & Johnson, 2001).

During their time in college, students engage in a continual and interactive process through which they assess how well their values align with the values of the institution, as they concurrently assess the feedback they receive on their social and academic achievement. Students assess their levels of social integration based on interactions with peers, their sense of fit within the student culture of an institution, and their engagement with formal student organizations. Assessment of academic integration is marked by feedback from faculty on academic performance and the students' comfort when interacting with faculty members about academic issues. These assessments lead students to some judgment about their social and academic integration. Based on their assessment of their social and academic integration, students revisit their initial goal and institutional commitments and make a decision about whether to proceed at the institution. This process of assessment and decision making continues throughout a student's college career (see Figure 8.1).

Although Tinto's model is widely used in the higher education literature (Braxton & Lien, 2000), researchers have expressed both empirical and theoretical concerns about it. Notably, in the early 2000s Braxton undertook a thorough examination of Tinto's model. He, along with others, completed a review of the empirical support of the model as a whole and the fifteen propositions that hypothesize the relationships between the components of Tinto's model (Braxton, Shaw Sullivan, & Johnson, 2001). Braxton also included in his book-length critique of Tinto's model several chapters addressing theoretical concerns. Although the authors included in Braxton's book examined Tinto's model from many theoretical and disciplinary lenses, the primary theoretical critique of Tinto's model has to do with its application of constructs and ideas, believed to be focused on the experiences of mainly white students (Rendon, Jalomo, & Nora, 2000; Tierney, 1999, 2000), to students from nonmajority cultures within the United States.

Empirical Critiques of Tinto's Model. Although a discussion of Braxton and colleagues' extensive review (2001) of Tinto's model of student departure

FIGURE 8.1 TINTO'S MODEL OF VOLUNTARY STUDENT DEPARTURE

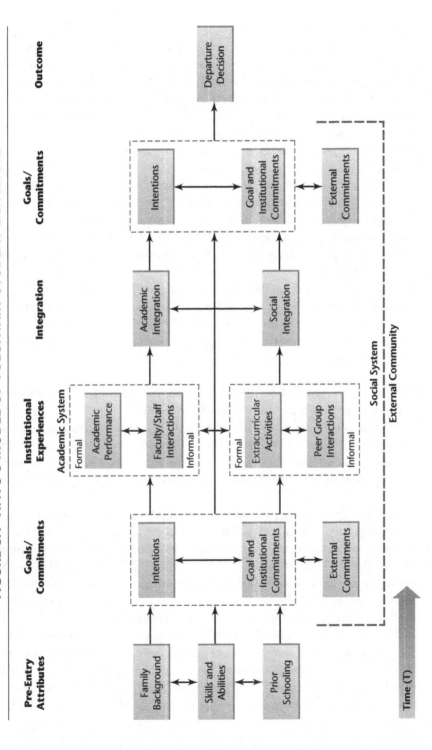

Source: Tinto, *Leaving College: Rethinking the Causes and Cures of Student Attrition* (2nd ed.), p. 114. Copyright 1987, 1993 by the University of Chicago. Used by permission.

is beyond the scope of this chapter, we note the authors' conclusion that the existing empirical evidence suggested only moderate support for Tinto's theory overall. Further, Braxton and his colleagues found that empirical evidence suggested only moderate support for Tinto's proposition related to the direct effects of academic integration on student commitment ("the greater the level of academic integration, the greater the level of subsequent commitment to the institution" [Braxton et al., 2001, p. 122]), calling into question a major construct within Tinto's model, academic integration, entirely (Braxton & Lien, 2000). Braxton and Lien went so far as to suggest the "abandonment of the construct of academic integration from further research" (p. 23) on student departure as an appropriate response to the lack of empirical evidence. Failing such abandonment, Braxton and Lien concluded that both the specification and measurement of the academic integration construct needed to be completely revised.

We would be remiss to leave the reader with the understanding that none of the propositions that make up Tinto's model were supported in the review by Braxton and colleagues (2001). In fact, Braxton and colleagues concluded that three propositions were strongly supported by empirical evidence:

- "The initial level of institutional commitment affects the subsequent level of institutional commitment" (p. 124).
- "The initial level of commitment to the goal of graduation affects the subsequent level of commitment to the goal of graduation" (p. 125).
- "Academic and social integration are mutually interdependent and reciprocal in their influence on student persistence" (p. 129).

Other propositions received moderately strong empirical support, including a proposition related to social integration: "the greater the level of social integration, the greater the level of subsequent commitment to the institution" (Braxton et al., 2001, p. 123). Strong and moderately strong empirical support for these propositions, however, was not enough to sway the authors from their conclusion that Tinto's model had only moderate empirical support in the research literature.

Finally, Braxton, Hirschy, and McClendon (2004) demonstrated that Tinto's model was better suited to explain student departure at residential colleges and universities than at commuter institutions. When studying the data from commuter students exclusively, none of the propositions discussed previously were well supported, suggesting that Tinto's model does not explain the departure decisions of commuter students. Braxton and Hirschy (2005) suggested that this discrepancy resulted from the combination of the general demographic characteristics of students who attend commuter institutions as well as the organizational characteristics and environments common at these institutions. This empirical critique also revealed a theoretical critique of Tinto's original model: the model fails to take into account the local context, an important influence on student learning and success we explored in Chapters Four, Five, and Six. We further develop theoretical critiques of Tinto's model in the next subsection.

Theoretical Critiques of Tinto's Model. In perhaps the first major critique of Tinto's original model, Tierney (1999) introduced the idea that Tinto's model did not represent the experiences of students from traditionally underrepresented and underserved racial and ethnic populations. Others echoed this critique (Kuh & Love, 2000; Rendon, Jalomo, & Nora, 2000). These theoretical critiques are based primarily on two assumptions of Tinto's model: (1) higher education in the United States serves as a "rite of passage" (Tierney, p. 82), and (2) students must sever ties from previous communities to integrate fully into their new college environments. Tierney called the process described by this latter assumption "cultural suicide" (p. 82) for college students of color.

Rather than build an understanding of student departure decisions based on cultural suicide, Tierney (1999) proposed that the concept of "cultural integrity" (p. 84) be incorporated into an understanding of student retention, suggesting that students of color who "refused to accept either assimilation or cultural rejection" (p. 84) when transitioning into higher education would perform better than those who assimilated. Kuh and Love (2000) built on this understanding, adding that a complete disconnection between students' home cultures and their higher education environments would be likely to result in isolation and eventual departure. We discussed these issues in more depth in Chapter Four.

The inability to incorporate the cultural meaning-making of students into a framework explaining departure decisions was a major shortcoming of Tinto's original model (Kuh & Love, 2000; Tierney 1999, 2000). The failure to understand student persistence from a cultural perspective diminishes the importance of students' cultures of origin; elevates assimilation into a presumably white, Western culture of higher education as the primary means to persistence; and negates the positive effects on student persistence of participation in culturally based student groups. Kuh and

Love suggested that "cultural enclaves" (p. 205) can serve as positive mediators between students' cultures of origin and higher education environments. Rendon and her colleagues (2000) suggested that successful students of color have become equipped with the skills to operate within both home and higher education cultures. The experiences of these students may point to ways to assist other underrepresented students in developing a similar set of skills. Finally, Palmer, Davis, and Maramba (2011), building on the work of Guiffrida (2005, 2006), suggested that the identification of social support for students of color, particularly the support given by family, is important to understanding students' persistence in college. These suggestions deemphasize the need for complete assimilation into the new higher education culture and allow students to succeed within two cultures.

Bean and Eaton's Psychological Model

Tinto's is not the only model to explain student persistence decisions. Beyond the critiques discussed earlier, other researchers have offered different models of student departure or persistence. Space does not allow a full discussion of multiple models, but because Tinto's model is clearly grounded in a sociological tradition, it seems appropriate to highlight a model from a different disciplinary tradition: Bean and Eaton's psychological model of college student retention (2000).

Building on Bean's earlier work (1982) and using Fishbein and Ajzen's theory of reasoned action (1975), Bean and Eaton (2000) synthesized several existing theories to propose a psychological lens through which to understand and explain student departure. Briefly, the model states that student departure is the direct result of students' intent to leave, which is influenced by precollege characteristics, interactions with the institutional and external environments, and attitudes about the school experience. Figure 8.2 offers a diagram of this model.

Bean and Eaton's model (2000) begins with a now familiar assumption: students come to college with an existing set of experiences, attitudes, and behaviors. Because this is a psychological model, however, the focus is clearly on students' preexisting attitudes about their institution and about being a student. Although precollege academic skills and abilities are a component of what a student brings to college, such measures as students' precollege academic self-efficacy, the value they place on education, and their ability to cope play equally important roles in understanding how students enter institutions of higher education.

FIGURE 8.2 BEAN AND EATON'S PSYCHOLOGICAL MODEL OF STUDENT DEPARTURE

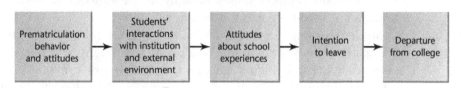

Source: Adapted from Bean, 2005.

After enrolling in higher education, students begin to assess their fit based on their interactions with the various parts of the institution and the external environment (Bean & Eaton, 2000). Although Bean and Eaton suggested four types of interactions—bureaucratic, academic, social, and external—academic interactions received considerable attention because of their direct connection to a student's sense of academic integration. According to Bean (2005),

> The combination of the student's background, interaction with the institution related to academic matters, and a belief in one's abilities to perform academic work [academic self-efficacy] have a cumulative mutual influence resulting in academic integration. When students' academic integration improves, so do their academic performance and their grades. (p. 226)

For Bean and Eaton, academic interactions comprise the interactions with courses, faculty members, academic advising, and other students.

Although academic interactions may be of primary importance, they are not the only influential type of interaction. Just as academic interactions reinforce or hinder a sense of academic integration, social interactions—students' interactions with and support from family and friends after enrolling in a higher education institution—influence a sense of social integration (Bean, 2005). Students also have interactions with the institution itself, what Bean and Eaton (2000) called "bureaucratic interactions" (p. 57). Bureaucratic interactions tend to be formal exchanges between the student and an institutional agent that are often related to resources, such as money or information. Finally, interactions with the environment outside of the institution influence students' sense of fit. Bean described this category of interaction as a "catch-all" (p. 232) meant to include any interactions outside of the institution that influence students. Financial worry, work off campus, family obligations, or stressful non-college life events fall in this category of interactions.

Students' interactions with these four components of the institutional and external environments are understood through psychological processes, result in psychological outcomes, and inform their sense of academic and social integration. Bean and Eaton (2000) grounded their model in the psychological theories of self-efficacy, coping mechanisms, and locus of control. Each interaction with the environment influences students' assessment of themselves in these areas and results in related outcomes. Academic interactions with faculty members, for example, can cause students to assess their academic self-efficacy and result in an increased (or decreased) sense of self-efficacy. This process of environmental interactions and assessments results in students' sense of academic and social integration—terms defined similarly to Tinto's definitions. Seen through an ecological lens (Bronfenbrenner, 1979, 1993, as described in Chapter Six), these interactions shape experiences and decisions about future engagement in the environment.

For Bean and Eaton (2000), integration leads to a sense of fit and to commitment, which directly influence students' intent to persist. In keeping with Fishbein and Ajzen's theoretical framework (1975), one's intention to behave in a certain manner is the best predictor of behavior. The strong connection between intent and behavior has some specific implications. Bean and Eaton based their psychological approach to student departure on the recognition that Tinto's sociological approach is not directly applicable to an individual student. Bean (2005) suggested that even though most research has found strong relationships between social integration and retention, this relationship may not hold true for every student at a particular institution at a particular time, rendering Tinto's model more meaningful on an institutional policy or multi-institutional research level than at the individual level. Bean and Eaton's model would suggest, on a simple level, that asking students how social integration (or lack thereof) is affecting their *intent* to persist would be effective in identifying who is likely to leave and to whom to direct institutional interventions.

Bean and Eaton (2000) summarized their model in this way:

Students enter college with a complex array of personal characteristics. As they interact within the institutional environment several psychological processes take place that, for the successful student, result in positive self-efficacy, reduced stress, increased efficacy, and internal locus of control. Each of these processes increases a student's scholarly motivation. These internal processes are reciprocal and iterative with continuous feedback and adjustment. (p. 58)

College Impact Models as Models of Retention

In their extensive reviews of empirical research related to higher education outcomes, Pascarella and Terenzini (1991, 2005) drew attention to a group of conceptual models they identified as "college impact models" (2005, p. 52). These models arise mainly from sociological traditions and explore how college environments interact with students' experiences and result in change. These models often begin with Astin's I-E-O model (1977, 1991, 1993b) as a foundation and attempt to elucidate the specific college experiences that produce student growth and learning. These models have been used extensively as conceptual frameworks to develop studies related to college student retention. Although multiple college impact models exist, two deserve special attention when discussing persistence: Astin's I-E-O model and John Weidman's model (1989) of undergraduate socialization. Finally, Patrick Terenzini and Robert Reason's Parsing the First Year of College model (2005, 2010) has been used both to study persistence and to frame an empirical literature review on the topic (Reason, 2009). The following subsections provide brief overviews of each of these models.

Astin's I-E-O Model Astin's Inputs-Environment-Outcomes model (1977, 1991, 1993b) serves as the methodological and conceptual foundation of many college impact models. As we described in the Preface, the model serves as the conceptual framework around which we have organized the content of this book. Astin's ideas, which can be traced back to 1970, can be seen as the underlying conceptual framework for Tinto's model (1987, 1993). The reach of Astin's model, particularly in relation to retention studies, is extensive.

As Pascarella and Terenzini (2005) discussed, Astin's model (1977, 1991, 1993b) is less a theoretical treatment of retention and more a methodological and conceptual model. Although Astin is a psychologist, his model can be adapted to study retention from multiple disciplinary perspectives. The model perhaps serves researchers best as a heuristic device to generate a conceptual framework for studying effects of individual characteristics, the campus environment, and students' experiences around the decision to persist in college.

Simply stated, Astin's model suggests that to understand fully what predicts college student outcomes, researchers must account for what the students bring with them to college (inputs) and the environments with which they interact while in college (environments). Input variables (race, sex, academic preparation, entrance test scores) are often considered control variables in retention studies. Including these in retention studies allows researchers to isolate the effects of these variables on students' persistence. Including input variables also allows researchers to make more certain conclusions about the effects of interventions designed to influence persistence. Isolating the effects of input variables permits an examination of the specific effects of environmental variables on student persistence.

The environment category in Astin's model should be understood broadly. Today we often use the term *environment* synonymously with *climate*, which is understood to be the feeling a student gets from the campus as a whole or places on campus (see Chapter Five for a discussion of campus climate). Researchers and practitioners alike may describe a campus climate as "friendly" or "inclusive" or "scholarly." Each of these terms is an attempt to capture the general feeling of a campus. Certainly, Astin's conception of the environment includes this conception of climate.

Astin's environment category should also be understood at the individual student level. Coupled with his involvement theory (Astin, 1984), the student-level conception of the environment suggests that the quality and quantity of student engagement with specific people, programs, and places on campus influence their outcomes. This postulation is similar to Kuh's more recent conception of "student engagement" (Terenzini & Reason, 2005, 2010).

Weidman's Undergraduate Socialization Model Although probably less widely recognized than Astin's model (1991), Weidman's model (1989) of undergraduate socialization (also described in Chapter Four) is helpful in furthering our understanding of the effects of campus environments on college student outcomes, including student persistence. Weidman's model focused greater attention than did previous college impact models on the influence of college contexts. That is, Weidman concentrated on the pressure that campus environments place on individual students to conform to widely accepted values. Reacting to the pressure to conform to these normative values, students either adapt (become socialized) to the college environment or remain apart from the environment. As with Tinto's assumptions, greater socialization into an environment is assumed to result in more positive outcomes, including a greater likelihood of persistence.

According to Pascarella and Terenzini (2005), Weidman's other major contribution was a more focused attention on the effects of non-college events and environments. As discussed previously, Tinto's model has been critiqued for ignoring the effects of non-college life events. Astin's I-E-O model offers little encouragement for researchers to include non-college events into their studies of student outcomes. Weidman's model is a reminder that non-college life events do affect students' persistence decisions. An ecological approach to student learning, development, and persistence is another way to consider factors outside the institution.

Terenzini and Reason's Parsing Model Terenzini and Reason (2005, 2010) offered a recent addition to the college impact models with their Parsing the First Year of College model. As the name implies, the model was developed to study individual effects of specific environments and experiences on first-year student outcomes. Terenzini and Reason suggested, however, that the model can serve as a conceptual framework to study any college student outcome for any group of students. For example, Reason (2009) used the framework to organize an extensive review of the retention literature. This model shares many characteristics with the models previously addressed, but it adds complexity to the understanding of how organizational and student climates affect student outcomes.

As with previous models, Terenzini and Reason's model assumes that students come to college with existing characteristics and experiences (inputs) that must be accounted for if a complete understanding of the effects of college is to be achieved. For these authors, however, the college experience component of the model is broken into three sections: the organizational context, the peer environment, and individual student experiences. Drawing on a conclusion by Pascarella and Terenzini (2005), who found that traditional measures of institutional characteristics (size, Carnegie Basic Classifications) are not predictive of most college student outcomes in well-designed research studies, Terenzini and Reason defined organizational characteristics as policies, practices, and faculty culture related to student learning and development. Owing much to Weidman's ideas, they posited that these organizational characteristics, along with peer environments, conveyed to students messages about values that in turn influenced how students behaved. Finally, drawing from previous

FIGURE 8.3 TERENZINI AND REASON'S PARSING THE FIRST YEAR OF COLLEGE MODEL

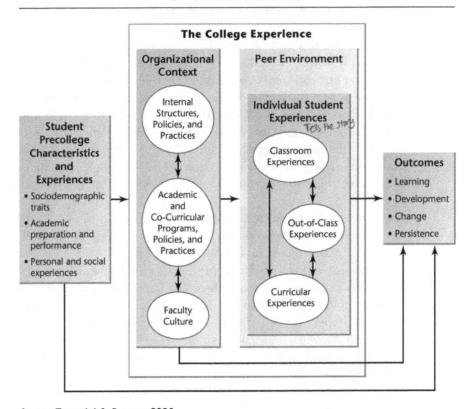

Source: Terenzini & Reason, 2005.

research by Terenzini (Terenzini, Springer, Yaeger, Pascarella, & Nora, 1996), Terenzini and Reason suggested that the individual student experiences that most directly affect student outcomes come from three main areas: classroom experiences; curricular experiences (course-taking patterns and major, for example); and out-of-class experiences. Figure 8.3 illustrates the Terenzini and Reason model.

Each of the three college impact models in this section can be used to study and understand student persistence behavior, though none of the three was originally designed to focus exclusively on this particular student outcome. Certainly, Astin's model is the most enduring, but Weidman's and Terenzini and Reason's advance and add complexity to an understanding of how institutions, and students' experiences within those institutions, can influence persistence behaviors.

Empirical Evidence Related to Retention and Persistence

We turn now from the theoretical treatment of retention to the empirical. Several comprehensive reviews of the empirical literature related to personal, organizational, and experiential predictors of college student persistence exist. Most notably, Pascarella and Terenzini (1991, 2005) included a chapter in each of their landmark *How College Effects Students* volumes on the subject. Tinto (2006–2007) and Reason (2003, 2009) have also completed reviews of the empirical literature. In this section we draw heavily from those existing reviews, supplemented by research published since 2009.

In keeping with the framework of this book, our presentation of empirical research follows Astin's I-E-O framework (1991), focusing on the input characteristics students bring with them to college, students' experiences within college, and environments that influence the outcome of persistence. Precollege experiences and personal characteristics that are related to students' persistence will be discussed in the subsection on inputs. The subsection on experiences comprises discussions of organizational characteristics, student cultures, and individual student experiences related to retention.

Inputs as Predictors

In summing up the empirical research related to persistence, Tinto (2005) concluded, "We can say with a good deal of confidence that academic preparation, commitments, and involvement matter" (p. ix). It is important to note that two of these three predictors of persistence—preparation and commitments—fall within the inputs category of predictors. Along with student demographic variables, such as race, sex, and socioeconomic status, these predictors present an interesting conundrum for higher education researchers and administrators: educational administrators must understand the predictive power of these characteristics, but there is little they can do to leverage that power.

Student Demographic Characteristics Student demographic characteristics, especially race, sex, and socioeconomic status (SES), have been found in numerous studies to be reliable predictors of student persistence behavior (Pascarella & Terenzini, 2005). Although there is little higher education professionals can do to enhance those input characteristics that positively influence persistence, or mitigate those that negatively influence it, student demographic characteristics remain important to understanding student persistence. As Pascarella and Terenzini (1991, 2005) noted, including student characteristics in persistence studies allows researchers to explore whether or not specific experiences or interventions affect groups of students differently. So, although one cannot make all female students attend residential colleges, one can understand that women might benefit more from residential colleges than do men, for example.

In general, research indicates that women persist at greater rates than men, white and Asian students at higher rates than students from other racial or ethnic groups, and wealthier students at higher rates than lower-SES students (Reason, 2009). But this oversimplification tells only part of the story. Exploring the interaction between race and SES, for example, reveals that differences in persistence rates by race might best be explained by differences in SES by race. That is, students of color are more likely than white peers to be from lower-SES families and thus less likely to persist.

Financial aid can certainly be used to mitigate some persistence obstacles for high-achieving, lower-SES students (Hu & St. John, 2001), but it is important to remember, as we transition to a discussion of academic preparation in the next subsection, the relationships among SES, race and ethnicity, and academic preparation in secondary schools in the United States. Students from lower-SES neighborhoods often attend elementary and secondary schools that fail to prepare them for postsecondary education (Chen, Wu, Tasoff, & Weko, 2010). The discussion of the importance of academic preparation that follows should be understood through a lens that incorporates this understanding of SES.

Academic Preparation Academic preparation, in terms of both the quality of secondary education and the types of courses taken during high school, is the strongest predictor of student success and persistence in college (Adelman, 2006; Astin & Oseguera, 2005). Astin and Oseguera found that students who entered college with an A average from high school were four times more likely to graduate than were students who entered with a C average. When coupled with students' entrance test scores (either ACT or SAT), this proxy for academic preparation in high school became the strongest predictor of student persistence in the Astin and Oseguera study.

Both high school grades and entrance test scores certainly are open to challenge as proxies for academic preparation. Grade inflation calls into question the reliability of high school grades to measure educational achievement (Burton & Ramist, 2001). The correlation between entrance test scores and SES also raises questions about the reliability of these assessments, to the point where a number of institutions have stopped requiring

SAT or ACT scores from applicants. These measurement concerns notwithstanding, the relationship between academic preparation and student persistence in college appears strong.

Adelman (1999, 2006), in two groundbreaking studies, found that the *quality* of the high school curriculum mattered a great deal in understanding how secondary school academic preparation related to postsecondary success. He concluded that the curriculum a student completed in high school was more predictive of persistence than were grades or test scores. In particular, Adelman (2006) found that students who completed advanced-level mathematics in high school were more likely to persist than students who did not complete such coursework. In a related finding, Astin and Oseguera (2005) found that students who completed foreign language study in high school were more likely to persist in college. Together these findings reinforce the importance to student persistence of college preparatory coursework in high school.

Commitments and Aspirations As noted earlier, Bean and Eaton's theoretical model (2000) of student persistence highlighted the importance of students' psychological characteristics, particularly their academic motivation and commitment to persist. Such psychological constructs as self-efficacy, conscientiousness (a student's relative tendency to carefully complete tasks), motivation, self-discipline, and clear definition of goals have all been related empirically to persistence (Reason, 2009).

Astin and Oseguera (2005) concluded that students who enter college with higher educational aspirations are more likely to persist. As with other student demographic and precollege characteristics, however, the interrelationship between educational aspirations and SES cannot be ignored. Astin and Oseguera found that higher educational aspirations were also related to higher SES, likely through parental education and occupations. Although the relationship between aspirations and persistence holds for lower-SES students, meaning that aspirations may help lower-SES students overcome obstacles to persistence, it is important to note that low aspirations, lower SES, and lower-quality academic preparation may combine to negatively influence persistence for some students.

Experiences as Predictors

If student demographic characteristics, academic preparation, and commitments are beyond the sphere of influence for higher education administrators, then how best do administrators positively influence student persistence? The types of predictors that fall within the experiences subsection of this chapter are more likely to be under the control of higher education administrators and policymakers. In the following paragraphs we present research related to organizational characteristics and organizational and student cultures within higher education institutions as well as individual student experiences within these contexts.

Organizational Characteristics and Cultures Most studies of student persistence include some control variables for institutional type (such as those we described in Chapter Five) and quality. Researchers often include variables for size, source of support (public versus private), and selectivity in admissions to control statistically for the influence of institutional characteristics on student outcomes. In well-designed studies, however, these types of organizational demographic characteristics have little or no relationship to most student outcomes, including persistence (Reason, 2009; Terenzini & Reason, 2005). Although selectivity (as measured by average test scores for entering first-year students) has been linked to student persistence, Pascarella and Terenzini (2005) suggested that this relationship is probably indirect through student environments and cultures, which we discuss later.

Researchers have moved beyond studying institutional characteristics and begun to focus on the effects of organizational behaviors and cultures on student persistence (Berger & Braxton, 1998; Braxton et al., 2004). Generally, this line of research suggests that organizations that encourage collaboration among students and include students in institutional decision-making processes increase students' levels of satisfaction and persistence (Berger, 2002). Similarly, institutions that focus on their history and traditions may generate a sense of belonging for students and increase students' persistence. However, institutions that are characterized by an emphasis on formality in bureaucratic processes or that are highly political and focused on hierarchies tend to impede student persistence.

Student Cultures It is likely that institutional behaviors and cultures influence student cultures and subcultures on campuses (Terenzini & Reason, 2005, 2010). Much of the research arising from the National Survey of Student Engagement and related projects is based on the assumption that institutional behaviors and cultures create environments that encourage or discourage student engagement in educationally purposeful activities; engagement in educationally purposeful activities, in turn, positively influences student outcomes, including persistence (for example, Kuh et al., 2005). Although little research exists to support this causal chain, particularly as it relates to student persistence, the assumption remains widely held among higher education professionals (Reason, 2009).

The negative effects on students of campus cultures that are racist or sexist are well established (see Chapters Five and Nine for further discussion). Racist climates on college campuses have been directly linked to lower persistence rates for both African American and white students (Cabrera, Nora, Terenzini, Pascarella, & Hagedorn, 1999). Similarly, a chilly climate for women can have deleterious effects on persistence, particularly within the traditionally male-specific fields of science, technology, mathematics, and engineering (Sax & Harper, 2007). Based on their review of empirical research, Pascarella and Terenzini (2005) concluded that negative effects of racism and sexism on persistence (and other student outcomes) are probably indirect through campus cultures and climates.

Individual Student Experiences Individual student experiences, whether inside or outside the classroom, are the most powerful influences on persistence. As we discussed in Chapter Three, students in the twenty-first century engage in nontraditional enrollment patterns (such as swirling and part-time enrollment) at greater rates than in the past. These enrollment patterns often cause students to take longer to graduate and, as one recent report concluded, "Time is the enemy of college completion" (Complete College America, 2011, p. 3). Extended time-to-graduation is a predictor of student attrition at both four-year institutions (Complete College America) and two-year institutions (Waller & Tietjen-Smith, 2009). Although nontraditional enrollment patterns may increase access to higher education by allowing students greater flexibility in how they attend, policymakers and institutional leaders must work to remove the obstacles to graduation created by these enrollment patterns.

In the classroom, students' exposure to active teaching methods encourages persistence (Braxton, Bray, & Berger, 2000; Pascarella, Salisbury, & Blaich, 2011). Recent research has demonstrated the positive effects of high-quality academic advising on student persistence, especially as academic advisers can assist students to enroll in courses that match their skills, abilities, and interests (Habley, Valiga, McClanahan, & Burkum, 2010; Lotkowski, Robbins, & Noeth, 2004). Not surprisingly, academic performance, especially in the first year of college, has profound effects on student persistence (Ishitani & DesJardins, 2002–2003).

Student engagement in intentional and positive out-of-class activities also increases the chance that students will persist (Pascarella & Terenzini, 2005). Participating in activities designed to increase engagement and ease transition to college increase a student's likelihood of persisting. As we noted in Chapter Four, attending first-year seminars, participating in learning communities, and living in residence halls have all been shown to increase student persistence (National Resource Center for the First-Year Experience and Students in Transition, 2002; National Study of Living-Learning Programs, 2007; Schuddle, 2011).

Finally, growing concern about students' ability to pay for college and its effect on student persistence is evident in the research literature. Students' concerns about their ability to pay for college, and the subsequent stress related to this concern, have been shown to interfere with academic performance and decrease the likelihood of persistence. Students who must work off campus to pay for college are less likely to persist than students who work on campus or who do not work (Pascarella & Terenzini, 2005). Financial aid, especially in the form of grants, reduces the risk that students will drop out (Ishitani & DesJardins, 2002–2003). Clearly, persistence is related to a host of individual factors, not all of which are within the student's or institution's control, though there is evidence to support meaningful efforts to increase persistence.

Conclusion

In this chapter we reviewed major theories and conceptual frameworks that guide current understandings of college student persistence. Increased access to college, the rising cost of attending college, and stagnant overall retention rates have served to focus continued attention on the study of student persistence. Policy goals from the federal government and new attention to performance-based funding at the state level suggest that student retention—particularly retention-to-graduation—will remain an issue for some time to come.

Points of Discussion

Implications for Students

- What can students and families do before college—as early as middle school—to lay a foundation for success in college?

- How important is it for students to know that they are in a group considered more or less likely to persist? Is there a risk of attaching a stigma to students from groups with generally lower persistence rates? Do students have a right to know persistence and graduation rates by demographic group (for example, sex, race, and SES) before deciding what institution to attend?

Implications for Institutions

- Because high school preparation and course-taking patterns of students appear to be the strongest predictors of student persistence in college, one obvious solution to any institutional persistence problem is to increase admissions standards. What are the implications of increasing admissions standards? How might such a policy affect the mission of an institution? How might such a policy affect student access?
- What are the implications of the ambiguity of language around issues of student persistence and retention? How are certain institutions affected negatively by assuming a retention-to-graduation goal for all of higher education? Is it ever appropriate to assume a "lesser" goal for students?
- What institution-level interventions related to student retention are likely to be most effective at a given institution? How does institutional context affect these recommendations?

Implications for Policy and National Discourse

- How would a shift from a retention perspective or a persistence perspective to a student success perspective (understood as assisting students to meet their own educational goals) change the emphasis of policymakers? Is such a shift feasible at the state or national policy level?
- Given the public policy interest in increasing the proportion of U.S. citizens with a bachelor's degree, what are the primary policy levers to improve persistence-to-graduation rates of college students? Knowing that increasing the proportion of U.S. citizens with a bachelor's degree can occur only if a larger percentage of high school graduates attend college, what can be done with high school students to increase their potential for success in pursuing a bachelor's degree?
- Given student swirling, double dipping, and other nonlinear enrollment patterns, what is the best way to determine institutional persistence and completion rates? What policy and privacy concerns arise from different approaches to calculating these rates?

Learning Activities

- Identify a prevalent nontraditional student group (for example, part-time students) or traditionally underrepresented student group (for example, lower-SES students) at your institution. Design an intervention, grounded in the empirical research discussed in this chapter and elsewhere, meant to support persistence among this specific group of students. Identify the research that justifies your intervention. How might this intervention differ from interventions that target other nontraditional or traditionally underrepresented student groups?
- Student persistence and retention are often incorrectly used interchangeably when the subject of student matriculation is brought up. How would this misinterpretation affect your institutional philosophy and policies concerning student persistence? Review your institutional programs designed to increase student persistence. Are they focused on persistence or retention? Now compare these programs to those of institutions your campus aspires to be like. Do they reflect different philosophies or attitudes about student persistence?

Resources Related to Student Retention and Persistence

Complete College America (www.completecollege.org)

Complete College America is a nonprofit organization working to improve college graduation rates in the United States. The organization's Web site focuses on several empirical reports and state-level data.

Lumina Foundation for Education (www.luminafoundation.org/)

The Lumina Foundation for Education's goal is "to increase the proportion of Americans with high-quality degrees and credentials to 60% by 2025." The Web site includes research-based and advocacy resources in support of this goal. The foundation is also a major funder of efforts to achieve this goal.

National Academic Advising Association (www.nacada.ksu.edu)

The National Academic Advising Association Web site maintains a comprehensive list of retention reports and retention-related links.

CHAPTER NINE

STUDENT OUTCOMES

Educators, legislators, and the American public concur that learning outcomes of higher education should include effective citizenship, critical thinking and complex problem solving, interdependent relations with diverse others, and mature decision making.

BAXTER MAGOLDA, 2007, P. 69

The third component—outcomes (the "O")—of the Astin's I-E-O model (1977, 1993b) is critical to understanding what happens to students as a result of having attended college. Outcomes are the focus of substantial research and debate about higher education, its value, who should attend and why, and who should pay. At the national and local levels, the debate is often framed around the concepts of "public good" and "private good." In brief, the former represents the benefits to society of having a more educated citizenry; the latter represents the benefits that accrue to individuals who gain more education. It is beyond the scope of this book to engage fully in this debate, but we believe it is important for individual students, higher education professionals, and society to understand what is known about college student outcomes. This knowledge informs the larger discourse about who benefits—individually and societally—when students go to college.

An obvious outcome of interest is persistence-to-graduation. In the previous chapter we presented theoretical models of student retention and persistence as well as data on student retention. Educators recognize that persistence is a necessary element for degree attainment; if a student does not persist, he or she does not complete the degree. The general public and policymakers focus less on persistence and more on degree completion. Institutional graduation rates seem like a simple measure to compare across institutions, for example, and postsecondary degree completion is a major focus of public policy discourse. Given what we have described throughout this book about student swirl and attendance patterns, however, graduation rates are not as simple a matter as they may at first appear to be. Even deciding which rate to use is up for debate. At bachelor's-degree-granting institutions, should we count the four-, five-, or six-year completion rate of first-time, full-time students? Certainly this measure tells something about the success of an institution in retaining and graduating those it admits as first-year students, but it provides at best an incomplete picture of institutional effectiveness. Students who transfer in are not counted; students who transfer to and complete at another institution are not counted. Institutions that admit a larger percentage of students with high academic risk get no acknowledgment of the extra efforts they make to help students succeed; highly selective institutions graduate nearly all of the students they admit, but these are students who would very likely graduate from any institution. Is it fair to evaluate institutional effectiveness only on graduation rates? We think not.

We turn then to outcomes that fall under the broad definition of student success. There are a number of definitions of student success that circulate in the higher education literature (see Hagedorn, 2005; Keeling, 2004; Kuh, 2011; Sedlacek, 2004; Seidman, 2005; Tinto, 1993). Consensus has emerged around the idea that "successful" students are "those who persist, benefit in desired ways from their college experiences, are satisfied with college, and graduate" (Kuh, Kinzie, Schuh, Whitt, & Associates, 2005, p. 8). This definition includes progress and completion measures (student persistence and graduation) as well as learning and developmental outcomes. A subset of literature includes student engagement as an indicator of student success, based on the sensible idea that students engaged in educationally and developmentally meaningful activities will benefit accordingly. We view engagement as an environmental process, not an outcome per se.

In terms of outcomes, there are competing pressures on and in higher education. A central example of these tensions relates to whether to provide liberal education for "well-rounded" learners or to provide career preparation. Educators have been asking this core question—Higher education for what purpose?—since nearly the beginning of higher education in the United States (see Thelin, 2011), and the tension between liberal education and career or vocational preparation has framed debates about curriculum; new institutional types (for example, land-grant institutions, normal schools, and technical colleges); and education for black

Americans after the Civil War. In the twenty-first century, the question is sharpened by economic pressures and the rising cost of postsecondary education. Will the investment of time and money pay off? The answer to that question depends to some degree on who is asking and what they consider a reasonable return on the investment. What outcomes do they seek as evidence that a college education—whether liberal arts or career focused—is worthwhile?

In considering what outcomes matter or matter most, educators are at a critical point in higher education history in terms of rethinking the student population in light of changing demographics. Educational leaders also face economic presses from both workforce needs and decreasing state appropriations as a proportion of the budgets of public institutions. In essence, the challenge of the twenty-first century is to educate more and increasingly diverse students for a wider range of careers, with increased reliance on funding from private sources (including students and families). In this context, what matters most in terms of college student outcomes may differ across and within institutions, as well as according to individual student interests and needs.

In this chapter, we provide a synthesis of research on student outcomes. We begin with a discussion of what matters most in producing outcomes, and then describe outcomes related to student learning and academic achievement. We discussed student development theories in Chapters Six and Seven, and we describe related outcomes here. We provide an overview of outcomes assessment. Finally, we argue for the use of student outcomes assessment in higher education practices meant to promote student success.

Key Influences on Student Outcomes

Researchers and scholars who have reviewed the bulk of the empirical research related to college student outcomes, and Pascarella and Terenzini (1991, 2005) in particular, consistently conclude that *where* students go to college has a much smaller effect on their learning and development than does *what happens* to them once they enroll. As Terenzini and Reason (2007) explained, the "where" in this statement includes the characteristics of institutions used by researchers to differentiate among schools, such as type, mission, size, and selectivity. They argued that these institutional characteristics are too distant from the actual experiences of students to influence learning. Further, Terenzini and Reason concluded that

when the characteristics of the students enrolled (e.g., secondary school
achievement, degree goals, motivation, and family background) are
taken into account . . . the conventional markers of educational
"quality" turn out to be rather poor (if not totally ineffective) predictors
of student learning and personal development. (p. 166)

Pascarella and Terenzini (2005) reviewed approximately 2,500 research
studies of college effects on students, examining both between-college
effects (comparing across institutions) and within-college effects (comparing students at one institution to one another). They argued:

Overall, no single institutional characteristic or set of characteristics
has a consistent impact across outcomes, but statistically reliable
between-college effects are apparent in certain outcome areas.
These between-college effects are more pronounced in the areas of
career and economic attainment after college than they are in the
developmental changes that occur during college (such as knowledge
acquisition, cognitive development, changes in values and attitudes, and
psychosocial development). These findings could be expected since in
the areas of career and economic achievement, the status allocating
aspects of a college, and what a degree from that college signals to
prospective employers about the characteristics of its students, may
count as much as if not more than the education provided. (p. 591)

Even in the areas of career and economic achievement, the evidence
of the effect of institutional characteristics on socioeconomic advantages
was underwhelming. Pascarella and Terenzini concluded that the socioeconomic advantages seen after graduation for students who attend highly
selective postsecondary institutions are related to the skills and abilities
these students bring to college, not to any institutional characteristic of
the college.

The effects of college on students' learning and development, therefore, are more directly related to what a student does while in college.
Researchers and scholars use the language of *within-college effects* (see Pascarella & Terenzini, 2005) when studying the differential effects of various
sets of experiences on students within the same institution. Studies of
within-college effects include those comparing how levels of involvement
in various activities (such as leading student organizations, studying, and
doing research with faculty members) can add to the learning and development of the students who engage in them. The overwhelming majority

of student outcomes research concludes that the more a student engages in educationally meaningful activities, the more that student will learn and develop. And, as the previous statement suggested, the effects of engagement in educationally meaningful activities supersede any effects that can be attributed to the type of institution a student attends.

Learning and Developmental Outcomes

As we discussed in the previous chapter, student retention and persistence are critical to student learning and achievement, but as already noted they are not the only indicators of student success. What do students actually learn in college? Scholars have been examining this question for some time, and the amount of research in this area has grown exponentially. In 1969 Kenneth Feldman and Theodore Newcomb published *The Impact of College on Students,* which reviewed forty years of research on college students, from the mid-1920s to the mid-1960s. They examined about 1,500 studies of college students to answer the question, "Do American students— regardless of who they are or where they go to college—change in definable ways during their undergraduate years?" (p. 5). In their 1991 volume *How College Affects Students,* Pascarella and Terenzini synthesized 2,600 studies "generally covering the time period 1967 to 1989" (Pascarella & Terenzini, 2005, p. 10). The 2005 volume of *How College Affects Students* covered 1989–1990 to 2001–2002 and includes "nearly 2500 studies" (p. xv). The trend is clear: studies of student outcomes increased from 1,500 studies in forty years, to 2,600 in twenty-two years, to 2,500 in thirteen years. To be sure, Internet searches have facilitated access to research reports that might not have appeared in searches conducted by hand in earlier decades, but even accounting for that access, interest in research on college student outcomes has increased over time.

Pascarella and Terenzini (1991, 2005) organized their volumes around eight major categories: (1) development of verbal, quantitative, and subject matter competence; (2) cognitive skills and intellectual growth; (3) psychosocial change; (4) attitudes and values; (5) moral development; (6) educational attainment and persistence; (7) career and economic impacts of college; (8) and quality of life after college. We focus in this chapter on six, drawing from the work of Pascarella and Terenzini and research from the 2000s, with educational attainment and persistence covered in the previous chapter. We add a seventh, holistic development toward self-authorship, an area of scholarship developed largely after the

2001–2002 cutoff for studies included in the second volume of *How College Affects Students.*

Development of Verbal, Quantitative, and Subject Matter Competence

Outcomes research in this category answers the question, *What do students learn in college?* in its most traditional form. When students leave college, are their knowledge and skills in reading, writing, math, and various academic subjects greater than they were when they began college? No matter the format or context (in person, online, hybrid, commuter, residential) in which a student learns, higher education's implicit promise is that students will learn something before they graduate. Ideally, they will learn many things. But do they?

For the most part, evidence shows that students do make gains in college. Pascarella and Terenzini (1991) reported gains from the first year to senior year on standardized tests of academic skills and subject matter. They estimated that students gained 21 percentile points on general verbal skills, 9.5 percentile points on general mathematics and quantitative skills, and 30.8 percentile points for specific subject matter. In other words, a student who entered at the 50th percentile in all areas would complete at the 71st, 59.5th, and 80.8th percentiles, respectively. Limited evidence from the 1990s reinforces evidence of gains, though the two longitudinal studies Pascarella and Terenzini (2005) examined were single-campus investigations with relatively small samples, which limited generalizability.

In general, students tend to gain more knowledge in the area of their academic major than outside it (Pascarella & Terenzini, 1991, 2005). This result is not surprising—and indeed may be considered positive—given the typical structure of the undergraduate curriculum, in which students may take lower-level courses across a broad range of general education areas and proceed to higher-level courses in the major. The difference is evident in the percentile gains noted in the previous paragraph.

When considering potential differences between institutions in regard to student gains, it is important to remember that student enrollment patterns come into play (see Chapter Three). In addition to complicating data collection efforts, student enrollment at more than one institution (simultaneously or sequentially) complicates the question of where students are gaining the knowledge and skills one might attempt to measure. Pascarella and Terenzini (2005) reported that in comparing subject matter gains across institutional types (including Historically Black Colleges and

Universities, women's colleges, and highly selective institutions) they found "inconsistent results" that indicated a "quite small magnitude" (p. 146) of between-college differences. Although institutional type does not play a large role in student gains, the institutional environment and campus climate appear to do so. Institutional cultures that support learning and scholarship result in modestly higher gains across the student population, and students of color at institutions with a more positive campus racial climate (see Chapter Five) gain more than their peers at institutions with a less positive racial climate.

Within institutions, there appear to be factors that may influence gains in verbal, quantitative, and subject matter knowledge. Pascarella and Terenzini (2005) summarized pedagogical approaches that promoted higher student gains compared to what they called "traditional" (p. 147) teaching methods. These approaches included learning for mastery (16–25 percentile point gains over traditional), active learning (10 points), cooperative and small group learning (19 points each), and constructivist-oriented approaches (6–16 points). Instructor behaviors (such as their organization, the quality and frequency of feedback they give students, and their availability and helpfulness) play a role in student gains, as do the nature of students' interactions with faculty outside the class. Student behaviors contribute significantly as well, with the unsurprising findings that students who use the library more, write more, and expend more effort on their academics typically learn more than students who do not. In the mid- to late 2000s, researchers with the Wabash National Study of Liberal Arts Education (Center for Inquiry, n.d.) supported these findings, as did the research team that conducted the Documenting Effective Educational Practices study (see Arum & Roksa, 2011; Kuh et al., 2005).

Cognitive Skills and Intellectual Growth

Many higher education institutions claim that in addition to teaching specific academic skills and knowledge they help students learn to be critical thinkers, lifelong learners, and problem solvers. These skills and abilities fall within the category of cognitive development that extends beyond (or parallel to) the acquisition of verbal, quantitative, or subject matter knowledge. We described this development in Chapter Seven and proposed that college educators could promote it. Here we define the category as an outcome and present evidence that students develop in this area during college.

Pascarella and Terenzini (2005) summarized their previous synthesis (Pascarella & Terenzini, 1991) of student outcomes research on intellectual growth as follows:

> compared with freshmen, college seniors have better oral and written communication skills, are better abstract reasoners or critical thinkers, are more skilled at using reason and evidence to address ill-structured problems for which there are no verifiably correct answers, have greater intellectual flexibility in that they are better able to understand more than one side of a complex issue, and can develop more sophisticated abstract frameworks to deal with complexity. (p. 156)

Percentile point gains across measures of these abilities ranged from 13 (for formal reasoning) to 38 (for the ability to deal with conceptual complexity).

For the 2005 synthesis, Pascarella and Terenzini found fewer studies in these areas and categorized them broadly into two categories: critical thinking and postformal reasoning. Critical thinking involves both skills and disposition. That is, a student must have the ability to think critically and the inclination to do so. Critical thinking skills are those necessary to identify and solve complex problems, including analyzing arguments and evidence, locating central issues in an argument, using data appropriately to make references, and evaluating the quality of evidence from authorities and others. A disposition toward critical thinking indicates a willingness to engage in problem solving through asking questions, analyzing evidence and its implications, tolerating new ideas, and seeing complexity. It is worth noting that this disposition is captured in a person's developmentally instigative characteristics represented in the Bronfenbrenner (1979, 1993) ecology model. A student's ability to think critically and his or her interest in engaging in critical thinking are both outcomes of development and contributors to it.

Postformal reasoning is so called because it relies on an individual's ability to think beyond the requirements of formal reasoning used to solve problems that have more or less knowable or "correct" answers (see King & Kitchener, 1994). Postformal reasoning skills are involved in puzzling through ill-structured problems for which a correct answer cannot be verified. Examples of these problems include those pertaining to the value and safety of genetically modified crops, the resolution of culturally bound violent conflicts, and the global security and preservation of water. King and Kitchener (1994) identified ill-structured problems as those with unclear boundaries; competing or conflicting information; and a number of potential solutions, none of which can be verified. Critical thinking skills are useful to a point in addressing such problems, but fall short when the student runs into unknown or unknowable information. The ability to engage in postformal reasoning takes over at this point.

A number of instruments have been used to measure cognitive and intellectual growth during college, with nearly all studies showing student gains. Kitchener, Wood, and Jensen (1999) used the Reflective Judgment Interview and the Reasoning About Current Issues Test. They found that seniors measured 26 percentile points above first-year students. In her early work, Baxter Magolda (1990) used semi-structured interviews and the Measure of Epistemological Reflection (MER), which is based on Perry's scheme (1970) of intellectual and ethical development (discussed in Chapter Seven). Kube and Thorndike (1991) also used the MER. Analyzing these longitudinal studies, Pascarella and Terenzini (2005) estimated gains on the order of 41 to 46 percentile points from the first year to junior year in the Baxter Magolda study and 49 percentile points from the first year to senior year in the Kube and Thorndike study. The evidence is clear: "Exposure to postsecondary education has a statistically significant, positive effect on critical thinking," and "Those who attend college make significantly greater gains in reflective judgment . . . than those who do not attend college" (Pascarella & Terenzini, 2005, p. 164).

Differences in students' intellectual and cognitive gains across institutions of varying type, selectivity, and environment are of interest to researchers and educators. Knowing what institutional characteristics are related to greater gains can guide educators and leaders in creating environments for maximum growth. The most significant variable in the promotion of students' cognitive and intellectual growth—even after controlling for student input characteristics, such as academic background and motivation—appears to be the nature of faculty-student interactions and faculty concern for student growth and development (Pascarella & Terenzini, 2005).

In 2003 the Council for Aid to Education (CAE, an independent subsidiary of the nonprofit RAND Corporation) launched the Collegiate Learning Assessment (CLA) to measure gains in learning (specifically, analytical and critical thinking) during college. CAE also offers a Community College Learning Assessment. Longitudinal studies are yielding data that may be useful to scholars, institutions, and students. Some of the news is not good. In their book *Academically Adrift*, Arum and Roksa (2011) reported that 45 percent of students did not demonstrate any significant improvement in critical thinking in their first two years in college; 36 percent did not do so in four years. These authors identified differences in critical thinking gains by major, with liberal arts students showing more improvement than peers in professional and some preprofessional majors (such as education, business, and engineering). It is not yet clear which findings from CLA-based research will support or contradict conclusions from Pascarella and Terenzini's synthesis (1991, 2005), but it is evident that attention to student learning and intellectual development is increasing among private and public sectors. We discuss the CLA itself in more detail at the end of this chapter in the section on assessing student outcomes.

As we noted earlier, within-college effects (that is, comparisons of students at the same institution) are the subject of substantial amounts of research, and for good reason. In short, the weight of evidence on student outcomes indicates that what a student does in college matters more than where he or she attends. Pascarella and Terenzini (2005) organized this research into six categories: academic major, coursework and curricular patterns, general pedagogical approaches, teacher behaviors, academic effort and involvement, and social and extracurricular activities. In summary, they found that academic major is not conclusively related to differences in gains in critical thinking; it does relate to the development of different kinds of reasoning skills, but not necessarily to differences in the *amount* of development or gain. In terms of coursework and curricular patterns, students with more exposure to core courses tended to have stronger gains than those with less exposure. Pedagogical approaches that involve collaborative and cooperative learning or academic controversy appear to promote greater problem-solving skills, though Pascarella and Terenzini noted that studies of purposeful interventions via pedagogy are varied and the evidence is not conclusive as to these interventions' benefit. Evidence of the effects of teacher behavior on the development of critical thinking is scant. Unsurprisingly, studies show that academic effort and involvement are closely related to gains in critical thinking and postformal reasoning. Finally, research on social and extracurricular activities shows that peer influence on cognitive and intellectual gains is high, and that experiences with service learning and diversity contribute to gains in this area. On- or off-campus work and on- or off-campus residence appeared not to have direct effects on cognitive growth.

Psychosocial Change

In Chapters Six and Seven we presented theories about how psychosocial change occurs across the lifespan and specifically in college. Here, we discuss evidence of the effects of college on psychosocial development, defined as increased understanding of self in society. Research in this area shows that generally, students undergo changes in identity, academic and social self-concepts, and self-esteem. They become more confident in their ability to think and make decisions independently and less reliant on authorities to provide answers for them. They typically "resolve identity issues and forge commitments to a personal identity" (Pascarella & Terenzini, 2005, p. 214). College student identities are studied holistically and in specific domains of identity (including race, gender, and sexual orientation).

Identity development as conceived by Erikson (1968) and Chickering and Reisser (1993) has been studied among college students. In particular, the Student Developmental Task and Lifestyle Inventory (Winston & Miller, 1987), now the Student Developmental Task and Lifestyle Assessment (Winston, Miller, & Cooper, n.d.), was developed to measure growth along Chickering and Reisser's revised seven vectors of identity development (see Chapter Seven). Thousands of studies have used these measures to show that, generally, college students do resolve the identity crisis of adolescence and show gains along the seven vectors. Academic and social self-concepts and self-esteem increase, students are more confident in their academic and leadership skills, and students are more independent thinkers. Studies using other measures, including self-reported gains (see Kuh, 1999), also indicate that students make progress in overall self-understanding. Large-scale representative studies indicate that "students make statistically significant freshman- to senior-year gains in leadership abilities, popularity, and social self-confidence" (Pascarella & Terenzini, 2005, p. 263).

Although there is a sizable body of literature on students from different racial and ethnic backgrounds, and although race and ethnicity are frequently used as variables in data analysis, there is less known about the effects of college on students' racial and ethnic identity development. Pascarella and Terenzini (2005) identified two studies from the late 1990s that examined racial identity in cross-sectional samples. Cokley (1999) found no differences between lower- and upper-division students in measurements of Cross's model (1991) of black identity formation. Using samples from a predominantly white institution and a historically black institution, McCowen and Alston (1998) found no freshman- to senior-year differences on the African Self-Consciousness Scale at either campus, but seniors at the historically black institution had higher scores in racial identity formation than did first-year students. Neither study included a control group of non-college-going young adults, so it is not clear to what extent these changes (or lack thereof) are an effect of the college environment. As noted in Chapter Five, the racial climate on campus is a significant factor in students' experiences and outcomes, though less is known about the effect of college on racial identity itself.

Vasti Torres (2003) selected entering college students to begin a longitudinal study of Latina identity. This qualitative study, reported over time as results have emerged (see Torres, 2003; Torres & Baxter Magolda, 2004; Torres & Hernandez, 2007), provides a model for examining the ways that a host of personal characteristics and experiences interact with and in the college environment to promote cognitive growth and the development of Latina identity. As Abes, Jones, and McEwen (2007) did in an analysis of multidimensional identity development, Torres has drawn from a self-authorship theoretical perspective (see Chapter Six) to present a portrait of identity development that entwines intrapersonal (psychosocial), interpersonal, and cognitive development. Torres and colleagues have been able to point out the features of campus life, as well as other important contexts of students' lives, that interact with racial identity. These features include peer culture, campus racial climate, academics, and faculty.

As with the racial identity literature, studies of sexual orientation identity development in college students tend to be more theoretical than longitudinal (Renn, 2010). Small-sample, single-campus studies predominate. They have been useful in providing empirical evidence of the experiences of lesbian, gay, and bisexual students and in illuminating some of the processes of sexual orientation identity development, but the lack of a comparison group makes it difficult to determine the effects of college as opposed to the effects of maturation. Pascarella and Terenzini (2005) concluded, "Attending college may indeed play a role in nonheterosexual students achieving a major psychological milestone: 'coming out,' or revelation of sexual orientation" (p. 218).

Pascarella and Terenzini (2005) found no evidence to support claims that institutional type (such as public institution compared to private institution or liberal arts college compared to research university) influences psychosocial outcomes, though there is evidence that institutional environments may play a role. For example, women at women's colleges reported greater increases in academic self-concept than did women at coeducational institutions (Kim & Alvarez, 1995). Similarly, black students at Historically Black Colleges and Universities had greater gains in academic self-concept than did their peers at predominantly white institutions, though additional factors included institutional selectivity and size (Berger, 2000; Berger & Milem, 2000; Kim, 1999; Miller-Bernal, 2000). Students on campuses that are more racially diverse show greater freshman- to senior-year gains in academic self-concept than do students at less diverse institutions (Chang, 1996, 1997; Szelenyi, 2002).

An increased inclination toward what the Higher Education Research Institute (1996) dubbed Socially Responsible Leadership may be considered a psychosocial outcome of college. Results of the Wabash National Study (Center for Inquiry, n.d.) indicate that liberal arts college students gained 0.36 standard deviations on a scale of Socially Responsible Leadership from their first to fourth year. Komives, Casper, Longerbeam, Mainella, and Osteen (2005) presented a grounded theory of leadership identity development, noting factors in the college environment that could enhance this type of development. These factors included opportunities for increasingly complex leadership responsibilities, exposure to diverse others, and effective mentoring.

Within institutions, specific sub-environments may also have differential effects on students' psychosocial development. Such factors as academic courses or major (Morris & Daniel, 2008; Torres & Baxter Magolda, 2004); participation in service learning (Jones & Abes, 2004; Simons & Cleary, 2005); involvement in extracurricular activities (Guardia & Evans, 2008; Inkelas, 2004); and friendship group composition (Antonio et al., 2004; Pope, 1998, 2000; Torres, 2003) may contribute to different outcomes. For example, feminist identity may be enhanced for women's studies majors (Bargad & Hyde, 1991; Luebke & Reilly, 1995). Students in identity-based student organizations (for example, the Black Student Alliance, Asian Student Association, or LGBT Caucus) may also experience development in those domains of identity (Harper & Quaye, 2007; Inkelas, 2004; Kezar & Moriarty, 2000; Renn, 2007; Renn & Ozaki, 2010). The lack of a comparison group in some of these studies (such as Renn & Ozaki) makes it difficult to attribute outcomes to these experiences, yet evidence does suggest that immersion in identity-based settings promotes psychosocial development in the relevant domain.

Attitudes and Values

Attitudes represent a state of mind or feeling with which an individual regards a matter, whether it is someone, something, or a group of people or things. Values represent a higher-order way of organizing generalized standards that transcend specific situations. A U.S. student may have an open-minded attitude concerning interacting with international peers and hold intercultural understanding as a value. Or she may have a negative attitude about a particular academic subject because of the way it was taught to her in high school, even if she has a broader value of intellectual exploration that leads her to try a course in this area during college. Her brother may hold social justice and human equality as values, which motivate him to try to change racist and sexist attitudes among his fraternity peers. College is a place where attitudes and values are evident, but does the college experience play a role in changing them?

In many categories, the answer is "yes"—attending college does appear to have an effect on students' attitudes and values. The inclusion of items related to attitudes and values on the Cooperative Institutional Research Program (CIRP) survey (Pryor, Hurtado, Sáenz, Santos, & Korn, 2007), among others, provides an effective means of measuring change over time in a large, representative sample of college students. For example, studies show that students gain 10 to 15 percentile points in "cultural, aesthetic, and intellectual sophistication while expanding their interests in the visual and performing arts in general" (Pascarella & Terenzini, 2005, p. 272). Students gain an appreciation for the liberal arts and become less extrinsically driven in educational and career areas. Over time, students become more open to others and to new ideas.

College graduates are more likely to participate in activities that are considered to be positive indicators of civic participation. U.S. citizens with a college degree are more likely to be registered to vote and to report voting in national elections (Baum, Ma, & Payea, 2010; Bowen & Bok, 1998). They are also more likely to support most civil liberties and to participate in community service (Baum et al., 2010; Bowen & Bok, 1998).

Going to college also appears to have a positive influence on attitudes about race and ethnicity. Over time, students become more egalitarian and less prejudiced, more culturally aware, and more committed to promoting racial understanding (see Pryor et al., 2007). Despite these changes in attitude, students appear to gain only slightly (4 percentile points) in understanding people of other racial and ethnic backgrounds (Pascarella & Terenzini, 2005), and Chang (2002a) found no clear differences in scores on the Modern Racism Scale for students taking courses designed to fulfill one university's diversity course requirement.

During college, students' attitudes and values concerning gender roles and sexual orientation also undergo a shift toward egalitarianism. Employing measures of attitudes about three key issues—sex equity in pay, date rape, and married women's role in work outside the home—Astin (1993b) found that seniors held more egalitarian views than they did in their first year. For example, the 2009 national aggregates of the College Senior

Survey indicate increasing acceptance of same-sex relationships: the number of college seniors who felt that there should be laws prohibiting "homosexual relationships" dropped from 23.8 percent at college entry to 14.9 percent (Frank, Ruiz, Sharkness, DeAngelo, & Pryor, 2010).

As we noted in Chapter One, much is made of the influence of college on students' religious attitudes and values, and evidence continues to support an overall decline in doctrinaire or traditional religious affiliation during college. In their 1991 review, Pascarella and Terenzini estimated this effect to be as much as 20 percentile points. Studies in the 1990s and 2000s show more mixed results, including Bryant, Choi, and Yasuno's study (2003) using CIRP data that showed a decrease in students' religious behaviors but an effort to integrate spirituality into their lives. Ongoing research from UCLA's Higher Education Research Institute spirituality study (www.spirituality.ucla.edu) confirms the continued importance of spirituality and spiritual quest in the lives of students. Bryant et al. suggested that what could look like a decrease in traditional religious values may instead reflect changes in how students think about religion. In sum, the effect of college on religion and spirituality is not completely clear, though declines in traditional religious activities and values may hold.

How does a college education affect attitudes and values? It appears that peers, faculty, and a variety of forms of campus involvement have the greatest effect (Astin, 1993b). There are some age cohort and external effects in play, but the college environment does seem to matter in regard to sociopolitical attitudes. Academic major, participation in diverse friendship groups, student-faculty interactions, and service learning appear to have effects when making comparisons within an institution, whereas across institutions there seems to be little influence of institutional type (Pascarella & Terenzini, 2005).

Moral Development

King (2009) argued persuasively for the holistic consideration of cognitive and moral development, yet she has also conducted substantive analyses of the abundant literature on morality, moral reasoning, and moral development in college students (see King & Mayhew, 2002, 2005; Mayhew & King, 2008). As described in Chapter Seven, moral development, sometimes called ethical development, represents increasing complexity in the ability to differentiate good (or right) behaviors, intentions, and decisions from those that are bad (or wrong). Long-standing claims that higher education promotes moral development date back to the origins of U.S.

higher education in the Massachusetts Bay Colony in 1636. In the twenty-first century there are renewed calls for higher education to assert this historical role. The Association of American Colleges and Universities (2002), for example, challenged its member institutions to

> foster intellectual honesty, responsibility for society's moral health and for social justice, active participation as a citizen of a diverse democracy, discernment of the ethical consequences of decisions and action and a deep understanding of one's self and respect for the complex identities of others, their histories and their cultures. (p. xii)

A substantial amount of evidence supports the claim that participation in higher education does, in fact, lead to increased moral development and the ability to use principled reasoning to resolve moral judgments. As described in Chapter Seven, a milestone in cognitive and moral development is the transition from conventional to postconventional thinking, and there is evidence that students do make this shift. In their 1991 and 2005 syntheses of research on student outcomes, Pascarella and Terenzini found that "the weight of evidence indicated that the college experience itself has a unique positive influence on increases in principled moral reasoning" (2005, p. 347). They also found that the development of moral reasoning is a necessary but not sufficient condition for moral action (see Rest, 1994).

King and Mayhew (2005) reviewed 157 studies of moral development in college students that used Rest's Defining Issues Test (DIT; 1979a, 1979b) and had been conducted since 1987. In an earlier review (King & Mayhew, 2002), they examined 174 studies using the DIT and conducted since 1980. The DIT measures moral development as theorized by Kohlberg, Levine, and Hewer (1984; see King & Mayhew, 2005, for a description and analysis of the DIT). In brief, King and Mayhew (2002, 2005) found evidence that student characteristics and college contexts interact to influence moral reasoning, which in turn influences cognitive, identity, and social outcomes. Specifically, they found that "being female, having higher aptitude/intelligence, being politically liberal, and being open to new experiences were found to be positively related to postconventional reasoning, but SES, ethnicity, and religious affiliation were not" (King & Mayhew, 2005, p. 422). Further, institutional types and academic disciplines were not useful for evaluating the effectiveness of the college environment in promoting moral development, but "pedagogical strategies such as experiential learning, reflection, group work, active learning and decision-making are more effective in promoting moral judgment than those that use more traditional pedagogies" (p. 422; see also Mayhew & King, 2008).

Like Mayhew and King (2008), Pascarella and Terenzini (2005) found support for differential within-college effects, though they did not find much evidence to support claims of between-college effects. They found that courses that provide explicit instruction in addressing dilemmas and those that emphasize personality development promote the development of moral reasoning. Ethics courses (such as those found in business and nursing curricula) can also be effective. Studies of service learning, academic major, and intercollegiate athletic involvement show mixed results. Interactions with faculty appear to promote moral development, and interactions with diverse peers may also contribute.

Holistic Development Toward Self-Authorship

In Chapter Six we discussed the importance of holistic development toward self-authorship (Baxter Magolda, 1998, 2001b), which includes the ability to balance internal and external needs and interests in defining self, making decisions, and taking action. As we consider outcomes in this chapter, we return to this important concept. Self-authorship is a relative newcomer to the literature on college student learning and development, and merited only a few paragraphs in Pascarella and Terenzini's tome (2005) based on research through 2002. Yet the holistic approach to cognitive, interpersonal, and intrapersonal development represented in the self-authorship literature gets to the heart of higher education's mission. Baxter Magolda (2007) put it plainly: "Twenty-first-century learning outcomes require self-authorship: the internal capacity to define one's belief system, identity, and relationships (Baxter Magolda, 2001b; Kegan, 1994)" (p. 69). Because it is such an important area of student learning and development, we include it here with other outcomes, even as research on self-authorship continues to develop.

Assessment of self-authorship as a higher education outcome is evolving. In the next part of this chapter we discuss assessment methods, but because techniques for measuring self-authorship are not as firmly established in the literature as are those for many other outcomes described in this chapter, we believe it is important to note some methodological issues here. Kegan (1982, 1994) used a technique called the Subject-Object Interview (SOI; Lahey, Souvaine, Kegan, Goodman, & Felix, 1988) to understand the extent to which individuals had reached different "orders of consciousness" (as he called the stages or phases in his model). Interview approaches are the most common in self-authorship research, including studies of college students (see, for example, Baxter Magolda, 2001b; King, Baxter Magolda, Barber, Kendall Brown, & Lindsay, 2009; Lewis et al., 2005; Pizzolato, 2003, 2004; Pizzolato, Chaudhari, Murrell, Podobnik, & Schaeffer, 2008; Torres & Hernandez, 2007), though most often research in higher education does not employ the SOI. Baxter Magolda and King (2007) described specific strategies for both promoting and assessing college students' self-authorship through interviews, and provided examples from their work on the Wabash National Study (King et al., 2009) and from Baxter Magolda's long-running study of self-authorship (Baxter Magolda, 2001b). A strength of this area of research is that there are, in addition to these examples, a number of longitudinal interview-based studies (Lewis et al., 2005; Torres & Hernandez) and mixed methods studies (Creamer & Laughlin, 2005; Seifert, Goodman, King, & Baxter Magolda, 2010). Some other areas of student development research that rely predominantly on qualitative measures rarely employ longitudinal designs.

Scholars working in the area have begun to develop and test quantitative measures of self-authorship. Creamer, Baxter Magolda, and Yue (2010) noted,

> As fits any scientific endeavor, there is a healthy amount of skepticism among members of the community of scholars conducting research about self-authorship about the feasibility of constructing a quantitative instrument that captures the complexity of the way self-authorship has been conceptualized. (p. 560)

Pizzolato (2007) introduced the Self-Authorship Survey (SAS), the quantitative half of a two-part survey. The other half was an open-ended Experience Survey (ES), which asked students to provide narratives about an important decision they had made. Together, the SAS and ES provide information about students' reasoning abilities and their self-reported actions in decision-making situations. Pizzolato found that although statistically significant, correlation between individual students' SAS scores and coded ES responses was "only modest" (p. 36). Pizzolato concluded:

> The ES builds on the SAS by providing insight into how the reasoning-action split may play out in individual students. Thus, until an even stronger measure of self-authorship is developed, using the two in

conjunction seems best able to serve the diverse needs (such as program evaluation, student outcome assessment, or diagnostic testing) of postsecondary institutions and programs attempting to facilitate self-authorship development in students. (p. 41)

Creamer et al. (2010) used the Career Decision Making Survey measure of self-authorship (CDMS-SA) to create a three-by-three matrix of scores across three phases of self-authorship development (External Formulas, Crossroads, Early Self-Authoring) and the three dimensions of the theory (epistemological, interpersonal, intrapersonal); results can be reported in a single score or in scores representing the three developmental phases. Creamer et al. (2010) reported that the measure has "strong enough reliability to support use in future research" (p. 557). Quantitative measures of self-authorship, which have the advantage over qualitative approaches in their scalability and practicality for widespread use in higher education, remain rare, and there are no published studies using the SAS or CDMS-SA in pre-post I-E-O research that allows for claims about specific effects of college on individual development and learning.

There is, however, evidence from qualitative studies that self-authorship can and does develop during college. In Baxter Magolda's longitudinal study that began with 101 first-year students in 1986, by graduation only two reached the point of cognitive development that she later asserted was necessary for self-authorship to emerge (Baxter Magolda, 1992, 1998, 2001b). Other studies have found a larger proportion of the sample achieving this developmental milestone. Using the SOI (Lahey et al., 1988) in a longitudinal study of West Point cadets, Lewis and colleagues (2005) found that zero out of thirty-eight cadets had advanced past Kegan's third order of consciousness in their first year, whereas six out of the thirty-two cadets (19 percent) remaining in the study were in transition to the fourth order of consciousness (self-authorship) in their final year at West Point (see Chapter Six for a description of Kegan's orders of consciousness). Comparing sophomore to senior measurements, eighteen of twenty-nine (62 percent) showed progression, though none reached a point of full self-authorship. Pizzolato (2004) found that students with a number of risk factors for attrition entered college with some ability to self-author, but many regressed to a stage of following (or seeking) external formulas once they arrived; some members of this group regained their self-authoring positions as they learned to cope with their new surroundings. Finally, a handful of studies examining psychosocial identities, which we described in a previous section (Abes & Jones, 2004; Abes, Jones, &

McEwen, 2007; Jones, 2009; Torres & Baxter Magolda, 2004; Torres & Hernandez, 2007), showed that college students can develop holistically in the cognitive, intrapersonal, and interpersonal domains of the self-authorship model.

At this time in the emergence of research on self-authorship it is not fully possible to assess differences in student outcomes across colleges and within colleges, though there is a growing literature on educational practices that are more likely than others to produce differential outcomes. The Wabash National Study (King et al., 2009; Seifert et al., 2010) showed that engagement in high-impact activities, such as taking challenging courses, studying abroad, and interacting closely with diverse peers, contributed to the development of a self-authoring mind. Pizzolato (2005) identified "provocative moments" (p. 628)—disorienting dilemmas in which students' existing meaning-making schemas failed to meet the challenge of the moment in a relationship or decision—in students' journey through the Crossroads on their way to authoring themselves. Elsewhere, Pizzolato (2006) pointed to opportunities for academic advisers to challenge and support students by asking questions about *why* they were making decisions as well as *what* those decisions were. A number of scholars have proposed and sometimes studied specific recommendations for promoting self-authorship (see Baxter Magolda & King, 2004; Bekken & Marie, 2007; Laughlin & Creamer, 2007), though the evidence for all of these potentially high-impact activities is not yet complete.

Career and Economic Impacts of College

At a time when 84.7 percent of entering students report that they are going to college to get a better job; when 71.2 percent report that making more money is a major motivation to attend (Pryor, Hurtado, DeAngelo, Palucki Blake, & Tran, 2011); and when the unemployment rate of college graduates is significantly lower than that of high school graduates, it may seem unnecessary to include a section on the career and economic impacts of college on those who attend. Yet there is evidence that attending college affects not only what jobs are available to graduates but also to some extent the careers to which students aspire. College attendance also has a measurable effect on lifetime earning potential, on the order of a 20 percent increase in lifetime earnings for college graduates over high school graduates (Hout & Janus, 2011). Degree completion—not just college attendance—seems critical to this difference (Pascarella

& Terenzini, 2005), pointing to the credentialing effect of the degree. Pascarella and Terenzini (2005) also concluded that, independent of individual student characteristics, attending an institution that selects a smaller percentage of applicants is related to higher earnings later in life.

The picture of college completion and career and economic benefit is not a simple one. Although there are measured differences in career and economic attainment across institutions, these findings are confounded in part by within-college differences in careers by academic major (Pascarella & Terenzini, 2005). So an Ivy League graduate who goes into public school teaching is not likely to benefit economically any more than the land-grant university alumnus who teaches across the hall, but their college classmates who majored in accounting may out-earn each of them. And the community college graduate who transfers into an urban comprehensive institution on her way to a moderately selective law school may do better still than the teachers and accountants. To be sure, effects of accumulated social capital from a lifetime of educational advantage cannot be discounted; an Ivy League degree carries privileges that most degrees from an urban comprehensive institution do not. Yet within-college differences in economic outcomes vary just as widely.

Other than the employment and economic benefits, does college confer other vocational benefits to those who attend? Some researchers would argue that in addition to helping students meet preestablished career goals, higher education also exposes students to careers they had not considered and helps them align career aspirations with self-assessed values, interests, and strengths (Kuh et al., 2005; Pascarella, & Terenzini, 1991, 2005). Although some people might argue that changing students' career choices is not the job of higher education, and indeed that such changes may interfere with timely completion of degree requirements, the student affairs profession in higher education has a long history of helping students clarify vocational goals and work toward them (see American Council on Education, 1937).

Assessing Student Outcomes

Discussing purported outcomes of college attendance is an empty exercise without assessment of those outcomes. The evidence presented in the previous sections was derived from research and assessment activities that focused on the impact of college on students. Higher education leaders and policymakers in the twenty-first century find themselves accountable for student outcomes, measured as completion rates, student learning, or student development. In institutions, assessing student outcomes often falls to student affairs professionals (for developmental outcomes) and academic affairs professionals (for learning outcomes). Offices responsible for institutional research and student tracking (for example, the registrar) typically aggregate and report data on persistence and completion, demographics, and financial aid. At an informal level, faculty and student affairs professionals conduct ongoing assessments of learning and development in the context of individual courses and cocurricular programming.

It is important to understand that *assessment* and *evaluation*, although sometimes used interchangeably, have different meanings in higher education practice. Upcraft and Schuh (1996) defined assessment as "any effort to gather, analyze, and interpret evidence which describes institutional, divisional, or agency effectiveness" (p. 18). Evaluation is "any effort to use assessment evidence to improve institutional, departmental, divisional, or agency effectiveness" (p. 19). Assessment is the process of collecting and interpreting evidence, whereas evaluation involves the use of that evidence to attempt to improve outcomes. Not all authors make this distinction, but it is important to keep in mind when considering the purposes of assessment activities. Very often, the goal of improving efficiency and outcomes is implied in the rationale for conducting assessment, but for some audiences it may be important to state explicitly that program improvement—not just monitoring—is the purpose behind assessment activities.

It is beyond the scope of this book to provide a detailed primer on assessing and evaluating student outcomes. We advise readers who are responsible for conducting substantive assessments of student outcomes to consult foundational resources in the field, including those by Schuh and Associates (2009); Bresciani (2009, 2011); Bresciani, Moore Gardner, and Hickmott (2009); Banta and Associates (2002); and Maki (2010). In this section, we provide an overview of assessment based on the I-E-O framework and a discussion of purposes of and approaches to outcomes assessment.

Assessment Based on the I-E-O Framework

As we noted in the Preface, Alexander Astin laid out the I-E-O framework in his 1991 book *Assessment for Excellence*. He advocated for careful empirical attention to the influence of both input characteristics and environments on student outcomes. He proposed the I-E-O model as a way to address the common problem of a lack of control groups (meaning matched comparison groups against whose outcomes those of students receiving the program, curriculum, or other intervention under assessment can be measured) in the "natural experiments" of higher education (Astin, 1991, p. 28). He argued against incomplete assessments that lacked one or more of the three components, pointing to "outcomes only" assessments as a growing but flawed measure of student gains in college. Useful in assessing overall levels of skill or achievement, these measures are not as useful in understanding why students score as they do.

I-E-O assessment entails measuring student inputs that may include demographics (sex, race, age, SES); precollege academic preparation and achievement (high school GPA, standardized test scores); family background (parents' education, generational status in the United States); special skills (athletic or artistic, for example); and any other factors that may be relevant to the outcomes one seeks to measure. Some of these input data are easily gleaned from admissions applications, assuming one can get permission to access them and protect student confidentiality; others may have to be collected explicitly for assessment purposes.

Assessment of inputs may also entail direct measurement, at college entry, of the outcome variables of interest. For example, if one is interested in the effects of a liberal arts education on students' inclination toward lifelong learning (see Seifert et al., 2010), one must measure students on this inclination at the start and the end of the liberal arts experience. Similarly, if development of athletic performance, leadership skills, or political attitudes as a result of going to college is of interest, then pre- and post-tests are necessary to say much about the effect of college on each of these outcomes. Needs assessments rely on input factors to determine what programs and services students may want or need.

Environmental variables constitute a host of factors, typically within the institution. Faculty, peers, curricula, extracurricular activities, work settings, and housing are a few examples. Frequency, duration, and quality of interactions with the environment make up a cluster of factors often called "engagement" (Kuh, 2008, 2011) or "involvement" (Astin, 1984). Nearly any aspect of the student experience could be considered as an environmental variable, which both creates exciting possibilities for research and assessment and introduces numerous obstacles to understanding what, exactly, leads to particular outcomes. Thousands of studies have used the I-E-O model to examine environmental variables, as, indeed, they hold the key to what institutions can do differently to improve student outcomes toward desired goals. Locally, assessments of an environment may include utilization studies (How many students use a program or service? Which students? How often?); satisfaction studies (How satisfied are students with programs and services?); and campus climate studies (How do students experience the gender, racial, or other climate?).

We believe that campus climate assessment is a critical feature of an overall assessment program, as it can reveal what students learn; why they stay (or leave); and what features of the environment (curriculum, peers, student-faculty interaction, learning support services) have an impact on student success. Campus climate, as we discussed in Chapter Five, is a product of multiple interactions of history, culture, and people within an organization. It is an environmental factor that acts on and is created by students, faculty, and staff. There is clear evidence that campus racial climate, for example, relates to retention and persistence of students of color (Hurtado, Milem, Clayton-Pedersen, & Allen, 1998) and to learning outcomes for all students (Hurtado, Dey, Gurin, & Gurin, 2003).

Outcomes, as summarized throughout this chapter, fall into a range of categories related to the goals of higher education. Content knowledge mastery, critical thinking, personal development, moral development, civic engagement, and values are among the many outcomes sought by educators. Students, families, and the public may have other outcomes in mind (such as job placement and increased earning potential), and certainly these are not unimportant, but outcomes desired of college graduates are broader than individual vocational advancement. Later in this chapter we discuss some standardized outcomes measurements, though local efforts at outcomes assessment need not rely solely on national studies.

Overall, the I-E-O framework seems to provide a sensible approach to conducting assessment in higher education. We caution, however, that such student enrollment patterns as swirling, double dipping, and stopping out, which we discussed in Chapter Three, introduce challenges to isolating environmental influences. Assessors must also adapt to increasingly diverse student populations, for whom some outcomes measures may not be normed. Assessment of online education is a growing field, but typically this assessment relates to learning outcomes of specific courses or programs of study and not to broader goals of higher education. We believe that the I-E-O framework can be adapted to emerging patterns of enrollment, diverse student populations, and different forms of accessing higher education.

Assessment Purposes and Approaches

Assessment can be conducted for many reasons. Bresciani (2011) identified program, department, or institutional improvement as key purposes for assessment. As higher education leaders attempt to redistribute resources in efforts to meet institutional goals under increasing financial strains, decisions about the discontinuation of programs or departments may come as a result of needs, utilization, or satisfaction assessments. It could be argued that such assessment-driven decisions are for the improvement of the overall institution, though the faculty, staff, and students most directly involved in reduced or discontinued programs may disagree.

Another key purpose of assessment in the twenty-first century is to provide data to meet external demands for accountability and to bolster institutional competitiveness in a crowded higher education market. Legislators and taxpayers want to know what they are getting for their investments in postsecondary education, whether those investments are directly to institutions or through student financial aid. Assessment data can aid in the case for maintaining public support for higher education. Being able to show the "value added" of attending a certain institution might help that institution compete for students and external support. Internal efforts to improve learning and developmental outcomes for students certainly provide a solid rationale for conducting assessments of different types, but there are external constituencies who may be audiences for assessment results as well.

The purpose of a given assessment may influence the approach chosen for data collection, analysis, and presentation. Some assessments are done solely with quantitative data, others solely with qualitative data, and still others with mixed methods (see Schuh & Associates, 2009). One way is not universally better than the others; when designing assessment processes, a key factor in the decision about what kinds of data to collect relates to the purpose of the inquiry. If what is sought is best measured numerically (for example, facility or program utilization assessment or degree of agreement with statements about campus climate), then quantitative measures should be included to answer how many, how much, how often, and with what measurable outcome. If what is sought relates to processes (for example, how students go about accessing certain campus services) or to meanings people make of some aspect of campus life (for example, to what institutional motivations students attribute changes in programs, services, or resources), then qualitative data are in order. Mixed methods designs provide strengths of both. Some mixed methods assessments lean more to one approach than the other, such as a survey that includes a number of items to be rated and only a few open-ended questions to answer, or extensive focus groups combined with a short demographic and utilization questionnaire.

Another determining factor in choosing the assessment method relates to the intended audiences of the assessment. If one seeks to persuade a notoriously "bottom line" board of trustees that students are using a program or service (such as the counseling center or academic advising) at its capacity and one needs more resources to expand the service, it would be wise to collect the kinds of so-called hard (usually meaning quantitative) data that can make a strong case to that board. It is also true that qualitative data presented through assessment can be persuasive, especially to "put a face on" the numbers. But anecdotes and even student testimony may not be persuasive if they are not gathered through a systematic assessment process. Understanding the multiple potential audiences for assessment findings can be very useful in the design process.

Throughout this book we have made note of instances in which studies of, for example, college choice, persistence, or outcomes have been limited by the use of single-time data collection. The ideal assessment would include data collection before and after the student experiences whatever phenomenon is of interest, as well as a matched control group that is not experiencing the phenomenon. Such instances are very rare in higher education research and program assessment, which operate more frequently on a quasi-experimental framework at best. Yet asking students after the fact about how a program or course changed them is not an adequate means of assessment; student self-reports of gains have been found to be less than reliable on their own (see Bowman, 2010, 2011). Practical matters, including many student affairs professionals' lack of "understanding of assessment, time, and resources" (Bresciani, 2010, p. 81), create barriers to conducting and using outcomes assessment to improve programs and services.

Assessment of cocurricular programs and of student affairs programs and services varies widely across institutions. Some assessment-driven divisions of student affairs or departments within divisions systematically collect data on student learning and development, program and resource utilization, and satisfaction related to cocurricular programs (residence hall activities, student leadership training). Yet in spite of abundant resources (including Schuh & Associates, 2009; Upcraft & Schuh, 1996) and frequent admonition (Bresciani, 2011; Keeling, 2004, 2006; Young & Janosik, 2007), assessment efforts at other institutions lag behind. The

American College Personnel Association and National Association of Student Personnel Administrators (2010) issued a joint report on professional competencies in student affairs, and assessment is a core element.

Still, within the constraints of time, knowledge, and resources, higher education administrators and policy bodies do conduct a significant amount of assessment. As calls for accountability to students, families, and the public increase, assessment of student outcomes is an essential addition to measurements of institutional productivity based solely on degree completion. To be sure, degree completion is an important goal and one on which higher education in the United States could significantly improve. But degree completion alone does not tell the full story of what happens to students when they attend higher education in any format (such as residential, commuter, online, public, private, or for-profit). Well-conducted assessments of meaningful outcomes are critical to understanding where higher education is doing well by students, where it can improve, and how it might do so.

A number of nationwide and multi-institutional studies, many longitudinal, provide a foundation for understanding and assessing higher education outcomes. The National Survey of Student Engagement, Cooperative Institutional Research Program, Coalition on the Finance of Higher Education, Wabash National Study, and Multi-Institutional Study of Leadership Development are examples. The National Center for Education Statistics (NCES) and National Science Foundation (NSF) have longstanding projects that include cohorts (or "panels") of student participants over time. NCES and NSF maintain and provide access to data sets that can be used in assessment, including the National Postsecondary Student Aid Survey (NPSAS), Beginning Postsecondary Students (BPS), and the National Educational Longitudinal Survey (NELS). Schuh and Associates (2009) listed twenty-two common assessment instruments in five categories: (1) entering undergraduates, (2) enrolled undergraduates, (3) student proficiencies and learning outcomes, (4) alumni, and (5) series of instruments. This list is a valuable resource when considering how to assess a given outcome.

Earlier in the chapter we noted that the Collegiate Learning Assessment is gaining ground as a measure of postsecondary outcomes. We predict that the CLA will feature heavily in discussions of student learning and institutional effectiveness in the next decade, and therefore believe it is important to discuss in more depth here. The CLA was, to say the least, an advance over existing large-scale learning assessments at the time of its introduction in 2003. The CLA is not without its critics (see Banta

& Pike, 2007; Borden & Young, 2008), however, and should be approached with a reasonable sense of scholarly skepticism, as should all advancements in measurement until they have been shown to be effective and psychometrically sound. The CLA assesses students' critical thinking skills, analytical reasoning, problem-solving skills, and written communication (Klein, Benjamin, Shavelson, & Bolus, 2007). The CLA does not assess students' content knowledge or procedural knowledge.

The CLA received much attention following the 2011 release of *Academically Adrift* (Arum & Roksa, 2011), which concluded, based in part on results of the CLA, that postsecondary education was not improving students' critical thinking skills. The conclusions from the Arum and Roksa book caused much attention to be focused on higher education and on the CLA. In a balanced analysis of the CLA, Klein and his colleagues (2007) raised several concerns. It is important to note here, in a chapter about *student* outcomes, that the CLA was designed to assess *institutions,* not individual student learning. Although Arum and Roksa used a pre-post design with individual students, the CLA was not intended to be used in such a way; the validity of any findings arising from the use of the CLA in this manner should be questioned (Banta & Pike, 2007; Klein et al.).

The CLA also has supporters (Klein et al., 2007; Paris, 2011). Paris painted a very positive picture of how several small, private liberal arts institutions used CLA results to create institutional changes and improve student learning. Indeed, Paris refuted Arum and Roksa's findings (2011), particularly those claims related to small, private colleges, highlighting the amount of learning the CLA was able to assess for students at such institutions. Further, Klein and colleagues touted the direct, objective, essay-based assessments of the CLA (as opposed to self-reported and multiple choice formats of other learning assessment instruments) as major strengths.

Conclusion

Student outcomes are and will remain an essential area of research. Understanding what happens to and for individuals who spend time and money on a college education is a matter of interest to educators, of course, but it is also of increasing importance in local, state, national, and international public policy and philanthropic circles. Given the worldwide investment of public and private funds in postsecondary education institutions and students, being able to explain what individuals *and* societies gain from this investment is not only a practical necessity but also a moral imperative.

This chapter concentrated on the outcomes portion of the I-E-O model, and showed that in a number of areas, people who go to college—and especially those who complete a degree—benefit in a many ways. We also pointed out college-related gains, such as skills, knowledge, attitudes, and behaviors, that have the potential to benefit the larger society. We noted that it matters more what students do in college than where they go, a finding that has persisted since Feldman and Newcomb (1969) synthesized research from the mid-1920s to the mid-1960s.

There is still much more that needs to be known about how to improve outcomes for all students, whether they attend in-person or online, non-profit or for-profit, highly selective or open access institutions. Institutional, state, and nationwide assessments have the potential to contribute to this effort by taking into account student input characteristics, learning environments, and measured outcomes. Without question, keeping intended outcomes in mind when planning, assessing, and improving educational programs will be critical to the success of postsecondary institutions in the twenty-first century.

Points of Discussion

Implications for Students

- How important is it for students to understand the institution's desired outcomes for them? If it is important, how would a student learn about the desired outcomes?
- What can students do to maximize their learning and development in college?

Implications for Institutions

- Whose responsibility is it to assess student outcomes in different domains?
- From an institutional perspective, what are the most important student outcomes?
- What data already exist at an institution that can be used for I-E-O assessment programs? How can these data be accessed? By whom? For what purposes?

- What resources are available to begin or expand an assessment program?
- Who will be interested in student outcomes assessment results? What does an institution do with results that paint it in a less than desirable light?
- How can an institution use assessment results to improve student services and programs, such as academic advising, career services, academic and social support, and community development?

Implications for Policy and National Discourse

- What student outcomes are most important for higher education and college graduates in the twenty-first century? How does the answer differ by institutional type or student-specific factors?
- To what extent should student outcomes be a matter of public concern and policy? If higher education institutions cannot demonstrate that they meet specific student outcomes of concern to the public, should they still be eligible to receive public funding in the form of, for example, state appropriations, research grants, and student financial aid?
- Is it acceptable for different sectors of higher education (for-profit, nonprofit, public, private, two-year, four-year) to have different goals for student outcomes? What is lost and what is gained through the diversity of goals for student outcomes? Is there a common set of goals that all should maintain and demonstrate?

Learning Activities

- Choose an institution of higher education. Locate its mission statement and, if possible, statements of intended learning outcomes for graduates (these may be universal statements for all students, or they might be broken down by academic program). How does the institution know if these outcomes are being achieved? Using an I-E-O approach, how would you assess one or more of these intended outcomes?
- Visit the Web site of one of your institution's accrediting bodies (visit www.chea.org/Directories/index.asp for a refresher). What do the relevant accrediting standards have to say about student outcomes? What outcomes are important, and which are missing? What kind of an impact could this have on the kinds of academic programs, student

services, or campus initiatives your institution implements? In what other ways does your campus demonstrate its commitment to student outcomes?

Resources Related to Student Outcomes

Collegiate Learning Assessment (www.collegiatelearningassessment.org/)

As discussed in this chapter, the CLA is a project of the Council for Aid to Education and is designed for institution-level assessment of student learning in the areas of critical thinking, analytical reasoning, and problem solving. CLA results are at the center of a number of policy discussions about higher education's goals and outcomes.

Cooperative Institutional Research Program at UCLA (www.heri.ucla.edu/cirpoverview.php)

CIRP is the world's longest-running and largest longitudinal study of college student characteristics, experiences, and outcomes. CIRP makes data available to researchers from outside its home institution (UCLA).

Integrated Postsecondary Education Data System (http://nces.ed.gov/ipeds)

The Integrated Postsecondary Education Data System (IPEDS) is an extensive national source for data on accredited postsecondary institutions in the United States. Much IPEDS data are free to the public and can be used for learning about students; faculty; staff; budgets; and such institutional characteristics as size, control (public, private, for-profit), and financial aid profile. It is a particularly valuable resource for institutional research and comparison to peer institutions.

Multi-Institutional Study of Leadership (www.leadershipstudy.net/)

The Multi-Institutional Study of Leadership (MSL), in partnership with the National Clearinghouse of Leadership Programs, is an annual, national survey of college student leadership development. In operation since 2006, the MSL now enrolls over seventy-five institutions, with a strong representation of private colleges and universities.

National Institute for Learning Outcomes Assessment (www.learningoutcomeassessment.org/index.html)

The National Institute for Learning Outcomes Assessment (NILOA) is a project based at Indiana University and the University of Illinois. NILOA's mission is to strengthen undergraduate education through the use of effective institutional assessment. The Web site provides reports, briefs, and papers that are useful for policymakers and educators.

National Survey of Student Engagement (www.nsse.iub.edu)

Since 2000, over 1,400 institutions in the United States and Canada have participated in the National Survey of Student Engagement (NSSE). Data are used by institutions for assessment and planning, and some data can be analyzed online via the NSSE Report Builder, at no cost to the public. These analyses are useful for benchmarking against one's own institution.

Wabash National Study of Liberal Arts Education (www.liberalarts.wabash.edu/study-overview/)

The Wabash National Study includes forty-nine institutions in a study designed to examine liberal arts outcomes. The Web site houses an extensive list of publications and resources on student outcomes.

CHAPTER TEN

SERVING COLLEGE STUDENTS IN THE UNITED STATES, TODAY AND TOMORROW

Quality in higher education must be defined in terms of student outcomes, particularly learning outcomes, and not by inputs or institutional characteristics. The value of degrees and credentials—both for the individual and society as a whole—ultimately rests on the skills and knowledge they represent . . . Today's 21st century students are far more diverse than at any time in history. They represent the full range of races and ethnicities, are of all ages, and come from all economic and social backgrounds. They need to develop skills and knowledge in a widely different range of fields. Since many are working adults, they need to attend college in very different ways than did their predecessors.

MATTHEWS, 2010, PP. 1, 5

As we stated at the outset of this book, there is no longer—if there ever was—a prototypical "American college student." College students in the United States come from a wide array of demographic categories, identities, and background characteristics. They choose to attend postsecondary institutions for a range of reasons and are influenced by geography, cost, and curriculum. They may swirl, double dip, stop out, or a combination of these on their way to an associate's or bachelor's degree, or they may not achieve their goals for educational attainment. College students attend diverse institutions—in person and online, nonprofit and, increasingly, for-profit. The diversity of U.S. college students is not evenly distributed across institutional types or within institutional environments. Learning and developmental outcomes are uneven across groups, though there are some gains that are more common. How, then, can a thoughtful educator or practitioner design programs, curricula, and policies that will best serve "college students in the United States"?

It should be clear at this point in the text that the challenge of twenty-first century higher education is to embrace the diversity of institutional types and environments while adapting to meet the needs of increasingly diverse students. We also cannot ignore the fiscal reality that costs are rising while the proportion of institutional funding provided directly by local, state, and federal sources is decreasing. How can knowledge of the I-E-O approach as we have presented it enhance the work of educators and improve the performance of higher education institutions? To guide this work, we propose eight guiding ideas based on the I-E-O framework.

Inputs

- Enrollment in all types of higher education institutions will continue to grow for the foreseeable future. Currently, 30 percent of adults in the United States hold a bachelor's degree, and another 9.5 percent hold an associate's degree (U.S. Census Bureau, 2012). Throughout this book we have pointed to the federal college completion agenda, which aims to increase the proportion of the U.S. population with a college degree to 60 percent in the next decade and a half. There are debates about whether a college degree is necessary for everyone, or if everyone is well suited for higher education (see Goldstein, 2011). We are convinced, however, that the postsecondary education system is not yet fulfilling its potential with the students who are already participating; with a national completion rate for bachelor's degrees hovering around 57 percent (National Center for Education Statistics, 2011g), it is difficult to contemplate providing effective programs and services to meet the educational goals of those students who are not yet even in the door. Yet we know that the student population will grow, and preparing our institutions to serve these students should be a priority.
- Student diversity will—and should—continue to increase to represent the dynamic nature of the U.S. population as well as to accommodate international students and scholars. We focused in this book on the known input characteristics of those students already attempting to achieve a college degree, and we know that this group is increasing in diversity along a number of dimensions we discussed. We also know that there are dimensions of diversity that are not yet visible or salient, but

that will emerge over the next decade. Being alert to these trends will be essential for creating environments for student success.

- The diversity of U.S. higher education is one of its strengths, but also one of its liabilities. We operate in a highly stratified ecosystem of institutions, in which selectivity and cost affect access and in which Minority-Serving Institutions and for-profit institutions take up a disproportionate responsibility for educating underrepresented minority students. Throughout the text we have discussed differences among institutional types. Although it is more common to think of institutions as environments in the I-E-O framework, they also represent inputs in terms of the preexisting conditions into which students enter. To be sure, individual institutions are dynamic entities, but the overall system of higher education is slower to change. Knowing how the mission, history, curriculum, type, and environment of one's institution fit into the overall context of higher education in the United States provides a firm base from which to consider policies and programs designed to increase student success.

Environments

- When an institution admits a student, it makes a commitment to that student's success. Even at open access or nonselective institutions, matriculating a student into a certificate or degree program implies that the institution is committed to the student's meeting his or her goals, as well as institutional goals for student learning. Policies, programs, curricula, and facilities are within the purview of institutional actors who bear responsibility for creating environments that support student success. These environments include programs designed to facilitate transition into the institution; teaching and learning settings; and programs that provide academic support, career advisement, and personal counseling. As important as these supports are, prematriculation communication and education are needed to help students understand the context that they are entering; students and their families deserve transparent communication about what financial, academic, social, physical, and psychological demands and supports they will encounter at the institution. Understanding the institution's role in facilitating student success and communicating clearly with prospective and matriculated students are foundational elements in the environment. Providing support for the success of diverse students is another. We believe that this support cannot be provided in a "one size fits all" approach, but must account for diverse needs and interests within the institution.

- Students must also do their part to be successful. It is not solely the institution's responsibility to ensure student success in the college environment. Yet many students come to college without the tacit knowledge required to be successful. Some do not know what programs and services are available, and others do not know how or are hesitant to access them. Based on a host of input characteristics (including academic background, family educational status, language, learning ability, and socioeconomic status), students access support services differentially, sometimes with the students who would benefit the most taking the least advantage of what the institution offers. Consequently, we believe it is incumbent on the institution to create an environment in which communication about student success and support for it are ubiquitous, in a culture that promotes student engagement in activities that foster success for diverse learners (see Harper & Quaye, 2009). Believing that students must do their part to succeed, and providing a culture and infrastructure in which they can, are critical aspects of creating an environment for student success.

Outcomes

- Institutions must identify desired student outcomes, articulate them clearly, measure them, and be transparent about the extent to which students meet them. As we have asserted throughout the book, desired outcomes will vary by student, institutional type, and mission. For example, leaving a community college before attaining a degree might be desirable if the student successfully transfers to a bachelor's degree program; leaving a bachelor's degree program might not be considered a sign of success by an undergraduate institution. Though definitions vary, degree completion, job placement, gainful employment, enrollment in graduate school, or some combination of these could be markers of desired outcomes at many institutions. As Arum and Roksa's headline-grabbing *Academically Adrift* (2011) pointed out, learning outcomes—what students can do better or know more about when they finish college—remain shrouded in mystery at many institutions. Stating desired outcomes, measuring them, and letting students and the public know about them are important ways that educators can hold themselves accountable to institutional mission and purpose.

- Students deserve equitable educational outcomes. Equitable does not necessarily mean that all students are treated exactly alike. It means that institutions ensure that regardless of students' input characteristics, they provide environments in which students from diverse backgrounds succeed at equal rates in meeting their educational goals. A commitment to equity pervades the student affairs and higher education literature, but it is not always clear how to achieve it in practice. Starting from this commitment and looking critically at outcomes for diverse students are starting points for working toward equity.
- Measurement and monitoring of I-E-O variables provide an important indicator of institutional success as well as individual student success. Student access, attendance patterns, campus climate, learning and developmental outcomes, persistence, and other factors can all be measured and monitored on an individual basis, but it is the aggregate that amounts to the success of the institution. How well does the institution meet its mission with regard to promoting success for all students? Answering this question while also attending to the needs of individual students points to the connection of policy, programs, and curriculum, all of which are critical facilitators of—or barriers to—student success.

Serving Twenty-First-Century Students

In the Preface we introduced "John," the imagined prototypical "American college student." We noted that there may have been a time when most students really were like him—a heterosexual white male Christian working ten hours a week on campus and taking courses at one institution on his way to a bachelor's degree in four years. Certainly, there still are students like John. Throughout this book, however, we have provided evidence that most students are not like John. It is folly to speak of the "American college student" in the twenty-first century when it is clear that college students in the United States defy simple categorization along lines of gender, race, socioeconomic status, religion, ability, and enrollment patterns.

We believe that it is important to acknowledge and celebrate the diversity of college students in the United States. It is as important, however, to acknowledge that postsecondary education as a whole and higher education institutions individually are not equitably serving students from different backgrounds. Depending on their precollege backgrounds, students have differential access to sectors of higher education and have different experiences once enrolled. They persist or drop out at different rates, depending on a host of input and environmental characteristics. Overall graduation rates serve as a blunt measure of institutional effectiveness; graduation rates disaggregated by race, sex, and socioeconomic status provide more information, but still cannot say anything about why some students persist and others do not. Graduation rates also cannot say anything about college student learning and development, which we contend are the central outcomes of interest. Examination of inputs, environments, and outcomes can help educators and educational leaders tease out some of the factors that are involved in retention, learning, and development for diverse students. This information can be used to improve campus climate, programs, services, and curricula to move toward a time when all students—those like John and those very different from him—can succeed.

Serving students in the twenty-first century will require knowledge, creativity, and dedication. Educators and administrators will have to respond to students on campus and online, as well as to families and other stakeholders. New opportunities for postsecondary education, in the form of massive online open courses (MOOCs), consortia-based online courses, and digital badges (see Kamenetz, 2010), will provide competition for older models of institution-based programs. The ability to meet students' needs and expectations will be a key determinant in what forms of postsecondary education endure through the middle of the century and which do not. We believe that a few decades from now, higher education in the United States will look very different from how it looks today.

Conclusion

College students in the United States—and the higher education system itself—are likely to continue to change over the next two decades. We are in a period of increased public scrutiny and accountability for college costs and outcomes, and college completion rates in particular. College costs have reached what many believe to be a "breaking point" that is forcing the middle class out of private higher education and the more expensive public institutions (Middle Class Task Force, 2009). Something will have to give on the institutional side. Yet on the student side, more students—and students from an increasingly wide range of academic preparation and socioeconomic backgrounds—seek a college education. Containing costs while meeting the needs of a larger population of students with more diverse backgrounds will be a substantial challenge. We believe that understanding student inputs, campus environments, and student outcomes is an essential starting point for leading U.S. higher education in the twenty-first century.

REFERENCES

Abes, E. S. (2009). Theoretical borderlands: Using multiple theoretical perspectives to challenge inequitable power structures in student development theory. *Journal of College Student Development, 50,* 151–156.

Abes, E. S., & Jones, S. R. (2004). Meaning-making capacity and the dynamics of lesbian college students' multiple dimensions of identity. *Journal of College Student Development, 45,* 612–632.

Abes, E. S., Jones, S. R., & McEwen, M. K. (2007). Reconceptualizing the model of multiple dimensions of identity: The role of meaning-making capacity in the construction of multiple identities. *Journal of College Student Development, 48,* 1–22.

Abes, E. S., & Kasch, D. (2007). Using queer theory to explore lesbian college students' multiple dimensions of identity. *Journal of College Student Development, 48,* 619–636.

About us. (n.d.). Retrieved from www.devryinc.com/about-us/history.jsp

Ackerman, R., & DiRamio, D. (Eds.). (2009). *Creating a veteran-friendly campus: Strategies for transition success* (New Directions for Student Services No. 126). San Francisco: Jossey-Bass.

ACT, Inc. (2004, December 13). U.S. colleges falling short on helping students stay in college. Retrieved from www.act.org/news/releawses/2004/2012-2013.html

Act 101 Program. (2011). Available from www.education.state.pa.us/portal /server.pt/community/act_101/8712

Adelman, C. (1999). *Answers in the toolbox: Academic intensity, attendance patterns, and bachelor's degree attainment.* Washington, DC: U.S. Department of Education.

Adelman, C. (2006). *The toolbox revisited: Paths to degree completion from high school through college.* Washington, DC: U.S. Department of Education.

Allen, I. E., & Seaman, J. (2008, November). *Staying the course: Online education in the United States, 2008.* Needham, MA: Sloan Consortium.

Allen, I. E., & Seaman, J. (2010, January). *Learning on demand: Online education in the United States, 2009.* Needham, MA: Sloan Consortium.

Allport, G. (1979). *The nature of prejudice* (25th anniversary ed.). Boston: Addison-Wesley.

Altbach, P. G., & Knight, J. (2007). Higher education's landscape of internationalization: Motivations and realities. In P. G. Altbach (Ed.), *Tradition and transition: The international imperative in higher education* (pp. 113–136). Rotterdam, The Netherlands: Sense.

American College Personnel Association. (1994). *The student learning imperative.* Washington, DC: Author.

American College Personnel Association. (n.d.). Vision, mission, and values. Retrieved from www2.myacpa.org/about-acpa/mission

American College Personnel Association & National Association of Student Personnel Administrators. (2010). Professional competency area for student affairs practitioners. Retrieved from www.naspa.org/regions/regioniii/Professional%20 Competency.pdf

American Council on Education. (1937). *The student personnel point of view.* Washington, DC: Author. Retrieved from www.myacpa.org/pub /documents/1937.pdf

American Indian Higher Education Consortium. (n.d.). Tribal colleges and universities. Retrieved from www.aihec.org/colleges/

Ancis, J. R., Sedlacek, W. E., & Mohr, J. J. (2000). Student perceptions of campus cultural climate by race. *Journal of Counseling & Development, 78,* 180–185.

Antonio, A. L., Chang, M. J., Hakuta, K., Kenny, D. A., Levin, S., & Milem, J. F. (2004). Effects of racial diversity on complex thinking in college students. *Psychological Science, 15,* 507–510.

Arnett, J. J. (2000). Emerging adulthood: A theory of development from the late teens through the twenties. *American Psychologist, 55,* 469–480.

Arum, R., & Roksa, J. (2011). *Academically adrift: Limited learning on college campuses.* Chicago: University of Chicago Press.

Association of American Colleges and Universities. (2002). *Greater expectations: A new vision for learning as a nation goes to college.* Washington, DC: Author.

Astin, A. W. (1968). *The college environment.* Washington, DC: American Council on Education.

Astin, A. W. (1970a). The methodology of research on college impact, Part I. *Sociology of Education, 43,* 223–254.

Astin, A. W. (1970b). The methodology of research on college impact, Part II. *Sociology of Education, 43,* 437–450.

Astin, A. W. (1977). *Four critical years.* San Francisco: Jossey-Bass.

Astin, A. W. (1984). Student involvement: A developmental theory for higher education. *Journal of College Student Personnel, 25,* 297–308.

Astin, A. W. (1985). *Achieving educational excellence: A critical assessment of priorities and practices in higher education.* San Francisco: Jossey-Bass.

Astin, A. W. (1991). *Assessment for excellence: The philosophy and practice of assessment and evaluation in higher education.* Phoenix, AZ: Oryx Press.

Astin, A. W. (1993a). An empirical typology of college students. *Journal of College Student Development, 34*, 36–46.

Astin, A. W. (1993b). *What matters in college? Four critical years revisited.* San Francisco: Jossey-Bass.

Astin, A. W., Astin, H. S., & Lindholm, J. A. (2011). *Cultivating the spirit: How college can enhance students' inner lives.* San Francisco: Jossey-Bass.

Astin, A. W., & Oseguera, L. (2005). Pre-college and institutional influences on degree attainment. In A. Seidman (Ed.), *College student retention: Formula for student success* (pp. 245–276). Westport, CT: Praeger.

Astin, A. W., & Sax, L. J. (1998). How undergraduates are affected by service participation. *Journal of College Student Development, 39*, 251–263.

Atkinson, D. R., Morten, G., & Sue, D. W. (1979). *Counseling American minorities.* Dubuque, IA: William C. Brown.

Aud, S., Fox, M., & KewalRamani, A. (2010). *Status and trends in the education of racial and ethnic groups* (NCES 2010-015). National Center for Education Statistics. Washington, DC: U.S. Government Printing Office.

Aud, S., Hussar, W. J., Planty, M., Snyder, T. D., Bianco, K., Fox, M., . . . Drake, L. (2010). *The condition of education 2010.* Washington, DC: National Center for Education Statistics.

Bailey, T. R., & Alfonso, M. (2005). *Paths to persistence: An analysis of research on program effectiveness at community colleges.* Indianapolis, IN: Lumina Foundation for Education. Retrieved from https://folio.iupui.edu /handle/10244/268

Banning, J. H. (Ed.). (1978). *Campus ecology: A perspective for student affairs.* Washington, DC: National Association of Student Personnel Administrators. Retrieved from www.campusecologist.org/files/Monograph.pdf

Banning, J. H., & Kaiser, L. (1974). An ecological perspective and model for campus design. *Personnel and Guidance Journal, 52*, 370–375.

Banta, T. W., & Associates. (2002). *Building a scholarship of assessment.* San Francisco: Jossey-Bass.

Banta, T. W., & Pike, G. R. (2007). Revisiting the blind alley of value-added. *Assessment Update, 19*(1), 1–2, 14–15.

Barefoot, B. O. (2000). *National survey of first-year curricular practices: Summary of findings.* Brevard, NC: Policy Center on the First Year of College. Retrieved from www.jngi.org/uploads/File/Final_Summary_Curricular.pdf

Barefoot, B. O. (2005). Current institutional practice in the first college year. In M. L. Upcraft, J. N. Gardner, B. O. Barefoot, & Associates (Eds.), *Challenging and supporting the first-year student: A handbook for improving the first year of college* (pp. 47–63). San Francisco: Jossey-Bass.

Barefoot, B. O., & Fidler, P. P. (1996). *The 1994 national survey of freshman seminar programs: Continuing innovations in the collegiate curriculum.* Columbia: University of South Carolina, National Resource Center for the First-Year Experience and Students in Transition.

Bargad, A., & Hyde, J. (1991). Women's studies: A study of feminist identity development in women. *Psychology of Women Quarterly, 15*, 181–201.

Barker, R. G. (1968). *Ecological psychology: Concepts and methods for studying the environment of human behavior.* Stanford, CA: Stanford University Press.

Bastedo, M. N., & Bowman, N. A. (2011). College rankings as an interorganizational dependency: Establishing the foundation for strategic and institutional accounts. *Research in Higher Education, 52,* 3–23.

Baum, S., Ma, J., & Payea, K. (2010). *Education pays 2010: The benefits of higher education for individuals and society.* New York: College Board.

Baxter Magolda, M. B. (1990). The impact of the freshmen year on epistemological development: Gender differences. *Review of Higher Education, 13,* 259–285.

Baxter Magolda, M. B. (1992). *Knowing and reasoning in college: Gender-related patterns in students' intellectual development.* San Francisco: Jossey-Bass.

Baxter Magolda, M. B. (1998). Developing self-authorship in young adult life. *Journal of College Student Development, 39,* 143–156.

Baxter Magolda, M. B. (2001a). A constructivist revision of the Measure of Epistemological Reflection. *Journal of College Student Development, 42,* 520–534.

Baxter Magolda, M. B. (2001b). *Making their own way: Narratives for transforming higher education to promote self-development.* Sterling, VA: Stylus.

Baxter Magolda, M. B. (2002). Epistemological reflection: The evolution of epistemological reflection assumptions from age 18–30. In B. K. Hofer & P. R. Pintrich (Eds.), *Personal epistemology: The psychology of beliefs about knowledge and knowing* (pp. 89–102). Mahwah, NJ: Erlbaum.

Baxter Magolda, M. B. (2004a). Evolution of a constructivist conceptualization of epistemological reflection. *Educational Psychologist, 39,* 31–42.

Baxter Magolda, M. B. (2004b). Self-authorship as the common goal of 21st-century education. In M. B. Baxter Magolda & P. M. King (Eds.), *Learning partnerships: Theory and modes of practice to educate for self-authorship* (pp. 1–35). Sterling, VA: Stylus.

Baxter Magolda, M. B. (2007). Self-authorship: The foundation for twenty-first-century education. In P. S. Meszaros (Ed.), *Self-authorship: Advancing students' intellectual growth* (New Directions for Teaching and Learning No. 109, pp. 69–83). San Francisco: Jossey-Bass.

Baxter Magolda, M. B. (2008). Three elements of self-authorship. *Journal of College Student Development, 49,* 269–284.

Baxter Magolda, M. B. (2009). The activity of meaning making: A holistic perspective on college student development. *Journal of College Student Development, 50,* 621–639.

Baxter Magolda, M. B., & King, P. M. (Eds.). (2004). *Learning partnerships: Theory and models of practice to educate for self-authorship.* Sterling, VA: Stylus.

Baxter Magolda, M. B., & King, P. M. (2007). Interview strategies for assessing self-authorship: Constructing conversations to assess meaning making. *Journal of College Student Development, 48,* 491–508.

Bean, J. P. (1982). Student attrition, intention, and confidence: Interaction effects in a path model. *Research in Higher Education, 17,* 291–320.

Bean, J. P. (2005). Nine themes of college student retention. In A. Seidman (Ed.), *College student retention: Formula for student success* (pp. 215–244). Westport, CT: Praeger.

Bean, J. P., & Eaton, S. B. (2000). A psychological model of college student retention. In J. M. Braxton (Ed.), *Reworking the student departure puzzle* (pp. 48–61). Nashville, TN: Vanderbilt University Press.

Beemyn, B. G. (2005). Making campuses more inclusive of transgender students. *Journal of Gay & Lesbian Issues in Education, 3*(1), 77–87.

Beemyn, B., Curtis, B., Davis, M., & Tubbs, N. J. (2005). Transgender issues on college campuses. In R. L. Sanlo (Ed.), *Gender identity and sexual orientation: Research, policy, and personal perspectives* (New Directions for Student Services No. 111, pp. 25–39). San Francisco: Jossey-Bass.

Beemyn, B. G., & Rankin, S. R. (2011). *The lives of transgender people.* New York: Columbia University Press.

Bekken, B., & Marie, J. (2007), Making self-authorship a goal of core curricula: The earth sustainability pilot project. In P. S. Meszaros (Ed.), *Self-authorship: Advancing students' intellectual growth* (New Directions for Teaching and Learning No. 109, pp. 53–67). San Francisco: Jossey-Bass.

Belenky, M. F., Clinchy, B. M., Goldberger, N. R., & Tarule, J. M. (1986). *Women's ways of knowing: The development of self, voice, and mind.* New York: Basic Books.

Bell-Scriber, M. J. (2008). Warming the nursing education climate for traditional-age students who are male. *Nursing Education Perspectives, 29,* 143–150.

Bem, S. L. (1981a). *Bem Sex-Role Inventory: Professional manual.* Palo Alto, CA: Consulting Psychologists Press.

Bem, S. L. (1981b).Gender schema theory: A cognitive account of sex typing. *Psychological Review, 88,* 354–364.

Bem, S. L. (1983). Gender schema theory and its implications for child development: Raising gender-aschematic children in a gender-schematic society. *Signs, 8,* 598–616.

Bennett, M. J. (1966). *When dreams came true: The GI Bill and the making of modern America.* Washington, DC: Brassey's.

Bensimon, E. M. (2004). The diversity scorecard: A learning approach to institutional change. *Change, 36*(1), 45–52.

Berger, J. B. (2000). Optimizing capital, social reproduction, and undergraduate persistence. In J. M. Braxton (Ed.), *Reworking the student departure puzzle* (pp. 95–124). Nashville, TN: Vanderbilt University Press.

Berger, J. B. (2002). Understanding the organizational nature of student persistence: Empirically-based recommendations for practice. *Journal of College Student Retention, 3,* 3–21.

Berger, J. B., & Braxton, J. M. (1998). Revising Tinto's interactionalist theory of student departure through theory elaboration: Examining the role of organizational attributes in the persistence process. *Research in Higher Education, 39,* 103–119.

Berger, J., & Milem, J. (2000). Exploring the impact of historically black colleges in promoting the development of undergraduates' self-concept. *Journal of College Student Development, 41,* 103–119.

Berkner, L., He, S., & Cataldi, E. (2002). *Descriptive summary of 1995–96 beginning postsecondary students: Six years later* (Statistical Analysis Report No. 2003–151). Washington, DC: Office of Educational Research and Improvement, National Center for Education Statistics.

Bevis, T. B., & Lucas, C. J. (2007). *International students in American colleges and universities: A history.* New York: Palgrave Macmillan.

Bial, D., & Rodriguez, A. (2007). Identifying a diverse student body: Selective college admissions and alternative approaches. In T. Crady & J. Sumner (Eds.), *Key issues in new student enrollment* (New Directions for Student Services No. 118, pp. 17–30). San Francisco: Jossey-Bass.

Bilodeau, B. L. (2005). Beyond the gender binary: A case study of two transgender students at a Midwestern university. *Journal of Gay & Lesbian Issues in Education, 3*(1), 29–46.

Bilodeau, B. L. (2009). *Genderism: Transgender students, binary systems, and higher education.* Saarbrücken, Germany: Verlag.

Bilodeau, B. L., & Renn, K. A. (2005). Analysis of LGBT identity development models and implications for practice. In R. L. Sanlo (Ed.), *Gender identity and sexual orientation: Research, policy, and personal perspectives* (New Directions for Student Services No. 111, pp. 25–39). San Francisco: Jossey-Bass.

Birnbaum, R. (1983). *Maintaining diversity in higher education.* San Francisco: Jossey-Bass.

Black, D., Gates, G., Sanders, S., & Taylor, L. (2000). Demographics of the gay and lesbian population in the United States: Evidence from available systematic data sources. *Demography, 37,* 139–154.

Borden, V.M.H. (2004). Accommodating student swirl: When traditional students are no longer the tradition. *Change, 36*(2), 10–17.

Borden, V.M.H., & Young, J. W. (2008). Measurement validity and accountability for student learning. In V.M.H. Borden & G. R. Pike (Eds.), *Assessing and accounting for student learning: Beyond the Spellings Commission* (New Directions for Institutional Research No. S1, pp. 19–36). San Francisco: Jossey-Bass.

Bourdieu, P. (1977). Cultural reproduction and social reproduction. In J. Karabel & A. H. Halsey (Eds.), *Power and ideology in education* (pp. 487–511). New York: Oxford University Press.

Bourdieu, P., & Passeron, J. C. (1977). *Reproduction in education, society and culture* (2nd ed.). London: Sage.

Bowen, W., & Bok, D. (1998). *The shape of the river: Long-term consequences of considering race in college and university admissions.* Princeton, NJ: Princeton University Press.

Bowman, N. A. (2010). Can first-year college students accurately report their learning and development? *American Educational Research Journal, 47,* 466–496.

Bowman, N. A. (2011). Validity of college self-reported gains at diverse institutions. *Educational Researcher, 40,* 22–24.

Braskamp, L. (2007). Three "central" questions worth asking. *Journal of College and Character, 9*(1), 1–7.

Braxton, J. M., Bray, N. J., & Berger, J. B. (2000). Faculty teaching skills and their influences on the student departure process. *Journal of College Student Development, 41,* 215–227.

Braxton, J. M., Brier, E. M., & Steele, S. L. (2007). Shaping retention from research to practice. *Journal of College Student Retention, 9,* 377–399.

Braxton, J. M., & Hirschy, A. S. (2005). Theoretical developments in the study of college student departure. In A. Seidman (Ed.), *College student retention: Formula for student success* (pp. 61–88). Westport, CT: Praeger.

Braxton, J. M., Hirschy, A. S., & McClendon, S. A. (2004). *Understanding and reducing college student departure* (ASHE-ERIC Higher Education Research Report Series No. 3). San Francisco: Jossey-Bass.

Braxton, J. M., & Lee, S. D. (2005). Toward reliable knowledge about college student departure. In A. Seidman (Ed.), *College student retention: Formula for student success* (pp. 107–128). Westport, CT: Praeger.

Braxton, J. M., & Lien, L. A. (2000). The viability of academic integration as a central construct in Tinto's interactionalist theory of college student departure. In J. M. Braxton (Ed.), *Reworking the student departure puzzle* (pp. 11–28). Nashville, TN: Vanderbilt University Press.

Braxton, J. M., Shaw Sullivan, A. V., & Johnson, R. M. (2001). Appraising Tinto's theory of college student departure. In J. C. Smart (Ed.), *Higher education: Handbook of theory and research* (Vol. 12, pp. 107–164). New York: Agathon Press.

Brayboy, B.M.J. (2005). Toward a tribal Critical Race Theory in education. *Urban Review, 37*, 425–446.

Bresciani, M. J. (2009). Implementing assessment to improve student learning and development. In G. McClellan & J. Stringer (Eds.), *The handbook of student affairs administration* (3rd ed., pp. 526–544). San Francisco: Jossey-Bass.

Bresciani, M. J. (2010). Understanding barriers to student affairs professionals' engagement in outcomes-based assessment of student learning and development. *Journal of Student Affairs, 14*, 81–90.

Bresciani, M. J. (2011). Assessment and evaluation. In J. H. Schuh, S. R. Jones, & S. R. Harper (Eds.), *Student services: A handbook for the profession* (5th ed., pp. 321–334). San Francisco: Jossey-Bass.

Bresciani, M. J., Moore Gardner, M., & Hickmott, J. (2009). *Demonstrating student success in student affairs.* Sterling, VA: Stylus.

Brint, S., & Karabel, J. (1989). *The diverted dream: Community colleges and the promise of educational opportunity in America, 1900–1985.* New York: Oxford University Press.

Brock, T., Jenkins, D., Ellwein, T., Miller, J. Gooden, S. Martin, K., . . . Pih, M. (2007). *Building a culture of evidence for community college student success: Early progress in the Achieving the Dream Initiative.* New York: Community College Research Center, Teachers College, Columbia University. Retrieved from http://eric.ed.gov/PDFS/ED496977.pdf

Bronfenbrenner, U. (1974). Developmental research and public policy and the ecology of childhood. *Child Development, 45*, 1–5.

Bronfenbrenner, U. (1979). *The ecology of human development: Experiments by nature and design.* Cambridge, MA: Harvard University Press.

Bronfenbrenner, U. (1993). The ecology of cognitive development: Research models and fugitive findings. In R. H. Wozniak & K. W. Fischer (Eds.), *Development in context: Acting and thinking in specific environments* (pp. 3–44). Mahwah, NJ: Erlbaum.

Bronfenbrenner, U. (1995). Developmental ecology through space and time: A future perspective. In P. Moen & G. H. Elder Jr. (Eds.), *Examining lives in context: Perspectives on the ecology of human development* (pp. 619–647). Washington, DC: American Psychological Association.

Bronfenbrenner, U. (Ed.). (2005). *Making human beings human: Bioecological perspectives on human development.* Thousand Oaks, CA: Sage.

Bronfenbrenner, U., & Morris, P. A. (2006). The bioecological model of human development. In W. Damon & R. M. Lerner (Eds.), *Handbook of child psychology* (6th ed., pp. 793–828). Hoboken, NJ: Wiley.

Brooks, F. E., & Starks, G. L. (Eds.). (2011). *Historically Black Colleges and Universities: An encyclopedia.* Santa Barbara, CA: ABC-CLIO.

Brown, J. S., Hitlin, S., & Elder, G. H., Jr. (2006). The greater complexity of lived race: An extension of Harris and Sim. *Social Science Quarterly, 87,* 411–431.

Brown, R. D., Clarke, B., Gortmaker, V., & Robinson-Keilig, R. (2004). Assessing the campus climate for gay, lesbian, bisexual and transgender (GLBT) students using a multiple perspectives approach. *Journal of College Student Development, 45,* 8–26.

Bryant, A. N. (2003). Changes in attitudes toward women's roles: Predicting gender-role traditionalism among college students. *Sex Roles, 48,* 131–142.

Bryant, A. N. (2006). Exploring religious pluralism in higher education: Non-majority religious perspectives among entering first-year college students. *Religion & Education, 33*(1), 1–25.

Bryant, A., Choi, J., & Yasuno, M. (2003, November). Understanding the religious and spiritual dimensions of students' lives in the first year of college. Paper presented at the 28th annual meeting of the Association for the Study of Higher Education, Portland, OR.

Bubolz, M. M., & Sontag, M. S. (1993). Human ecology theory. In P. G. Boss, W. J. Doherty, R. LaRossa, W. R. Schumm, & S. K. Steinmetz (Eds.), *Sourcebook of family theories and methods: A contextual approach* (pp. 419–448). New York: Plenum Press.

Burton, N. W., & Ramist, L. (2001). *Predicting success in college: SAT studies of classes graduating since 1980* (College Board Report No. 2001-02). New York: College Entrance Examination Board.

Cabrera, A. F., Burkum, K. R., & La Nasa, S. M. (2005). Pathways to a four-year degree: Determinants of transfer and degree completion. In A. Seidman (Ed.), *College student retention: A formula for student success* (ACE/Praeger Series on Higher Education, pp. 154–214). Westport, CT: Greenwood Press.

Cabrera, A. F., & La Nasa, S. M. (2000a). Editors' notes. In A. F. Cabrera & S. M. La Nasa (Eds.), *Understanding the college choice of disadvantaged students* (New Directions for Institutional Research No. 107, pp. 1–3). San Francisco: Jossey-Bass.

Cabrera, A. F., & La Nasa, S. M. (2000b). Overcoming the tasks on the path to college for America's disadvantaged. In A. F. Cabrera & S. M. La Nasa (Eds.), *Understanding the college choice of disadvantaged students* (New Directions for Institutional Research No. 107, pp. 31–43). San Francisco: Jossey-Bass.

Cabrera, A. F., & La Nasa, S. M. (2000c). Understanding the college-choice process. In A. F. Cabrera & S. M. La Nasa (Eds.), *Understanding the college choice of disadvantaged students* (New Directions for Institutional Research No. 107, pp. 5–22). San Francisco: Jossey-Bass.

Cabrera, A. F., & La Nasa, S. M. (2001). On the path to college: Three critical tasks facing America's disadvantaged. *Research in Higher Education, 42,* 119–149.

Cabrera, A. F., Nora, A., Terenzini, P. T., Pascarella, P. T., & Hagedorn, L. S. (1999). Campus racial climate and the adjustment of students to college: A comparison between white students and African American students. *Journal of Higher Education, 70,* 134–160.

Carnegie Foundation for the Advancement of Teaching. (n.d.). The Carnegie Classification of institutions of higher education. Retrieved from http://classifications.carnegiefoundation.org/

Carpenter, C. S. (2009). Sexual orientation and outcomes in college. *Economics of Education Review, 28,* 693–703.

Cass, V. C. (1979). Homosexual identity formation: A theoretical model. *Journal of Homosexuality, 4,* 219–235.

Cass, V. C. (1984). Homosexual identity formation: Testing a theoretical model. *Journal of Sex Research, 20,* 143–167.

Cawthon, T. W., & Jones, C. (2004). A description of traditional and contemporary campus ministries. *College Student Affairs Journal, 23,* 158–172.

Center for Collegiate Mental Health. (2012, January). *2011 annual report* (Publication No. STA 12-59). Retrieved from http://ccmh.squarespace.com/storage/CCMH_AnnualReport_2011.pdf

Center for Inquiry. (n.d.). *Summary of four-year change.* Wabash, IN: Wabash National Study. Retrieved from www.liberalarts.wabash.edu/storage/4-year-change-summary-website.pdf

Chaney, B., Muraskin, L., Cahalan, M., & Goodwin, D. (1998). Helping the progress of disadvantaged students in higher education: The federal Student Support Services program. *Educational Evaluation and Policy Analysis, 20,* 197–215.

Chang, M. (1996). *Racial diversity in higher education: Does a racially mixed student population affect educational outcomes?* (Unpublished doctoral dissertation). University of California: Los Angeles.

Chang, M. (1997, November). Racial diversity: A compelling interest for higher education. Paper presented at the 22nd annual meeting of the Association for the Study of Higher Education, Albuquerque, NM.

Chang, M. J. (1999). Does racial diversity matter? The educational impact of a racially diverse undergraduate population. *Journal of College Student Development, 40,* 377–395.

Chang, M. J. (2002a). The impact of an undergraduate diversity course requirement on students' racial views and attitudes. *Journal of General Education, 51,* 21–42.

Chang, M. J. (2002b). Racial dynamics on campus: What student organizations can tell us. *About Campus, 7*(1), 2–8.

Chang, M. J., Astin, A. W., & Kim, D. (2004). Cross-racial interaction among undergraduates: Some causes and consequences. *Research in Higher Education, 45,* 529–553.

Chang, M. J., Cerna, O., Han, J., & Sáenz, V. (2008). The contradictory roles of institutional status in retaining underrepresented students in biomedical and behavioral science majors. *Review of Higher Education, 31,* 433–464.

Chang, M. J., Denson, N., Sáenz, V., & Misa, K. (2006). The educational benefits of cross-racial interaction among undergraduates. *Journal of Higher Education, 77,* 430–455.

Chang, M. J., & Kiang, P. N. (2002). New challenges of representing Asian American students in higher education. In W. A. Smith, P. G. Altbach, & K. Lomotey (Eds.), *The racial crisis in American higher education: Continuing challenges for the twenty-first century* (Rev. ed., pp. 137–158). Albany: State University of New York Press.

Chen, X., Wu, J., Tasoff, S., & Weko, T. (2010). *Academic preparation for college in the high school senior class of 2003–04* (NCES 2010-169). Washington, DC: National Center for Education Statistics.

Chickering, A. W. (1969). *Education and identity.* San Francisco: Jossey-Bass.

Chickering, A. W., & Reisser, L. (1993). *Education and identity* (2nd ed.). San Francisco: Jossey-Bass.

Choney, S. K., Berryhill-Paapke, E., & Robbins, R. R. (1995). The acculturation of American Indians: Developing frameworks for research and practice. In J. G. Ponterotto, J. M. Casas, L. A. Suzuki, & C. M. Alexander (Eds.), *Handbook of multicultural counseling* (pp. 73–92). Thousand Oaks, CA: Sage.

Chow, P. (2010). *Open doors 2010: Report on international education exchange.* New York: Institution of International Education.

Choy, S. P. (2001). *Students whose parents did not go to college: Postsecondary access, persistence, and attainment* (NCES 2001-126). Washington, DC: National Center for Education Statistics.

Choy, S. P. (2002). Nontraditional undergraduates: A special analysis. Washington, DC: National Center for Education Statistics.

Clark, B. R., & Trow, M. (1966). The organizational context. In T. M. Newcomb & E. K. Wilson (Eds.), *College peer groups: Problems and prospects for research* (pp. 17–70). Chicago: Aldine.

Cohen, A. M., & Brawer, F. B. (2008). *The American community college* (5th ed.). San Francisco: Jossey-Bass.

Cokley, K. (1999). Reconceptualizing the impact of college racial composition on African-American students' racial identity. *Journal of College Student Development, 40*, 235–246.

Colby, A., Ehrlich, T., Beaumont, E., & Stephens, J. (2003). *Educating citizens: Preparing America's undergraduates for lives of moral and civic responsibility.* San Francisco: Jossey-Bass.

College Board. (2009, September). *Distribution of grant aid by income level and institution type* (Trends in Higher Education Series). Retrieved from http://professionals.collegeboard.com/profdownload/trends-2009-distribution-of-aid-one-page.pdf

Collins, J. F. (2000). Biracial-bisexual individuals: Identity coming of age. *International Journal of Sexuality and Gender Studies, 5*, 221–253.

Committee on Measures of Student Success. (2011, December). *Committee on Measures of Student Success: A report to Secretary of Education Arne Duncan.* Washington, DC: U.S. Department of Education. Retrieved from www2.ed.gov/about/bdscomm/list/cmss-committee-report-final.pdf

Complete College America. (2011). *Time is the enemy: The surprising truth about why today's college students aren't graduating . . . and what needs to change.* Washington, DC: Author. Retrieved from www.completecollege.org/docs/Time_Is_the_Enemy.pdf

Compton, J. I., Cox, E., & Santos-Laanan, F. (2006). Adult learners in transition. In F. Santos-Laanan (Ed.), *Understanding students in transition: Trends and Issues* (New Directions for Student Services No. 114, pp. 73–80). San Francisco: Jossey-Bass.

Cook, B. J., Young, K., & Associates. (2009). *From soldier to student: Easing the transition of service members on campus.* Washington, DC: American Council on Education.

Creamer, E. G., Baxter Magolda, M. B., & Yue, J. (2010). Preliminary evidence of the reliability and validity of a quantitative measure of self-authorship. *Journal of College Student Development, 51,* 550–562.

Creamer, E. G., & Laughlin, A. (2005). Self-authorship and women's career decision making. *Journal of College Student Development, 46,* 13–27.

Cremonini, L., Westerheijden, D., & Enders, J. (2008). Disseminating the right information to the right audience: Cultural determinants in the use (and misuse) of rankings. *Higher Education, 55,* 373–385.

Crenshaw, K. W. (1991). Mapping the margins: Intersectionality, identity politics, and violence against women of color. *Stanford Law Review, 43,* 1241–1299.

Cress, C. M., & Ikeda, E. K. (2003). Distress under duress: The relationship between campus climate and depression in Asian American college students. *Journal of Student Affairs Research and Practice, 40,* 74–97.

Cross, W. E., Jr. (1971). Toward a psychology of black liberation: The Negro-to-black conversion experience. *Black World, 20*(9), 13–27.

Cross, W. E., Jr. (1991). *Shades of black: Diversity in African American identity.* Philadelphia: Temple University Press.

Cross, W. E., Jr., & Fhagen-Smith, P. (2001). Patterns in African American identity development: A life span perspective. In C. L. Wijeyesinghe & B. W. Jackson III (Eds.), *New perspectives on racial identity development: A theoretical and practical anthology* (pp. 243–270). New York: New York University Press.

Cureton, S. R. (2003). Race-specific college student experiences on a predominately white campus. *Journal of Black Studies, 33,* 295–311.

Dalton, J. C. (2001). Career and calling: Finding a place for the spirit in work and community. In M. A. Jablonski (Ed.), *The implications of student spirituality for student affairs practice* (New Directions for Student Services No. 95, pp. 17–26). San Francisco: Jossey-Bass.

D'Augelli, A. R. (1994). Identity development and sexual orientation: Toward a model of lesbian, gay, and bisexual identity development. In E. J. Trickett, R. J. Watts, & D. Birman (Eds.), *Human diversity: Perspectives on people in context* (pp. 312–333). San Francisco: Jossey-Bass.

Davis, J. (2010). *The first-generation student experience: Implications for campus practice, and strategies for improving persistence and success.* Sterling, VA: Stylus.

Davis, P. A. (2008). *A formative evaluation of the student support services TRIO program for low income and first generation college bound students self-efficacy at Butte-Glenn Community College District.* Los Angeles: University of Southern California. Retrieved from http://gradworks.umi.com/33/25/3325179.html

Davis, T. L. (2002). Voices of gender role conflict: The social construction of college men's identity. *Journal of College Student Development, 43,* 508–521.

de Anda, D. (1984). Bicultural socialization: Factors affecting the minority experience. *Social Work, 29,* 101–107.

Debard, R. (2004). Millennials coming to college. In M. D. Coomes & R. Debard (Eds.), *Serving the millennial generation* (New Directions for Student Services No. 106, pp. 33–46). San Francisco: Jossey-Bass.

de los Santos, J. A., & Wright, I. (1990). Maricopa's swirling students: Earning one-third of Arizona State's bachelor's degrees. *Community, Technical, and Junior College Journal, 60*(6), 32–34.

DesJardins, S. L., & McCall, B. P. (2010). Simulating the effects of financial aid packages on college student stopout, reenrollment spells, and graduation chances. *Review of Higher Education, 33,* 513–541.

DeVoe, J. F., & Darling-Churchill, K. E. (2008). *Status and trends in the education of American Indians and Alaska Natives: 2008* (NCES 2008-084). Washington, DC: National Center for Education Statistics.

Dey, E. L., & Associates. (2009). *Civic responsibility: What is the campus climate for learning?* Washington, DC: Association of American Colleges and Universities.

Dill, B. T., & Zambrana, R. E. (Eds.). (2009). *Emerging intersections: Race, class, and gender in theory, policy and practice.* New Brunswick, NJ: Rutgers University Press.

Dilley, P. (2005). Which way out? A typology of non-heterosexual male collegiate identities. *Journal of Higher Education, 76,* 56–88.

DiRamio, D., Ackerman, R., & Mitchell, R. L. (2008). From combat to campus: Voices of student-veterans. *NASPA Journal, 45,* 73–102.

Donaldson, J. F., & Townsend, B. K. (2007). Higher education journals' discourse about adult undergraduate students. *Journal of Higher Education, 78,* 27–50.

DuBois, W.E.B. (1903). The talented tenth. In B. T. Washington (Ed.), *The Negro problem: A series of articles by representative Negroes of today* (pp. 33–75). New York: James Pott. Retrieved from http://teachingamericanhistory.org/library/index.asp?document=174

Duquaine-Watson, J. (2007). "Pretty darned cold": Single mothers in the community college climate in post–welfare reform America. *Equity & Excellence in Education, 40,* 229–240.

Eaton, S., & Bean, J. (1995). An approach/avoidance behavioral model of college student retention. *Research in Higher Education, 36,* 617–645.

Edwards, K. E., & Jones, S. R. (2009). "Putting my man face on": A grounded theory of college men's gender identity development. *Journal of College Student Development, 50,* 210–228.

Eimers, M. T., & Pike, G. R. (1997). Minority and nonminority adjustment to college: Differences or similarities? *Research in Higher Education, 38,* 77–97.

Ekstrom, R. B. (1985). *A descriptive study of public high school guidance: Report to the Commission for the Study of Precollegiate Guidance Counseling.* Princeton, NJ: Educational Testing Service.

Engberg, M. E., Hurtado, S., & Smith, G. (2007). Developing attitudes of acceptance toward lesbian, gay, and bisexual peers: Enlightenment, contact, and the college experience. *Journal of Gay & Lesbian Issues in Education, 4*(3), 49–77.

Engle, J., & Tinto, V. (2008). *Moving beyond access: College success for low-income, first-generation students.* Washington, DC: Pell Institute for the Study of Opportunity in Higher Education.

Ennis, S. R., Ríos-Vargas, M., & Albert, N. G. (2011). *The Hispanic population: 2010.* (2010 Census Briefs). Washington, DC: U.S. Department of Commerce.

Erikson, E. H. (1963). *Childhood and society* (2nd ed.). New York: Norton.

Erikson, E. H. (1968). *Identity: Youth and crisis.* New York: Norton.

Erikson, E. H. (1980). *Identity and the life cycle.* New York: Norton. (Original work published 1959)

Erisman, W., & Looney, S. (2007). *Opening the door to the American dream: Increasing higher education access and success for immigrants.* Washington, DC: Institute for Higher Education Policy.

Evans, N. J., & DeVita, J. M. (in press). Diversity in higher education. In L. Hogan (Ed.), *Student affairs for academic administrators*. Sterling, VA: Stylus.

Evans, N. J., Forney, D. S., Guido, F. M., Patton, L. D., & Renn, K. A. (2010). *Student development in college: Theory, research, and practice* (2nd ed.). San Francisco: Jossey-Bass.

Fain, P. (2011, September 7). Success by another name. *Inside Higher Ed*. Retrieved from www.insidehighered.com/news/2011/09/07/education_department _committee_weighs_in_on_measuring_community_college_success

Fassinger, R. E. (1998). Lesbian, gay, and bisexual identity and student development theory. In R. L. Sanlo (Ed.), *Working with lesbian, gay, bisexual, and transgender college students: A handbook for faculty and administrators* (pp. 13–22). Westport, CT: Greenwood Press.

Fassinger, R. E., & Miller, B. A. (1997). Validation of an inclusive model of homosexual identity formation in a sample of gay men. *Journal of Homosexuality, 32*, 53–78.

Feagin, J. R., Vera, H., & Imani, N. (1996). *The agony of education: Black students at white colleges and universities*. New York: Routledge.

Feldman, K. A., & Newcomb, T. M. (1969). *The impact of college on students* (Vols. 1–2). San Francisco: Jossey-Bass.

Ferdman, B. M., & Gallegos, P. I. (2001). Racial identity development and Latinos in the United States. In C. L. Wijeyesinghe & B. W. Jackson III (Eds.), *New perspectives on racial identity development: A theoretical and practical anthology* (pp. 32–66). New York: New York University Press.

Fike, D. S., & Fike, R. (2008). Predictors of first-year student retention in the community college. *Community College Review, 36*(2), 68–88.

Fischer, M. J. (2007). Settling into campus life: Differences by race/ethnicity in college involvement and outcomes. *Journal of Higher Education, 78*, 125–161.

Fishbein, M., & Ajzen, I. (1975). *Belief, attitude, intention, and behavior: An introduction to theory and research*. Boston: Addison-Wesley.

Ford, M. R., & Lowery, C. R. (1986). Gender differences in moral reasoning: A comparison of the use of justice and care orientations. *Journal of Personality and Social Psychology, 50*, 777–783.

Foundational Dimensions transfer focus (four-year college version). (2010). John N. Gardner Institute for Excellence in Undergraduate Education. Retrieved from www.fyfoundations.org/transferdimensions.aspx

Foundations of Excellence in the First College Year. (n.d.). John N. Gardner Institute for Excellence in Undergraduate Education. Retrieved from www.fyfoundations.org/firstyearselfstudy.aspx

Fox, M. A., Connolly, B. A., & Snyder, T. D. (2005). *Youth indicators 2005: Trends in the well-being of American youth*. Washington, DC: National Center for Education Statistics.

Frank, R., Ruiz, S., Sharkness, J., DeAngelo, L., & Pryor, J. (2010). *Findings from the 2009 administration of the College Senior Survey*. Los Angeles: Higher Education Research Institute.

Freeman, C. E. (2004). *Trends in educational equity of girls and women: 2004* (NCES 2005-016). Washington, DC: National Center for Education Statistics.

Freeman, K., & Thomas, G. (2002). Black colleges and college choice: Characteristics of students who choose HBCUs. *Review of Higher Education, 25*, 349–358.

Fry, R. (2011). *Hispanic college enrollment spikes: Narrowing gaps with other groups.* Washington, DC: Pew Hispanic Center.

Gardner, J. N., Upcraft, M. L., & Barefoot, B. O. (2005). Principles of good practice for the first college year and summary of recommendations. In M. L. Upcraft, J. N. Gardner, B. O. Barefoot, & Associates (Eds.), *Challenging and supporting the first-year student: A handbook for improving the first year of college* (pp. 515–524). San Francisco: Jossey-Bass.

Gasman, M. (2008). Minority-Serving Institutions: A historical backdrop. In M. Gasman, B. Baez, & C.S.V. Turner (Eds.), *Understanding Minority-Serving Institutions* (pp. 18–27). Albany: State University of New York Press.

Geiger, R. L. (2005). The ten generations of American higher education. In R. O. Berdahl, P. G. Altbach, & P. J. Gumport (Eds.), *Higher education in the twenty-first century* (2nd ed., pp. 38–69). Baltimore: Johns Hopkins University Press.

Gelb, J., & Palley, M. L. (1982). *Women and public policies.* Princeton, NJ: Princeton University Press.

Gildersleeve, R. E., Rumann, C., & Mondragón, R. (2010). Serving undocumented students: Current law and policy. In J. Price (Ed.), *Understanding and supporting undocumented students* (New Directions for Student Services No. 131, pp. 5–18). San Francisco: Jossey-Bass.

Gilligan, C. (1977). In a different voice: Women's conception of self and morality. *Harvard Educational Review, 47,* 482–517.

Gilligan, C. (1982). *In a different voice: Psychological theory and women's development.* Cambridge, MA: Harvard University Press.

Gilligan, C. (1993). *In a different voice: Psychological theory and women's development* (2nd ed.). Cambridge, MA: Harvard University Press.

Gloria, A. M., Castellanos, J., Scull, N. C., & Villegas, F. J. (2009). Psychological coping and well-being of male Latino undergraduates: "Sobreviviendo la Universidad." *Hispanic Journal of Behavioral Sciences, 31,* 317–339.

Goldrick-Rab, S. (2006). Following their every move: An investigation of social-class differences in college pathways. *Sociology of Education, 79,* 61–79.

Goldrick-Rab, S., Carter, D. F., & Winkle Wagner, R. (2007). What higher education has to say about the transition to college. *Teachers College Record, 109,* 2444–2481.

Goldrick-Rab, S., & Pfeffer, F. T. (2009). Beyond access: Explaining socioeconomic differences in college transfer. *Sociology of Education, 82,* 101–125.

Goldstein, D. (2011, June 15). Should all kids go to college? *Nation.* Retrieved from www.thenation.com/article/161463/should-all-kids-go-college

Gonyea, R. M., & Moore, J. V. (2007, November). Gay, lesbian, bisexual, and transgender students and their engagement in educationally purposeful activities in college. Paper presented at the 32nd annual meeting of the Association for the Study of Higher Education, Louisville, KY.

Guardia, J. R., & Evans, N. J. (2008). Factors influencing the ethnic identity development of Latino fraternity members at a Hispanic Serving Institution. *Journal of College Student Development, 49,* 163–181.

Guiffrida, D. A. (2005). To break away or strengthen ties to home: A complex question for African American students attending a predominantly white institution. *Equity and Excellence in Education, 38,* 49–60.

Guiffrida, D. A. (2006). Toward a cultural advancement of Tinto's theory. *Review of Higher Education, 29,* 451–472.

Guillory, J. P., & Ward, K. (2008). Tribal colleges and universities: Identity, invisibility, and current issues. In M. Gasman, B. Baez, & C.S.V. Turner (Eds.), *Understanding Minority-Serving Institutions* (pp. 91–110). Albany: State University of New York Press.

Gump, L. S., Baker, R. C., & Roll, S. (2000). Cultural and gender differences in moral judgment: A study of Mexican Americans and Anglo-Americans. *Hispanic Journal of Behavioral Sciences, 22,* 78–93.

Gurin, P., Lehman, J. S., Lewis, E., Dey, E. L., Gurin, G., & Hurtado, S. (2004). *Defending diversity: Affirmative action at the University of Michigan.* Ann Arbor: University of Michigan Press.

Habley, W., Valiga, M., McClanahan, R., & Burkum, K. (2010). *What works in student retention.* Iowa City, IA: ACT.

Hagedorn, L. S. (2005). How to define retention: A new look at an old problem. In A. Seidman (Ed.), *College student retention: Formula for student success* (pp. 89–106). Westport, CT: Praeger.

Hall, R. M., & Sandler, B. R. (1982). *The classroom climate: A chilly one for women?* Project on the Status and Education of Women. Washington, DC: Association of American Colleges.

Hall, R. M., & Sandler, B. R. (1984). *Out of the classroom: A chilly campus climate for women?* Project on the Status and Education of Women. Washington, DC: Association of American Colleges.

Hamrick, F. A., & Stage, F. K. (2004). College predisposition at high–minority enrollment, low-income schools. *Review of Higher Education, 27,* 151–168.

Harbour, W. S., & Madaus, J. W. (2011). Editor's notes. In W. S. Harbour & J. W. Madaus (Eds.), *Disability services and campus dynamics* (New Directions for Higher Education No. 154, pp. 1–3). San Francisco: Jossey-Bass.

Harper, S. R. (2009). Niggers no more: A critical race counternarrative on black male student achievement at predominantly white colleges and universities. *International Journal of Qualitative Studies in Education, 22,* 697–712.

Harper, S. R., Harris, F., III, & Mmeje, K. A. (2005). A theoretical model to explain the overrepresentation of college men among campus judicial offenders: Implications for campus administrators. *Journal of Student Affairs Research and Practice, 42,* 565–588.

Harper, S. R., & Quaye, S. J. (2007). Student organizations as venues for black identity expression and development among African American male student leaders. *Journal of College Student Development, 48,* 127–144.

Harper, S. R., & Quaye, S. J. (Eds.). (2009). *Student engagement in higher education: Theoretical perspectives and practical approaches for diverse populations.* New York: Routledge.

Harper, S. R., Wardell, C. C., & McGuire, K. M. (2011). Man of multiple identities: Complex individuality and identity intersectionality among college men. In J. A. Laker & T. Davis (Eds.), *Masculinities in higher education: Theoretical and practical considerations* (pp. 81–96). New York: Routledge.

Harris, D. R., & Sim, J. J. (2002). Who is multiracial? Assessing the complexity of lived race. *American Sociological Review, 67,* 614–627.

Harris, F., III. (2010). College men's conceptualizations of masculinities and contextual influences: Toward a conceptual model. *Journal of College Student Development, 51*, 297–318.

Harris, F., III, & Edwards, K. E. (2010). College men's experiences as men: Findings and implications from two grounded theory studies. *Journal of Student Affairs Research and Practice, 47*, 43–62.

Harris, F., III, & Harper, S. R. (2008). Masculinities go to community college: Understanding male identity socialization and gender role conflict. In J. Lester (Ed.), *Gendered perspectives on community colleges* (New Directions for Community Colleges No. 142, pp. 25–35). San Francisco: Jossey-Bass.

Hart, J., & Fellabaum, J. (2008). Analyzing campus climate studies: Seeking to define and understand. *Journal of Diversity in Higher Education, 1*, 222–234.

Heckman, J. J., & LaFontaine, P. A. (2007). *The American high school graduation rate: Trends and levels* (Institute for the Study of Labor Discussion Paper No. 3216). Bonn, Germany: Institute for the Study of Labor.

Heller, D. E. (2006, March). Merit aid and college access. Paper presented at the Symposium on the Consequences of Merit-Based Student Aid, Wisconsin Center for the Advancement of Postsecondary Education, Madison.

Heller, D. E., & Marin, P. (2001, December). Who should we help? The negative social consequence of merit scholarships. Cambridge, MA: Civil Rights Project, Harvard University.

Heller, D. E., & Rasmussen, C. J. (2001, December). Merit scholarships and college access: Evidence from two states. Paper presented at the State Merit Programs: College Access and Equity symposium, Cambridge, MA.

Helms, J. E. (1990). *Black and white racial identity: Theory, research, and practice.* Westport, CT: Greenwood Press.

Helms, J. E. (1992). *A race is a nice thing to have: A guide to being a white person or understanding the white persons in your life.* Topeka, KS: Content Communications.

Helms, J. E. (1995). An update of Helms's white and people of color racial identity models. In. J. G. Ponterotto, J. M. Casas, L. A. Suzuki, & C. M. Alexander (Eds.), *Handbook of multicultural counseling* (pp. 181–198). Thousand Oaks, CA: Sage.

Hendel, D. D. (2007). Efficacy of participating in a first-year seminar on student satisfaction and retention. *Journal of College Student Retention, 8*, 413–423.

Henry, G. T., & Rubenstein, R. (2002). Paying for grades: Impact of merit-based financial aid on educational quality. *Journal of Policy Analysis and Management, 21*, 93–109.

Higher Education Research Institute. (1996). *A social change model of leadership development: Guidebook version III.* Los Angeles: Author.

Hill, J. P. (2009). Higher education as moral community: Institutional influences on religious participation during college. *Journal for the Scientific Study of Religion, 48*, 515–534.

Holland, J. L. (1966). *The psychology of vocational choice: A theory of personality types and model environments.* Waltham, MA: Blaisdell.

Hood, A. B. (Ed.). (1986). *The Iowa Student Development Inventories.* Iowa City, IA: Hitech Press.

Hood, A. B. (1997). *The Iowa Student Development Inventories* (2nd ed.). Iowa City, IA: Hitech Press.

Horn, L. J., & Carroll, C. D. (1996). *Nontraditional undergraduates: Trends in enrollment from 1986 to 1992 and persistence and attainment among 1989–90 beginning postsecondary students* (NCES 97-578). Postsecondary Education Descriptive Analysis Reports. Washington, DC: Office of Educational Research and Improvement, National Center for Education Statistics.

Horn, L. J., & Carroll, C. D. (1998). *Stopouts or stayouts? Undergraduates who leave college in their first year* (NCES 1999-087). Washington, DC: Office of Educational Research and Improvement, National Center for Education Statistics.

Horowitz, H. L. (1988). *Campus life: Undergraduate cultures from the end of the eighteenth century to the present.* Chicago: University of Chicago Press.

Horse, P. G. (2001). Reflections on American Indian identity. In C. L. Wijeyesinghe & B. W. Jackson III (Eds.), *New perspectives on racial identity development: A theoretical and practical anthology* (pp. 91–107). New York: New York University Press.

Hossler, D., Braxton, J. M., & Coopersmith, G. (1989). Understanding student college choice. In J. C. Smart (Ed.), *Higher education: Handbook of theory and research* (Vol. 5, pp. 231–288). New York: Agathon Press.

Hossler, D., & Foley, E. M. (1995). Reducing the noise in the college choice process: The use of college guidebooks and ratings. In R. D. Walleri & M. K. Moss (Eds.), *Evaluating and responding to college guidebooks and rankings* (New Directions for Institutional Research No. 88, pp. 21–30). San Francisco: Jossey-Bass.

Hossler, D., & Gallagher, K. S. (1987). Studying college choice: A three-phase model and the implications for policymakers. *College & University, 62*(3), 207–221.

Hossler, D., Schmit, J., & Vesper, N. (1999). *Going to college: How social, economic, and educational factors influence the decisions students make.* Baltimore: Johns Hopkins University Press.

Hout, M., & Janus, A. (2011). Educational mobility in the United States since the 1930s. In R. Murnane & G. J. Duncan (Eds.), *Socioeconomic inequality and educational disadvantage* (pp. 165–186). Washington, DC: Brookings Institution.

Howard-Hamilton, M. F., Hinton, K. G., & Hughes, R. L. (2010). Critical borders: Student development theoretical perspectives applied to culture centers. In L. D. Patton (Ed.), *Culture centers in higher education: Perspectives on identity, theory, and practice* (pp. 105–118). Sterling, VA: Stylus.

Howe, N., & Strauss, W. (2000). *Millennials rising: The next great generation.* New York: Vintage.

Howe, N., & Strauss, W. (2003). *Millennials go to college.* Washington, DC: American Association of Collegiate Registrars and Admissions Officers.

Hoyt, J. E., & Winn, B. A. (2004). Understanding retention and college student bodies: Differences between drop-outs, stop-outs, opt-outs, and transfer-outs. *Journal of Student Affairs Research and Practice, 41,* 395–417.

Hu, S., & St. John, E. P. (2001). Student persistence in a public higher education system: Understanding racial and ethnic differences. *Journal of Higher Education, 72,* 265–286.

Huisman, J. (1995). *Differentiation, diversity, and decentralization in higher education.* Utrecht, The Netherlands: Lemma.

Humes, K. R., Jones, N. A., & Ramirez, R. R. (2011). *Overview of race and Hispanic origin: 2010.* (2010 Census Briefs). Washington, DC: U.S.

Department of Commerce, Economics and Statistics Administration, U.S. Census Bureau.

Hunter, M. S., & Linder, C. W. (2005). First-year seminars. In M. L. Upcraft, J. N. Gardner, B. O. Barefoot, & Associates (Eds.), *Challenging and supporting the first-year student: A handbook for improving the first year of college.* San Francisco: Jossey-Bass.

Hurtado, S. (1992). The campus racial climate: Contexts of conflict. *Journal of Higher Education, 63,* 539–569.

Hurtado, S. (2005). The next generation of diversity and intergroup relations research. *Journal of Social Issues, 61,* 595–610.

Hurtado, S., & Carter, D. F. (1997). Effects of college transition and perceptions of the campus racial climate on Latino college students' sense of belonging. *Sociology of Education, 70,* 324–345.

Hurtado, S., Dey, E. L., Gurin, P. Y., & Gurin, G. (2003). College environments, diversity, and student learning. In J. C. Smart (Ed.), *Higher education: Handbook of theory and research* (Vol. 18, pp. 145–190). Dordrecht, The Netherlands: Kluwer Academic.

Hurtado, S., Engberg, M. E., Ponjuan, L., & Landreman, L. (2002). Students' precollege preparation for participation in a diverse democracy. *Research in Higher Education, 43,* 163–186.

Hurtado, S., Griffin, K. A., Arellano, L., & Cuellar, M. (2008). Assessing the value of climate assessments: Progress and future directions. *Journal of Diversity in Higher Education, 1,* 204–221.

Hurtado, S., Han, J. C., Sáenz, V. B., Espinosa, L., Cabrera, N., & Cerna, O. (2007). Predicting transition and adjustment to college: Biomedical and behavioral science aspirants' and minority students' first year of college. *Research in Higher Education, 43,* 841–887.

Hurtado, S., Milem, J. F., Clayton-Pedersen, A. R., & Allen, W. R. (1998). Enhancing campus climates for racial/ethnic diversity: Educational policy and practice. *Review of Higher Education, 21,* 279–302.

Hurtado, S., & Ponjuan, L. (2005). Latino educational outcomes and the campus climate. *Journal of Hispanic Higher Education, 4,* 235–251.

Hussar, W. J., & Bailey, T. M. (2009). *Projections of education statistics to 2018* (NCES 2009-062). Washington, DC: National Center for Education Statistics.

Indiana Commission for Higher Education. (2008, June). *Reaching higher with college completion: Moving from access to success.* Indianapolis: Author. Retrieved from www.in.gov/che/files/3-College_Completion-7-7.pdf

Inkelas, K. K. (2004). Does participation in ethnic cocurricular activities facilitate a sense of ethnic awareness and understanding? A study of Asian Pacific American undergraduates. *Journal of College Student Development, 45,* 285–302.

Inkelas, K. K., Daver, Z. E., Vogt, K. E., & Leonard, J. B. (2007). Living-learning programs and first-generation college students' academic and social transition to college. *Research in Higher Education, 48,* 403–434.

Inkelas, K. K., Vogt, K. E., Longerbeam, S., Owen, J., & Johnson, D. (2006). Measuring outcomes of living-learning programs: Examining college environments and student learning and development. *Journal of General Education, 55,* 294–328.

Inkelas, K. K., & Weisman, J. (2003). Different by design: An examination of outcomes associated with three types of living-learning programs. *Journal of College Student Development, 44,* 335–368.

Ishitani, T. T., & DesJardins, S. L. (2002–2003). A longitudinal investigation of dropout from college in the United States. *Journal of College Student Retention, 4,* 173–201.

Jablonski, M. A. (Ed.). (2001). *The implications of student spirituality for student affairs practice* (New Directions for Student Services No. 95). San Francisco: Jossey-Bass.

Jackson, B. W. (1976). Black identity development. In L. H. Golubchick & B. Persky (Eds.), *Urban social and educational issues* (pp. 158–164). Dubuque, IA: Kendall Hunt.

Jackson, B. W., & Wijeyesinghe, C. L. (Eds.). (2012). *New perspectives on racial identity development* (2nd ed.). New York: New York University Press.

Jaschik, S. (2006, August 8). An end to picking one box. *Inside Higher Ed.* Retrieved from www.insidehighered.com/news/2006/08/08/race

Jessup-Anger, J. E. (2012). Examining how residential colleges inspire the life of the mind. *Review of Higher Education, 35,* 431–462.

Jones, S. R. (2009). Constructing identities at the intersections: An autoethnographic exploration of multiple dimensions of identity. *Journal of College Student Development, 50,* 287–304.

Jones, S. R., & Abes, E. S. (2004). Enduring influences of service-learning on college students' identity development. *Journal of College Student Development, 45,* 134–148.

Jones, S. R., & Abes, E. S. (2011). The nature and uses of theory. In J. S. Schuh, S. R. Jones, S. R. Harper, & Associates (Eds.), *Student services: A handbook for the profession* (pp. 149–167). San Francisco: Jossey-Bass.

Jones, S. R., & McEwen, M. K. (2000). A conceptual model of multiple dimensions of identity. *Journal of College Student Development, 41,* 405–413.

Junco, R., & Salter, D. W. (2004). Improving the campus climate for students with disabilities through the use of online training. *Journal of Student Affairs Research and Practice, 41,* 263–276.

Kamenetz, A. (2010). *DIY U: Edupunks, edupreneurs, and the coming transformation of higher education.* White River Junction, VT: Chelsea Green.

Kanellos, N. (1997). *Hispanic firsts: 500 years of extraordinary achievement.* Detroit: Visible Ink Press.

Keeling, R. P. (Ed.). (2004). *Learning reconsidered: A campus-wide focus on the student experience.* Washington, DC: American College Personnel Association & National Association of Student Personnel Administrators.

Keeling, R. P. (Ed.). (2006). *Learning reconsidered 2: Implementing a campus-wide focus on the student experience.* Washington, DC: American College Personnel Association & National Association of Student Personnel Administrators.

Kegan, R. (1982). *The evolving self.* Cambridge, MA: Harvard University Press.

Kegan, R. (1994). *In over our heads: The mental demands of modern life.* Cambridge, MA: Harvard University Press.

Kegan, R., & Lahey, L. L. (2009). *Immunity to change: How to overcome it and unlock the potential in yourself and your organization.* Boston: Harvard Business School.

Keller, G. (2001). The new demographics of higher education. *Review of Higher Education, 24,* 219–235.

Kellom, G. E. (Ed.). (2004). *Developing effective programs and services for college men* (New Directions for Student Services No. 107). San Francisco: Jossey-Bass.

Kent, C. A., & Sowards, K. N. (2008). Property taxation and equity in public school finance. *Journal of Property Tax Assessment & Administration, 6*(1), 25–42.

Kezar, A. J., & Moriarty, D. (2000). Expanding our understanding of student leadership development: A study exploring gender and ethnic identity. *Journal of College Student Development, 41,* 55–69.

Kilson, M. (2001). *Claiming place: Biracial young adults of the post–civil rights era.* Westport, CT: Bergin and Garvey.

Kim, J. (2001). Asian American identity development theory. In C. L. Wijeyesinghe & B. W. Jackson III (Eds.), *New perspectives on racial identity development: A theoretical and practical anthology* (pp. 67–90). New York: New York University Press.

Kim, M. (1999, November). A comparative analysis of academic development among African-American students in historically black versus predominantly white institutions. Paper presented at the 24th annual meeting of the Association for the Study of Higher Education, San Antonio, TX.

Kim, M., & Alvarez, R. (1995). Women-only colleges: Some unanticipated consequences. *Journal of Higher Education, 66,* 641–668.

Kimmel, M. (2008). *Guyland: The perilous world where boys become men.* New York: HarperCollins.

King, A. R. (2011). Environmental influences on the development of female college students who identify as multiracial/biracial-bisexual/pansexual. *Journal of College Student Development, 52,* 440–455.

King, J. E. (2003). *2003 status report on the Pell Grant program.* Washington, DC: American Council on Education.

King, P. M. (1978). William Perry's theory of intellectual and ethical development. In L. L. Knefelkamp, C. Widick, & C. A. Parker (Eds.), *Applying new developmental findings* (New Directions for Student Services No. 4, pp. 35–51). San Francisco: Jossey-Bass.

King, P. M. (2009). Principles of development and developmental change underlying theories of cognitive and moral development. *Journal of College Student Development, 50,* 597–620.

King, P. M., & Baxter Magolda, M. B. (2005). A developmental model of intercultural maturity. *Journal of College Student Development, 46,* 571–592.

King, P. M., Baxter Magolda, M. B., Barber, J. P., Kendall Brown, M., & Lindsay, N. K. (2009). Developmentally effective experiences for promoting self-authorship. *Mind, Brain, and Education, 3,* 108–118.

King, P. M., Kendall Brown, M., Lindsay, N. K., & VanHecke, J. R. (2007). Liberal arts student learning outcomes: An integrated perspective. *About Campus, 12*(4), 2–9.

King, P. M., & Kitchener, K. S. (1994). *Developing Reflective Judgment: Understanding and promoting intellectual growth and critical thinking in adolescents and adults.* San Francisco: Jossey-Bass.

King, P. M., & Kitchener, K. S. (2002). The Reflective Judgment model: Twenty years of research on epistemic cognition. In B. K. Hofer & P. R. Pintrich (Eds.), *Personal epistemology: The psychology of beliefs about knowledge and knowing* (pp. 37–61). Mahwah, NJ: Erlbaum.

King, P. M., & Kitchener, K. S. (2004). Reflective Judgment: Theory and research on the development of epistemic assumptions through adulthood. *Educational Psychologist, 39,* 5–18.

King, P. M., & Mayhew, M. J. (2002). Moral judgment development in higher education: Insights from the Defining Issues Test. *Journal of Moral Education, 31,* 247–270.

King, P. M., & Mayhew, M. J. (2005). Theory and research on the development of moral reasoning among college students. In J. C. Smart (Ed.), *Higher education: Handbook of theory and research* (Vol. 19, pp. 375–440). Dordrecht, The Netherlands: Kluwer Academic.

Kinzie, J., Palmer, M., Hayek, J., Hossler, D., Jacob, S. A., & Cummings, H. (2004). Fifty years of college choice: Social, political and institutional influences on the decision-making process. *Lumina Foundation for Education New Agenda Series, 5*(3), 1–66.

Kirst, M. W., & Venezia, A. (2004). *From high school to college: Improving opportunities for success in postsecondary education.* San Francisco: Jossey-Bass.

Kitchener, K. S., Wood, P. K., & Jensen, L. (1999, August). Curricular, co-curricular, and institutional influences on real-world problem solving. Paper presented at the 107th annual meeting of the American Psychological Association, Boston.

Klein, S., Benjamin, R., Shavelson, R., & Bolus, R. (2007). The Collegiate Learning Assessment: Facts and fantasies. *Evaluation Review, 31,* 415–439.

Kleinfeld, J. (2009). No map to manhood: Male and female mindsets behind the college gender gap. *Gender Issues, 26,* 171–182.

Klymyshyn, A.M.U., Green, D. O., & Richardson, C. (2010). Diversity at Central Michigan University: A case study of achieving diversity at a predominantly white public university. In H. A. Neville, M. B. Huntt, & J. Chapa (Eds.), *Implementing diversity: Contemporary challenges and best practices at predominantly white universities* (pp. 125–144). Urbana: University of Illinois at Urbana-Champaign, Center on Democracy in a Multiracial Society.

Knapp, L. G., Kelly-Reid, J. E., & Ginder, S. A. (2010). *Enrollment in postsecondary institutions, fall 2008; graduation rates, 2002 and 2005 cohorts; and financial statistics, fiscal year 2008* (NCES 2010-152). Washington, DC: National Center for Education Statistics.

Knapp, L. G., Kelly-Reid, J. E., & Whitmore, R. W. (2006). *Enrollment in postsecondary institutions, fall 2004; graduation rates, 1998 and 2001; and financial statistics, fiscal year 2004* (NCES 2006-155). Washington, DC: National Center for Education Statistics.

Knefelkamp, L. L., Widick, C., & Parker, C. A. (1978). Editors' notes: Why bother with theory? In L. L. Knefelkamp, C. Widick, & C. A. Parker (Eds.), *Applying new developmental findings* (New Directions for Student Services No. 4, pp. vii–xvi). San Francisco: Jossey-Bass.

Kodama, C. M., McEwen, M. K., Liang, C.T.H., & Lee, S. (2001). A theoretical examination of psychosocial issues for Asian Pacific American students. *NASPA Journal, 38,* 411–437.

Kodama, C. M., McEwen, M. K., Liang, C.T.H., & Lee, S. (2002). An Asian American perspective on psychosocial student development theory. In M. K. McEwen, C. M. Kodama, A. Alvarez, S. Lee, & C.T.H. Liang (Eds.), *Working with Asian American college students* (New Directions for Student Services No. 97, pp. 45–59). San Francisco: Jossey-Bass.

Kohlberg, L. (1969). Stage and sequence: The cognitive developmental approach
to socialization. In D. A. Goslin (Ed.), *Handbook of socialization theory and research*
(pp. 347–480). Skokie, IL: Rand McNally.

Kohlberg, L. (1976). Moral stages and moralization: The cognitive-developmental
approach. In T. Lickona (Ed.), *Moral development and behavior: Theory, research, and
social issues* (pp. 31–53). New York: Holt McDougal.

Kohlberg, L., Levine, C., & Hewer, A. (1984). The current formulation of the
theory. In L. Kohlberg (Ed.), *Essays on moral development: Vol. 2. The psychology of
moral development* (pp. 212–319). San Francisco: Harper & Row.

Komives, S. R., Casper, J. O., Longerbeam, S., Mainella, F. C., & Osteen, L. (2005).
Developing a leadership identity: A grounded theory. *Journal of College Student
Development, 46,* 593–611.

Komives, S. R., Longerbeam, S., Owen, J. E., Mainella, F. C., & Osteen, L. (2006). A
leadership identity development model: Applications from a grounded theory.
Journal of College Student Development, 47, 401–418.

Kotok, A. (2008, June 6). Student-veterans come marching home: Their return to
studies. *Science.* Retrieved from http://sciencecareers.sciencemag.org/career
_development/previous_issues/articles/2008_06_06/caredit_a0800082

Kreider, R. M., & Ellis, R. (2011). *Number, timing, and duration of marriages and
divorces: 2009.* Washington, DC: U.S. Census Bureau. Retrieved from
www.census.gov/prod/2011pubs/p70-125.pdf

Kube, B., & Thorndike, R. (1991, April). Cognitive development during college:
A longitudinal study measured on the Perry scheme. Paper presented at
the annual meeting of the American Educational Research Association,
Chicago.

Kuh, G. D. (1999). How are we doing? Tracking the quality of the undergraduate
experience, 1960s to the present. *Review of Higher Education, 22,* 99–119.

Kuh, G. D. (2008). *High impact educational practices: What they are, who has access to
them, and why they matter.* Washington, DC: Association of American Colleges and
Universities.

Kuh, G. D. (2009). Understanding campus environments. In G. S. McClellan, J.
Stringer, & Associates (Eds.), *The handbook of student affairs administration* (3rd ed.,
pp. 59–80). San Francisco: Jossey-Bass.

Kuh, G. D. (2011). Student success. In J. H. Schuh, S. R. Jones, & S. R. Harper
(Eds.), *Student services: A handbook for the profession* (5th ed., pp. 257–269). San
Francisco: Jossey-Bass.

Kuh, G. D., Hu, S., & Vesper, N. (2000). "They shall be known by what they do": An
activities-based typology of college students. *Journal of College Student Development,
41,* 228–244.

Kuh, G. D., Kinzie, J., Schuh, J. H., Whitt, E. J., & Associates. (2005). *Student success
in college: Creating conditions that matter.* San Francisco: Jossey-Bass.

✴ Kuh, G. D., & Love, P. G. (2000). A cultural perspective on student departure. In
J. M. Braxton (Ed.), *Reworking the student departure puzzle* (pp. 196–212). Nashville,
TN: Vanderbilt University Press.

Ladson-Billings, G. (1998). Just what is Critical Race Theory and what's it doing in a
nice field like education? *Qualitative Studies in Education, 11,* 7–24.

Lahey, L. L., Souvaine, E., Kegan, R., Goodman, R., & Felix, S. (1988). *A guide to the Subject-Object Interview: Its administration and interpretation.* Cambridge, MA: Subject-Object Research Group, Harvard Graduate School of Education.

Lamport, M. A., & Bulgin, R. (2010, September 18). The education and miseducation of boys in cultural, political, and Christian perspective. *Christian Perspectives in Education, 3*(2). Retrieved from http://digitalcommons.liberty.edu/cgi/viewcontent.cgi?article=1046&context=cpe

Lareau, A. (1987). Social class differences in family-school relationships: The importance of cultural capital. *Sociology of Education, 60,* 73–85.

Laufgraben, J. L. (2005). Learning communities. In M. L. Upcraft, J. N. Gardner, B. O. Barefoot, & Associates (Eds.), *Challenging and supporting the first-year student: A handbook for improving the first year of college* (pp. 371–387). San Francisco: Jossey-Bass.

Laughlin, A., & Creamer, E. G. (2007). Engaging differences: Self-authorship and the 'decision-making process. In P. S. Meszaros (Ed.), *Self-authorship: Advancing students' intellectual growth* (New Directions for Teaching and Learning No. 111, pp. 43–51). San Francisco: Jossey-Bass.

Lemann, N. (2010, October 6). Schoolwork: Comment about public education and education reform. *New Yorker Magazine.* Retrieved from www.newyorker.com/talk/comment/2010/09/27/100927taco_talk_lemann

Lester, J. (2006). Who will we serve in the future? The new student in transition. In F. Santos-Laanan (Ed.), *Understanding students in transition: Trends and issues* (New Directions for Student Services No. 114, pp. 47–62). San Francisco: Jossey-Bass.

Lev, A. I. (2004). *Transgender emergence: Therapeutic guidelines for working with gender variant people and their families.* New York: Haworth Clinical Practice Press.

Levine, A., & Cureton, J. S. (1998). Student politics: The new localism. *Review of Higher Education, 21,* 137–150.

Levine, A., & Dean, D. (2012). *Generation on a tightrope: A portrait of today's college student.* San Francisco: Jossey-Bass.

Levine, A., & Nidiffer, J. (1996). *Beating the odds: How the poor get to college.* San Francisco: Jossey-Bass.

Levine, H., & Evans, N. J. (1991). The development of gay, lesbian, and bisexual identities. In N. J. Evans & V. A. Wall (Eds.), *Beyond tolerance: Gays, lesbians and bisexuals on campus* (pp. 1–24). Alexandria, VA: American College Personnel Association.

Lewis, P., Forsythe, G. B., Sweeney, P., Bartone, P. T., Bullis, C., & Snook, S. (2005). Identity development during the college years: Findings from the West Point longitudinal study. *Journal of College Student Development, 46,* 357–373.

Lillard, D., & Gerner, J. (1999). Getting to the Ivy League: How family composition affects college choice. *Journal of Higher Education, 70,* 706–730.

Locks, A. M., Hurtado, S., Bowman, N. A., & Oseguera, L. (2008). Extending notions of campus climate and diversity to students' transition to college. *Review of Higher Education, 31,* 257–285.

Long, B. T. (2004). How have college decisions changed over time? An application of the conditional logistic choice model. *Journal of Econometrics, 121,* 271–296.

Lopez, J. D. (2005). Race-related stress and sociocultural orientation among Latino students during their transition into a predominantly white, highly selective institution. *Journal of Hispanic Higher Education, 4,* 354–365.

López Turley, R. N., Santos, M., & Ceja, C. (2007). Social origin and college opportunity expectations across cohorts. *Social Science Research, 36,* 1200–1218.

Lotkowski, V. A., Robbins, S. B., & Noeth, R. J. (2004). *The role of academic and non-academic factors in improving college retention.* Iowa City, IA: ACT.

Love, P. G., & Guthrie, V. L. (1999). *Understanding and applying cognitive development theory* (New Directions for Student Services No. 88). San Francisco: Jossey-Bass.

Lucas, R. (1970). The right to higher education. *Journal of Higher Education, 41,* 55–64.

Lucozzi, E. A. (1998). A far better place: Institutions as allies. In R. L. Sanlo (Ed.), *Working with lesbian, gay, bisexual, and transgender college students: A handbook for faculty and administrators* (pp. 47–52). Westport, CT: Greenwood Press.

Luebke, B., & Reilly, M. (1995). *Women's studies graduates: The first generation.* New York: Teachers College Press.

Lyons, N. P. (1983). Two perspectives: On self, relationships, and morality. *Harvard Educational Review, 53,* 125–145.

MacDonald, V. M., & García, T. (2003). Historical perspectives on Latino access to higher education, 1848–1990. In J. Castellanos & L. Jones (Eds.), *The majority in the minority: Expanding the representation of Latina/o faculty, administrators and students in higher education* (pp. 15–43). Sterling, VA: Stylus.

Maki, P. L. (2010). *Assessing for learning: Building a sustainable commitment across the institution* (2nd ed.). Sterling, VA: Stylus.

Manski, E. F., & Wise, D. A. (1983). *College choice in America.* Cambridge, MA: Harvard University Press.

Marcia, J. E. (1966). Development and validation of ego-identity status. *Journal of Personality and Social Psychology, 3,* 551–558.

Marcia, J. E. (1975). Identity six years after: A follow-up study. *Journal of Youth and Adolescence, 5,* 145–160.

Marcia, J. E. (1980). Identity in adolescence. In J. Adelson (Ed.), *Handbook of adolescent psychology* (pp. 159–187). Hoboken, NJ: Wiley.

Marcia, J. E. (1994). The empirical study of ego-identity. In H. A. Bosma, T.L.G. Graafsma, H. D. Grotevant, & D. J. de Levita (Eds.), *Identity and development: An interdisciplinary approach* (pp. 67–80). Thousand Oaks, CA: Sage.

Martínez Alemán, A. M., & Wartman, K. L. (2008). *Online social networking on campus: Understanding what matters in student culture.* New York: Routledge.

Mattanah, J. F., Ayers, J. F., Brand, B. L., Brooks, L. J., Quimby, J. L., & McNary, S. W. (2010). A social support intervention to ease the college transition: Exploring main effects and moderators. *Journal of College Student Development, 51,* 93–108.

Mattanah, J. F., Lopez, F. G., & Govern, J. M. (2011). The contributions of parental attachment bonds to college student development and adjustment: A meta-analytic review. *Journal of Counseling Psychology, 58,* 565–596.

Matthews, D. (2010). *A stronger nation through higher education: How and why Americans must achieve the "big goal" for college attainment.* Indianapolis, IN: Lumina Foundation for Education.

Mayhew, M. J., & DeLuca Fernández, S. L. (2007). Pedagogical practices that contribute to social justice outcomes. *Review of Higher Education, 31*, 55–80.

Mayhew, M. J., & King, P. (2008). How curricular content and pedagogical strategies affect moral reasoning development in college students. *Journal of Moral Education, 37*, 17–40.

McCarn, S. R., & Fassinger, R. E. (1996). Revisioning sexual minority identity formation: A new model of lesbian identity and its implications for counseling and research. *Counseling Psychologist, 24*, 508–534.

McCormick, A. C. (2003). Swirling and double-dipping: New patterns of student attendance and their implications for higher education. In J. E. King, E. L. Anderson, & M. E. Corrigan (Eds.), *Changing student attendance patterns: Challenges for policy and practice* (New Directions for Higher Education No. 121, pp. 13–24). San Francisco: Jossey-Bass.

McCowen, C., & Alston, R. (1998). Racial identity, African self-consciousness, and career decision making in African-American women. *Journal of Multicultural Counseling and Development, 26*(1), 28–38.

McDonough, P. M. (1994). Buying and selling higher education: The social construction of the college applicant. *Journal of Higher Education, 65*, 427–446.

McDonough, P. M. (1997). *Choosing college: How social class and schools structure opportunity.* New York: State University of New York Press.

McDonough, P. M. (2004). The school-to-college transition: Challenges and prospects. *Informed practice: Syntheses of higher education research for campus leaders* (pp. 1–43). Washington, DC: American Council on Education, Center for Policy Analysis.

McGuire, M. D. (1995). Validity issues for reputational studies. In P. G. Love & V. L. Guthrie (Eds.), *Understanding and applying cognitive development theory* (New Directions for Student Services No. 88, pp. 45–59). San Francisco: Jossey-Bass.

McKevitt, G. (1990–1991, Winter). Hispanic Californians and Catholic higher education: The diary of Jesús María Estudillo, 1857–1864. *California History, 69*, 320–331.

McEwen, M. K. (2003). The nature and uses of theory. In S. R. Komives, D. B. Woodard Jr., & Associates (Eds.), *Student services: A handbook for the profession* (4th ed., pp. 153–178). San Francisco: Jossey-Bass.

McPherson, M., & Shapiro, M. O. (1998). *The student aid game: Meeting need and rewarding talent in American higher education.* Princeton, NJ: Princeton University Press.

Mercer, C. J., & Stedman, J. B. (2008). Minority-Serving Institutions: Selected institutional and student characteristics. In M. Gasman, B. Baez, & C.S.V. Turner (Eds.), *Understanding Minority-Serving Institutions* (pp. 28–42). Albany: State University of New York Press.

Meszaros, P. S. (2007). The journey of self-authorship: Why is it necessary? In P. S. Meszaros (Ed.), *Self-authorship: Advancing students' intellectual growth* (New Directions for Teaching and Learning No. 109, pp. 5–14). San Francisco: Jossey-Bass.

Middle Class Task Force. (2009). *Financing the dream: Securing college affordability for the middle-class.* (Staff report). Washington, DC: Author, Office of the Vice President of the United States. Retrieved from www.whitehouse.gov/assets/documents /staff_report_college_affordability1.pdf

Midwestern Higher Education Compact. (2009). *Completion-based funding for higher education.* Minneapolis, MN: Author.

Milem, J. F. (2003). The educational benefits of diversity: Evidence from multiple sectors. In M. Chang, D. Witt, J. Jones, & K. Hakuta (Eds.), *Compelling interest: Examining the evidence on racial dynamics in higher education* (pp. 126–169). Stanford, CA: Stanford University Press.

Miller-Bernal, L. (2000). *Separate by degree: Women students' experiences in single-sex and coeducational colleges.* New York: Peter Lang.

Mohr, J., & Fassinger, R. (2000). Measuring dimensions of lesbian and gay male experience. *Measurement and Evaluation in Counseling and Development, 33,* 66–90.

Moodie, A. (2011, November 13). US: For-profits controversial but driving growth. *University World News,* (197). Retrieved from www.universityworldnews.com /article.php?story=20111111215528267

Moore, J. M. (2003). *Booker T. Washington, W.E.B. DuBois, and the struggle for racial uplift.* Lanham, MD: Scholarly Resources.

Moos, R. H. (1973). Conceptualizations of human environments. *American Psychologist, 28,* 652–665.

Moos, R. H. (1979). *Evaluating educational environments: Procedures, measures, findings, and policy implications.* San Francisco: Jossey-Bass.

Moos, R. H., & Insel, P. (Eds.). (1974). *Issues in social ecology.* Palo Alto, CA: National Press Books.

Morales, E. E. (2010). Legitimizing hope: An exploration of effective mentoring for Dominican American male college students. *Journal of College Student Retention, 11,* 385–406.

Morphew, C. C., & Hartley, M. (2006). Mission statements: A thematic analysis of rhetoric across institutional type. *Journal of Higher Education, 77,* 456–471.

Morris, L. K., & Daniel, L. G. (2008). Perceptions of a chilly climate: Differences in traditional and non-traditional majors for women. *Research in Higher Education, 49,* 256–273.

Mueller, J. A., & Cole, J. (2009). A qualitative examination of heterosexual consciousness among college students. *Journal of College Student Development, 50,* 320–336.

Mullendore, R. H., & Banahan, L. A. (2005). Designing orientation programs. In M. L. Upcraft, J. N. Gardner, B. O. Barefoot, & Associates (Eds.), *Challenging and supporting the first-year student: A handbook for improving the first year of college* (pp. 319–409). San Francisco: Jossey-Bass.

Muraskin, L., & Lee, J. (2004). *Raising the graduation rates of low-income college students.* Washington, DC: Pell Institute for the Study of Opportunity in Higher Education.

Museus, S. D., & Kiang, P. N. (2009). Deconstructing the model minority myth and how it contributes to the invisible minority reality in higher education research. In S. D. Museus (Ed.), *Conducting research on Asian Americans in higher education* (New Directions for Institutional Research No. 142, pp. 5–15). San Francisco: Jossey-Bass.

Museus, S. D., & Quaye, S. J. (2009). Toward an intercultural perspective of racial and ethnic minority college student persistence. *Review of Higher Education, 33,* 67–94.

Nakanishi, D. T. (1995). Asian Pacific Americans and colleges and universities. In J. A. Banks & C. A. McGee Banks (Eds.), *Handbook of research on multicultural education* (pp. 683–695). San Francisco: Jossey-Bass.

Nash, R. J., & Murray, M. C. (2010). *Helping college students find purpose: The campus guide to meaning-making.* San Francisco: Jossey-Bass.

National Association of State Universities and Land-Grant Colleges. (2008). *The land-grant tradition.* Washington, DC: VMW Printing.

National Association of Student Personnel Administrators. (n.d.). About us. Retrieved from www.naspa.org/about/default.cfm

National Center for Education Statistics (NCES). (2011a). *Digest of education statistics, 2010* (NCES 2011-015). Table 5. Retrieved from http://nces.ed.gov/programs /digest/d10/tables/dt10_005.asp

National Center for Education Statistics (NCES). (2011b). *Digest of education statistics, 2010* (NCES 2011-015). Table 205. Retrieved from http://nces.ed.gov/programs /digest/d10/tables/dt10_205.asp

National Center for Education Statistics (NCES). (2011c). *Digest for education statistics, 2010* (NCES 2011-015). Table 206. Retrieved from http://nces.ed.gov /programs/digest/d10/tables/dt10_206.asp

National Center for Education Statistics (NCES). (2011d). *Digest for education statistics, 2010* (NCES 2011-015). Table 235. Retrieved from http://nces.ed.gov /programs/digest/d10/tables/dt10_235.asp

National Center for Education Statistics (NCES). (2011e). *Digest for education statistics, 2010* (NCES 2011-015). Table 249. Retrieved from http://nces.ed.gov /programs/digest/d10/tables/dt10_249.asp

National Center for Education Statistics (NCES). (2011f). *Digest for education statistics, 2010* (NCES 2011-015). Table 250. Retrieved from http://nces.ed.gov/programs /digest/d10/tables/dt10_250.asp

National Center for Education Statistics (NCES). (2011g). *Digest of education statistics, 2010* (NCES 2011-015). Table 341. Retrieved from http://nces.ed.gov/programs /digest/d10/tables/dt10_341.asp

National Commission on Asian American and Pacific Islander Research in Education. (2010). *Federal higher education policy priorities and the Asian American and Pacific Islander community.* Retrieved from www.nyu.edu/projects/care/docs/2010_CARE_Report.pdf

National Resource Center for the First-Year Experience and Students in Transition. (2002). *The 2000 national survey of first-year seminar programs: Continuing innovations in the collegiate curriculum.* Columbia: University of South Carolina, Author.

National Study of Living-Learning Programs. (2007). *2007 report of findings.* College Park: University of Maryland, Author. Retrieved from http://drum.lib.umd.edu /bitstream/1903/8392/1/2007%20NSLLP%20Final%20Report.pdf

Nelson, L. A. (2011, September 8). No success on success measures. *Inside Higher Ed.* Retrieved from www.insidehighered.com/news/2011/09/08/committee_on _measures_of_student_success_to_meet_one_more_time

Niskey, L. T. (2007). The critical state of college access and affordability in the United States. *College & University, 83*(2), 61–68.

Niu, S., & Tienda, M. (2008). Choosing colleges: Identifying and modeling choice sets. *Social Science Research, 37,* 416–433.

Nunez, A., & Cuccaro-Alamin, S. (1998). *First-generation students: Undergraduates whose parents never enrolled in postsecondary education* (NCES 98-082). Washington, DC: National Center for Education Statistics.

Obama, B. H. (2009a, July 14). Remarks by the president on the American graduation initiative. Speech presented at Macomb Community College, Warren, MI.

Retrieved from www.whitehouse.gov/the_press_office/Remarks-by-the-President
-on-the-American-Graduation-Initiative-in-Warren-MI

Obama, B. H. (2009b, February 24). Remarks of President Barack Obama—as
prepared for delivery. Address to Joint Session of Congress. Retrieved from
www.whitehouse.gov/the_press_office/Remarks-of-President-Barack-Obama
-Address-to-Joint-Session-of-Congress/

Office of Management and Budget. (1997, October 30). Revisions to the standards
for the classification of federal data on race and ethnicity. (*Federal Register* notice).
Retrieved from www.whitehouse.gov/omb/fedreg_1997standards

Ogren, C. (2003). Rethinking the "nontraditional" student from a historical
perspective: State normal schools in the late nineteenth and early twentieth
centuries. *Journal of Higher Education, 74,* 640–664.

Omi, M., & Winant, H. (2004). Racial formation. In L. Heldke & P. O'Connor
(Eds.), *Oppression, privilege, and resistance: Theoretical perspectives on racism, sexism,
and heterosexism* (pp. 115–142). New York: McGraw-Hill.

Pagano, M., & Roselle, L. (2009). Beyond reflection through an academic lens:
Refraction and international experiential education. *Frontiers: The Interdisciplinary
Journal of Study Abroad, 18,* 217–229.

Palmer, R. T., Davis, R. J., & Maramba, D. C. (2011). The impact of family support
on the success of black men at an historically black university: Affirming the
revision of Tinto's theory. *Journal of College Student Development, 52,* 577–597.

Paris, D. C. (2011). *Catalyst of change: The CIC/CLA Consortium.* Washington, DC:
Council for Independent Colleges. Retrieved from www.cic.edu/publications
/books_reports/CLA2011_report_WEB.pdf

Parker, K., Lenhart, A., & Moore, K. (2011). *The digital revolution and higher education:
College presidents, public differ on value of online learning.* Washington, DC: Pew
Research Center. Retrieved from http://pewinternet.org/~/media//Files
/Reports/2011/PIP-Online-Learning.pdf

Parks, S. D. (2000). *Big questions, worthy dreams: Mentoring young adults in their search
for meaning, purpose, and faith.* San Francisco: Jossey-Bass.

Parks, S. D. (2011). *Big questions, worthy dreams: Mentoring emerging adults in their search
for meaning, purpose, and faith* (Rev. ed.). San Francisco: Jossey-Bass.

Parsad, B., & Lewis, L. (2008). *Distance education at degree-granting postsecondary institutions:
2006–07* (NCES 2009-044). Washington, DC: National Center for Education Statistics.

Pascarella, E. T., Edison, M., Nora, A., Hagedorn, L. S., & Terenzini, P. T. (1996).
Influences on students' openness to diversity and challenge in the first year of
college. *Journal of Higher Education, 67,* 174–195.

Pascarella, E. T., Hagedorn, L. S., Whitt, E. J., Yeager, P. M., Edison, M. I., Terenzini,
P. T., & Nora, A. (1997). Women's perceptions of a "chilly climate" and their
cognitive outcomes during the first year of college. *Journal of College Student
Development, 38,* 109–124.

Pascarella, E. T., Pierson, C. T., Wolniak, G. C., & Terenzini, P. T. (2004). First-
generation college students: Additional evidence on college experiences and
outcomes. *Journal of Higher Education, 75,* 249–284.

Pascarella, E. T., Salisbury, M. H., & Blaich, C. (2011). Exposure to effective
instruction and college student persistence: A multi-institutional replication and
extension. *Journal of College Student Development, 52,* 4–18.

Pascarella, E. T., & Terenzini, P. T. (1991). *How college affects students.* San Francisco: Jossey-Bass.

Pascarella, E. T., & Terenzini, P. T. (2005). *How college affects students* (2nd ed.). San Francisco: Jossey-Bass.

Pascarella, E. T., Terenzini, P. T., & Wolfe, L. M. (1986). Orientation to college and freshman year persistence/withdrawal decisions. *Journal of Higher Education, 57,* 155–175.

Pasque, P. A., & Murphy, R. (2005). The intersections of living-learning programs and social identity factors of academic achievement and intellectual engagement. *Journal of College Student Development, 46,* 429–441.

Patton, L. D. (Ed.). (2010). *Culture centers in higher education: Perspectives on identity, theory, and practice.* Sterling, VA: Stylus.

Patton, L. D. (2011a). Perspectives on identity, disclosure, and the campus environment among African American gay and bisexual men at one historically black college. *Journal of College Student Development, 52,* 77–100.

Patton, L. D. (2011b). Promoting critical conversations about identity centers. In P. Magolda & M. B. Baxter Magolda (Eds.), *Contested issues in student affairs* (pp. 255–260). Sterling, VA: Stylus.

Paulsen, M. B., & St. John, E. P. (2002). Social class and college costs: Examining the financial nexus between college choice and persistence. *Journal of Higher Education, 73,* 189–236.

Pavel, D. M., Ingelbret, E., & Banks, S. R. (2001). Tribal colleges and universities in an era of dynamic development. *Peabody Journal of Education, 76,* 50–72.

Perkins, L. M. (1983). The impact of the "cult of true womanhood" on the education of black women. *Journal of Social Issues, 39*(3), 17–28.

Perkins, L. M. (1997). The African American female elite: The early history of African American women in the seven sister colleges, 1880–1960. *Harvard Educational Review, 67,* 718–756.

Perna, L. W. (2002). Precollege outreach programs: Characteristics of programs serving historically underrepresented groups of students. *Journal of College Student Development, 43,* 64–83.

Perna, L. W., & Titus, M. A. (2004). Understanding differences in the choice of college attended: The role of state public policies. *Review of Higher Education, 27,* 501–525.

Perry, W. G., Jr. (1970). *Forms of intellectual and ethical development in the college years: A scheme.* New York: Holt, Rinehart and Winston.

Perry, W. G., Jr. (1981). Cognitive and ethical growth: The making of meaning. In A. W. Chickering (Ed.), *The modern American college* (pp. 76–116). San Francisco: Jossey-Bass.

Pervin, L. A. (1967). Satisfaction and perceived self-environment similarity: A semantic differential study of student-college interaction. *Journal of Personality, 35,* 623–634.

Pervin, L. A. (1968). Performance and satisfaction as a function of individual-environment fit. *Psychological Bulletin, 69,* 56–68.

Peter, K., & Horn, L. (2005). *Gender differences in participation and completion of undergraduate education and how they have changed over time* (NCES 2005-169). Washington, DC: National Center for Education Statistics.

Pewewardy, C., & Frey, B. (2002). Surveying the landscape: Perceptions of multicultural support services and racial climate at a predominantly white university. *Journal of Negro Education, 71,* 77–95.

Phinney, J. S. (1990). Ethnic identity in adolescents and adults: Review of research. *Psychological Bulletin, 108,* 499–514.

Piaget, J. (1932). *The moral judgment of the child* (M. Gabain, Trans.). Harmondsworth, England: Penguin.

Piaget, J. (1977). *The moral judgment of the child* (2nd ed.; M. Gabain, Trans.). Harmondsworth, England: Penguin.

Pike, G. R., & Kuh, G. D. (2006). Relationships among structural diversity, informal peer interactions and perceptions of the campus environment. *Review of Higher Education, 29,* 425–450.

Pizzolato, J. E. (2003). Developing self-authorship: Exploring the experiences of high-risk college students. *Journal of College Student Development, 44,* 797–811.

Pizzolato, J. E. (2004). Coping with conflict: Self-authorship, coping, and adaptation to college in first-year high-risk students. *Journal of College Student Development, 45,* 425–442.

Pizzolato, J. E. (2005). Creating crossroads for self-authorship: Investigating the provocative moment. *Journal of College Student Development, 46,* 624–641.

Pizzolato, J. E. (2006). Complex partnerships: Self-authorship and provocative academic advising practices. *NACADA Journal, 26*(1), 32–46.

Pizzolato, J. E. (2007). Assessing self-authorship. In P. S. Meszaros (Ed.), *Self-authorship: Advancing students' intellectual growth* (New Directions for Teaching and Learning No. 109, pp. 31–42). San Francisco: Jossey-Bass.

Pizzolato, J. E. (2010). What is self-authorship? A theoretical exploration and construct. In M. B. Baxter Magolda, E. G. Creamer, & P. S. Meszaros (Eds.), *Development and assessment of self-authorship: Exploring the concept across cultures* (pp. 187–206). Sterling, VA: Stylus.

Pizzolato, J. E., Chaudhari, P., Murrell, E. D., Podobnik, S., & Schaeffer, Z. (2008). Ethnic identity, epistemological development, and achievement among students from disadvantaged backgrounds. *Journal of College Student Development, 49,* 301–318.

Pizzolato, J. E., Hicklen, S., Brown, B. L., & Chaudhari, P. (2009). Student development, student learning: Examining the relation between learning and epistemological development. *Journal of College Student Development, 50,* 475–490.

Plank, S. B., & Jordan, W. J. (2001). Effects of information, guidance, and actions on postsecondary destinations: A study of talent loss. *American Educational Research Journal, 38,* 947–979.

Planty, M., Hussar, W., Snyder, T., Kena, G., KewalRamani, A., Kemp, J., . . . Dinkes, R. (2009). *The condition of education 2009* (NCES 2009-081). Washington, DC: National Center for Education Statistics.

Pope, R. L. (1998). The relationship between psychosocial development and racial identity of black college students. *Journal of College Student Development, 39,* 273–282.

Pope, R. L. (2000). The relationship between psychosocial development and racial identity of college students of color. *Journal of College Student Development, 41,* 302–312.

Pope, R. L., Reynolds, A. L., & Mueller, J. (2004). *Multicultural competence in student affairs*. San Francisco: Jossey-Bass.

Posse Foundation. (2010). *Celebrating twenty years: 2009 annual report*. Retrieved from www.possefoundation.org/m/posse-annual-report-09.pdf

Poston, W.S.C. (1990). The biracial identity development model: A needed addition. *Journal of Counseling & Development, 69*, 152–155.

Pratt, M. W., Hunsberger, B., Pracer, S. M., Alisat, S., Bowers, C., Mackey, K., . . . Thomas, N. (2000). Facilitating the transition to university. Evaluation of a social support discussion intervention program. *Journal of College Student Development, 41*, 427–441.

Provasnik, S., & Planty, M. (2008). *Community colleges: Special supplement to* The Condition of Education 2008 (NCES 2008–033). Washington, DC: National Center for Education Statistics.

Pryor, J. H., Hurtado, S., DeAngelo, L., Palucki Blake, L., & Tran, S. (2009). *The American freshman: National norms 2009*. Los Angeles: Higher Education Research Institute.

Pryor, J. H., Hurtado, S., DeAngelo, L., Palucki Blake, L., & Tran, S. (2011). *The American freshman: National norms fall 2010*. Los Angeles: Higher Education Research Institute.

Pryor, J. H., Hurtado, S., Sáenz, V. B., Santos, J. L., & Korn, W. S. (2007). *The American freshman: Forty year trends, 1966–2006*. Los Angeles: Higher Education Research Institute.

Rankin, S. R., & Reason, R. D. (2005). Differing perceptions: How students of color and white students perceive campus climate for underrepresented groups. *Journal of College Student Development, 46*, 43–61.

Rankin, S. R., & Reason, R. D. (2008). Transformational tapestry model: A comprehensive approach to transforming campus climate. *Journal of Diversity in Higher Education, 1*, 262–274.

Rankin, S. R., Weber, G., Blumenfeld, W., & Frazer, S. (2010). *2010 state of higher education for lesbian, gay, bisexual and transgender people*. Charlotte, NC: Campus Pride.

Reason, R. D. (2003). Student variables that predict retention: Recent research and new developments. *NASPA Journal, 40*, 172–191.

Reason, R. D. (2009). An examination of the persistence research through the lens of a comprehensive conceptual framework. *Journal of College Student Development, 50*, 659–682.

Reason, R. D., Cox, B. E., McIntosh, K., & Terenzini, P. T. (2011, February). What they're doing: A profile of first-year initiatives. Paper presented at the 30th annual First-Year Experience Conference, Atlanta.

Reason, R. D., Evensen, D. H., & Heller, D. E. (2009). *Evaluation of Pennsylvania's Act 101 programs* (Working Paper No. 2). University Park, PA: Center for the Study of Higher Education.

Reason, R. D., Terenzini, P. T., & Domingo, R. J. (2006). First things first: Developing academic competence in the first year of college. *Research in Higher Education, 47*, 149–175.

Reason, R. D., Terenzini, P. T., & Domingo, R. J. (2007). Developing social and personal competence in the first year of college. *Review of Higher Education, 30*, 271–299.

Reisser, L. (1995). Revisiting the seven vectors. *Journal of College Student Development, 36*, 505–511.

Rendon, L., Jalomo, R., & Nora, A. (2000). Theoretical considerations in the study of minority student retention in higher education. In J. M. Braxton (Ed.), *Reworking the student departure puzzle* (pp. 127–156). Nashville, TN: Vanderbilt University Press.

Renn, K. A. (2000). Patterns of situational identity among biracial and multiracial college students. *Review of Higher Education, 23*, 399–420.

Renn, K. A. (2003). Understanding the identities of mixed race college students through a developmental ecology lens. *Journal of College Student Development, 44*, 383–403.

Renn, K. A. (2004). *Mixed race students in college: The ecology of race, identity, and community on campus.* Albany: State University of New York Press.

Renn, K. A. (2007). LGBT student leaders and queer activists: Identities of lesbian, gay, bisexual, transgender, and queer-identified college student leaders and activists. *Journal of College Student Development, 48*, 311–330.

Renn, K. A. (2010). LGBT and queer research in higher education: The state and status of the field. *Educational Researcher, 39*, 132–141.

Renn, K. A. (2011). Identity centers: An idea whose time has come . . . and gone? In P. Magolda & M. B. Baxter Magolda (Eds.), *Contested issues in student affairs* (pp. 244–254). Sterling, VA: Stylus.

Renn, K. A., & Arnold, K. D. (2003). Reconceptualizing research on college student peer culture. *Journal of Higher Education, 74*, 261–291.

Renn, K. A., & Ozaki, C. C. (2010). Psychosocial and leadership identity development among leaders of identity-based campus organizations. *Journal of Diversity in Higher Education, 3*, 14–26.

Renn, K. A., & Patton, L. (2010). Campus ecology and environments. In J. D. Schuh, S. R. Jones, & S. L. Harper (Eds.), *Student services: A handbook for the profession* (5th ed., pp. 242–256). San Francisco: Jossey-Bass.

Renn, K. A., & Shang, P. (Eds.). (2008). *Biracial and multiracial college students: Theory, research, and best practices in student affairs* (New Directions for Student Services No. 123). San Francisco: Jossey-Bass.

Rest, J. R. (1979a). *Development in judging moral issues.* Minneapolis: University of Minnesota Press.

Rest, J. R. (1979b). *The impact of higher education on moral judgment development* (Moral Research Projects Technical Report No. 5). Minneapolis: University of Minnesota Press.

Rest, J. R. (1994). Background: Theory and research. In J. Rest & D. Navarez (Eds.), *Moral development in the professions: Psychology and applied ethics* (pp. 1–25). Mahwah, NJ: Erlbaum.

Rest, J. R., Narvaez, D., Thoma, S. J., & Bebeau, M. J. (2000). A Neo-Kohlbergian approach to morality research. *Journal of Moral Education, 29*, 381–395.

Reynolds, A. L. (2009). *Helping college students: Developing essential support skills for student affairs practice.* San Francisco: Jossey-Bass.

Rist, R. C. (2000). Student social class and teacher expectations: The self-fulfilling prophecy in ghetto education. *Harvard Educational Review, 70*, 257–302.

Rockquemore, K. A., & Brunsma, D. L. (2002). *Beyond black: Biracial identity in America.* Thousand Oaks, CA: Sage.

Rodgers, R. F. (1990). Student development. In U. Delworth, G. R. Hanson, & Associates (Eds.), *Student services: A handbook for the profession* (2nd ed., pp. 117–164). San Francisco: Jossey-Bass.

Roksa, J. (2009). Building bridges for student success: Are higher education articulation policies effective? *Teachers College Record, 111,* 2444–2478.

Roksa, J., & Calcagno, J. C. (2010). Catching up in community colleges: Academic preparation and transfer to four-year institutions. *Teachers College Record, 112,* 260–288.

Root, M.P.P. (2003a). Five mixed-race identities. In L. I. Winter & H. L. DeBose (Eds.), *New faces in a changing America: Multiracial identity in the 21st century* (pp. 3–20). Thousand Oaks, CA: Sage.

Root, M.P.P. (2003b). Racial identity development and persons of mixed race heritage. In M.P.P. Root & M. Kelley (Eds.), *Multiracial child resource book: Living complex identities* (pp. 34–41). Seattle: MAVIN Foundation.

Rumann, C. B., & Hamrick, F. A. (2009). Supporting student veterans in transition. In R. Ackerman & D. DiRamio (Eds.), *Creating a veteran-friendly campus: Strategies for transition success* (New Directions for Student Services No. 126, pp. 25–34). San Francisco: Jossey-Bass.

Rumann, C. B., & Hamrick, F. A. (2010). Student veterans in transition: Re-enrolling after war zone deployments. *Journal of Higher Education, 81,* 431–458.

Russell, S. T., Muraco, A., Subramaniam, A., & Laub, C. (2009). Youth empowerment and high school gay-straight alliances. *Journal of Youth and Adolescence, 38,* 891–903.

Sáenz, V. B. (2005). *Breaking the cycle of segregation: Examining students' pre-college racial environments and their diversity experiences in college.* (Doctoral dissertation). Retrieved from ProQuest (UMI 31883367)

Sáenz, V. B., Ngai, H. N., & Hurtado, S. (2007). Factors influencing positive interactions across race for African-American, Asian-American, Latino, and white college students. *Research in Higher Education, 64,* 434–452.

Sáenz, V. B., & Ponjuan, L. (2009). The vanishing Latino male in higher education. *Journal of Hispanic Higher Education, 8,* 54–89.

Saez, P. A., Casado, A., & Wade, J. C. (2009). Factors influencing masculinity ideology among Latino men. *Journal of Men's Studies, 17,* 116–128.

Sanford, N. (1966). *Self and society.* New York: Atherton Press.

Sanford, N. (1967). *Where colleges fail: The study of the student as a person.* San Francisco: Jossey-Bass.

Sanlo, R., Rankin, S. R., & Schoenberg, R. (Eds.). (2002). *Our place on campus: Lesbian, gay, bisexual, transgender services and programs in higher education.* Westport, CT: Greenwood Press.

Savin-Williams, R. C. (1988). Theoretical perspectives accounting for adolescent homosexuality. *Journal of Adolescent Health, 9,* 95–104.

Savin-Williams, R. C. (1990). Gay and lesbian adolescents. *Marriage and Family Review, 14,* 197–216.

Sax, L. J. (2001). Undergraduate science majors: Gender differences in who goes on to graduate school. *Review of Higher Education, 24,* 153–172.

Sax, L. J., Bryant, A. N., & Harper, C. E. (2008). The differential effects of student-faculty interaction on college outcomes for women and men. *Journal of College Student Development, 46*, 642–657.

Sax, L. J., & Harper, C. E. (2007). Origins of the gender gap: Pre-college and college influences on differences between men and women. *Research in Higher Education, 48*, 669–694.

Schneider, M., & Yin, L. M. (2011). *The high costs of low graduation rates: How much does dropping out of college really cost?* Washington, DC: American Institutes for Research.

Schudde, L. T. (2011). The causal effect of campus residency on college student retention. *Review of Higher Education, 34*, 581–610.

Schuh, J. H., & Associates. (2009). *Assessment methods for student affairs.* San Francisco: Jossey-Bass.

Seal, K. H., Bertenthal, D., Miner, C. R., Saunak, S., & Marmar, C. (2007). Bringing the war back home: Mental health disorders among 103,788 US veterans from Iraq and Afghanistan seen at Department of Veterans Affairs facilities. *Archives of Internal Medicine, 167*, 476–482.

Sedlacek, W. E. (2004). *Beyond the big test: Noncognitive assessment in higher education.* San Francisco: Jossey-Bass.

Seggie, F. N., & Sanford, G. (2010). Perceptions of female Muslim students who veil: Campus religious climate. *Race, Ethnicity and Education, 13*, 59–82.

Seidman, A. (Ed.). (2005). *College student retention: Formula for student success.* Westport, CT: ACE/Praeger.

Seifert, T. A. (2007). Understanding Christian privilege: Managing the tensions of spiritual plurality. *About Campus, 12*(2), 10–17.

Seifert, T. A., Goodman, K., King, P. M., & Baxter Magolda, M. B. (2010). Using mixed methods to study first-year college impact on liberal arts learning outcomes. *Journal of Mixed Methods Research, 4*, 248–267.

Shang, P. (2008). An introduction to social and historical factors affecting multiracial college students. In K. R. Renn & P. Shang (Eds.), *Biracial and multiracial students* (New Directions for Student Services No. 123, pp. 5–12). San Francisco: Jossey-Bass.

Shaw, E., Kobrin, J., Packman, S., & Schmidt, A. (2009). Describing students involved in the search phase of the college choice process: A cluster analysis study. *Journal of Advanced Academics, 20*, 662–700.

Shipp Meeks, J. (2009). *The impact of TRIO's Upward Bound and student support services: A qualitative case study of students who participated in both programs.* Memphis, TN: University of Memphis. Retrieved from http://gradworks.umi.com/34/00 /3400165.html

Silverschanz, P., Cortina, L., Konik, J., & Magley, V. (2007). Slurs, snubs, and queer jokes: Incidence and impact of heterosexist harassment in academia. *Sex Roles, 58*, 179–191.

Simons, L., & Cleary, B. (2005). Student and community perceptions of the "value added" for service-learners. *Journal of Experiential Education, 28*, 164–188.

Skinner, R. R. (2005). *Institutional eligibility and the Higher Education Act: Legislative history of the 90/10 rule and its current status.* (CRS Report for Congress). Washington, DC: Congressional Research Service, Library of Congress.

Smart, J., Feldman, K., & Ethington, C. (2000). *Academic disciplines: Holland's theory and the study of college students and faculty.* Nashville, TN: Vanderbilt University Press.

Smedley, A., & Smedley, B. D. (2005). Race as biology is fiction, racism as a social problem is real: Anthropological and historical perspectives on the social construction of race. *American Psychologist, 60,* 16–26.

Snyder, T. D., & Dillow, S. A. (2009). *Digest of education statistics 2009* (NCES 2010-013). Washington, DC: National Center for Education Statistics.

Snyder, T. D., & Dillow, S. A. (2011, April). *Digest of education statistics 2010* (NCES 2011-015). Washington, DC: National Center for Education Statistics.

Solomon, B. M. (1985). *In the company of educated women: A history of women and higher education in America.* New Haven: Yale University Press.

Solórzano, D., Ceja, M., & Yosso, T. (2000). Critical Race Theory, racial microaggressions, and campus racial climate: The experiences of African American college students. *Journal of Negro Education, 69,* 60–73.

Spirituality in Higher Education. (2010). A national study of college students' search for meaning and purpose. Los Angeles: Higher Education Research Institute. Retrieved from www.spirituality.ucla.edu

Stern, G. G. (1970). *People in context: Measuring person-environment congruence in education and industry.* Hoboken, NJ: Wiley.

Stiller, N. J., & Forrest, L. (1990). An extension of Gilligan's and Lyons' investigation of morality: Gender differences in college students. *Journal of College Student Development, 31,* 54–63.

Strange, C. C. (2003). Dynamics of campus environments. In S. Komives, D. Woodard Jr., & Associates (Eds.), *Student services: A handbook for the profession* (4th ed., pp. 297–316). San Francisco: Jossey-Bass.

Strange, C. C., & Banning, J. H. (2001). *Educating by design: Creating campus learning environments that work.* San Francisco: Jossey-Bass.

Strayhorn, T. L. (2008). "Sentido de Pertenencia": A hierarchical analysis predicting sense of belonging among Latino college students. *Journal of Hispanic Higher Education, 7,* 301–320.

Strayhorn, T. L. (2010). When race and gender collide: Social and cultural capital's influence on the academic achievement of African American and Latino males. *Review of Higher Education, 33,* 307–332.

Suarez-Balcazar, Y., Orellana-Damacela, L., Portillo, N., Rowan, J. M., & Andrews-Guillen, C. (2003). Experiences of differential treatment among college students of color. *Journal of Higher Education, 74,* 428–444.

Sue, D. W., & Sue, D. (2003). *Counseling the culturally diverse: Theory and practice* (4th ed.). Hoboken, NJ: Wiley.

Szelenyi, K. (2002, November). Diverse viewpoints on American college campuses: Do students benefit? An exploratory study. Paper presented at the 27th annual meeting of the Association for the Study of Higher Education, Sacramento, CA.

Tamura, E. H. (2001). Asian Americans in the history of education. *History of Education Quarterly, 41*(1), 58–71.

Tanner, J. L., Arnett, J. J., & Leis, J. A. (2008). Emerging adulthood: Learning and development during the first stage of adulthood. In M. C. Smith &

N. DeFrates-Densch (Eds.), *Handbook of research on adult learning and development* (pp. 34–67). New York: Routledge.

Taylor, K. B. (2008). Mapping the intricacies of young adults' development journey from socially prescribed to internally defined identities, relationships, and beliefs. *Journal of College Student Development, 49,* 215–234.

Terenzini, P. T., Cabrera, A. F., & Bernal, E. (2001). *Swimming against the tide: The poor in American higher education* (College Board Research Report No. 2001-3). New York: College Board.

Terenzini, P. T., & Reason, R. D. (2005, November). Parsing the first-year of college: A conceptual framework for studying college impacts. Paper presented at the 30th Annual Meeting of the Association for the Study of Higher Education, Philadelphia.

Terenzini, P. T., & Reason, R. D. (2007). Bad rap or regrettable truth: Engagement and student learning at public research universities. In R. L. Geiger, C. L. Colbeck, R. L. Williams, & C. K. Anderson (Eds.), *The future of the American public research university* (pp. 165–186). Rotterdam, The Netherlands: Sense.

Terenzini, P. T., & Reason, R. D. (2010, June). Toward a more comprehensive understanding of college effects on student learning. Paper presented at the 23rd Annual Conference of the Consortium of Higher Education Researchers, Oslo, Norway.

Terenzini, P. T., Springer, L., Yaeger, P. M., Pascarella, E. T., & Nora, A. (1996). First-generation college students: Characteristics, experiences, and cognitive development. *Research in Higher Education, 37,* 1–22.

Thelin, J. R. (2011). *A history of American higher education* (2nd ed.). Baltimore: Johns Hopkins University Press.

Thomas, R., & Chickering, A. W. (1984). Education and identity revisited. *Journal of College Student Personnel, 25,* 392–399.

Thorne, A. C. (1985). *Visible and invisible women in land-grant colleges, 1890–1940.* Logan: Utah State University Press.

Tierney, W. G. (1999). Models of minority college-going and retention: Cultural integrity versus cultural suicide. *Journal of Negro Education, 68,* 80–91.

Tierney, W. G. (2000). Power, identity, and the dilemma of college student departure. In J. M. Braxton (Ed.), *Reworking the student departure puzzle* (pp. 213–234). Nashville, TN: Vanderbilt University Press.

Tierney, W. G., & Dilley, P. (1998). Constructing knowledge: Educational research and gay and lesbian studies. In W. F. Pinar (Ed.), *Queer theory in education* (pp. 49–72). New York: Routledge.

Tilghman, S. M. (2007). Expanding equal opportunity: The Princeton experience with financial aid. *Harvard Educational Review, 77,* 435–441, 529.

Tinto, V. (1987). *Leaving college: Rethinking the causes and cures of student attrition.* Chicago: University of Chicago Press.

Tinto, V. (1993). *Leaving college: Rethinking the causes and cures of student attrition* (2nd ed.). Chicago: University of Chicago Press.

Tinto, V. (1997). Classrooms as communities: Exploring the educational character of student persistence. *Journal of Higher Education, 68,* 599–623.

Tinto, V. (2005). Foreword. In A. Seidman (Ed.), *College student retention: Formula for student success* (pp. ix–x). Westport, CT: Praeger.

Tinto, V. (2006–2007). Research and practice of student retention: What next? *Journal of College Student Retention, 8,* 1–18.

Torres, V. (1999). Validation of a bicultural orientation model for Hispanic college students. *Journal of College Student Development, 40,* 285–298.

Torres, V. (2003). Influences on ethnic identity development of Latino college students in the first two years of college. *Journal of College Student Development, 44,* 532–547.

Torres, V., & Baxter Magolda, M. B. (2004). Reconstructing Latino identity: The influence of cognitive development on the ethnic identity process of Latino students. *Journal of College Student Development, 45,* 333–347.

Torres, V., & Hernandez, E. (2007). The influence of ethnic identity on self-authorship: A longitudinal study of Latino/a college students. *Journal of College Student Development, 48,* 558–573.

Torres, V., Howard-Hamilton, M. F., & Cooper, D. L. (2003). *Identity development of diverse populations: Implications for teaching and administration in higher education.* San Francisco: Jossey-Bass.

Torres, V., Jones, S. R., & Renn, K. A. (2009). Identity development theories in student affairs: Origins, current status, and new approaches. *Journal of College Student Development, 50,* 577–596.

Troiden, R. R. (1979). Becoming homosexual: A model of gay identity acquisition. *Psychiatry, 42,* 362–373.

Troiden, R. R. (1988). Homosexual identity development. *Journal of Adolescent Health Care, 9,* 105–113.

Upcraft, M. L., & Schuh, J. H. (1996). *Assessment in student affairs.* San Francisco: Jossey-Bass.

U.S. Census Bureau. (2012, February 23). Educational attainment in the United States: 2011. Retrieved from www.census.gov/newsroom/releases/archives/education/cb12-33.html

U.S. Department of Education. (2010, September). *Web tables—profile of undergraduate students: 2007–08.* Retrieved from http://nces.ed.gov/pubs2010/2010205.pdf

U.S. Department of Education. (2011). *Funding education beyond high school: The guide to federal student aid—2011–12.* Washington, DC: Author.

U.S. Department of Veterans Affairs. (2009a). Over 25,000 post-9/11 GI Bill applications received in first two weeks. Retrieved from www1.va.gov/opa/pressrel/pressrelease.cfm?id=1675

U.S. Department of Veterans Affairs. (2009b). Participation in the new post-9/11 GI Bill continues to grow. Retrieved from www1.va.gov/opa/pressrel/pressrelease.cfm?id=1778

Van Der Werf, M., & Sabatier, G. (2009, June). *The college of 2020: Students.* Washington, DC: Chronicle Research Services.

Wallace, K. R. (2001). *Relative/outsider: The art and politics of identity among mixed heritage students.* Westport, CT: Ablex.

Waller, L. R., & Tietjen-Smith, T. (2009). A national study of community college retention rates segmented by institutional degree of urbanization. *Academic Leadership Journal, 7*(1). Retrieved from www.academicleadership.org/article/a-national-study-of-community-college-retention-rates-segmented-by-institutional-degree-of-urbanization

Walsh, W. B. (1978). Person/environment interaction. In J. H. Banning (Ed.), *Campus ecology: A perspective for student affairs* (pp. 7–18). Washington, DC: National Association of Student Personnel Administrators. Retrieved from www.campusecologist.org/files/Monograph.pdf

Wechsler, H. (2005). *Harvard School of Public Heath college alcohol study, 2001.* Harvard School of Public Health. Ann Arbor: Inter-university Consortium for Political and Social Research.

Weidman, J. (1984). Impacts of campus experiences and parental socialization on undergraduates' career choices. *Research in Higher Education, 20,* 445–476.

Weidman, J. C. (1989). Undergraduate socialization: A conceptual approach. In J. C. Smart (Ed.), *Higher education: Handbook of theory and research* (Vol. 5, pp. 289–322). New York: Agathon Press.

Whitt, E. J., Nora, A., Edison, M. I., Terenzini, P. T., & Pascarella, E. T. (1999). Women's perceptions of a "chilly climate" and cognitive outcomes in college: Additional evidence. *Journal of College Student Development, 40,* 163–177.

Wijeyesinghe, C. L. (2001). Racial identity in multiracial people: An alternative paradigm. In C. L. Wijeyesinghe & B. W. Jackson III (Eds.), *New perspectives on racial identity development* (pp. 129–152). New York: New York University Press.

Winston, R. B., Jr., & Miller, T. K. (1987). *Student Developmental Task and Lifestyle Inventory manual.* Athens, GA: Student Development Associates.

Winston, R. B., Jr., Miller, T. K., & Cooper, D. L. (1999a). *Student Developmental Task and Lifestyle Assessment (SDTLA).* Athens, GA: Student Development Associates.

Winston, R. B., Jr., Miller, T. K., & Cooper, D. L. (1999b). *Technical manual for the Student Developmental Task and Lifestyle Assessment.* Athens, GA: Student Development Associates.

Winston, R. B., Jr., Miller, T. K., & Cooper, D. L. (n.d.). Student Developmental Task and Lifestyle Assessment. Retrieved from http://sdtla.appstate.edu/index.php ?andMMN_position=1:1

Wolf-Wendel, L. E., Toma, J. D., & Morphew, C. C. (2001). How much difference is too much difference? Perceptions of gay men and lesbians in intercollegiate athletics. *Journal of College Student Development, 42,* 465–479.

Wolniak, G., & Engberg, M. (2007). The effects of high school feeder networks on college enrollment. *Review of Higher Education, 31,* 27–53.

Woo, J. H., Choy, S. P., & Weko, T. (2011, October). *Merit aid for undergraduates: Trends from 1995–96 to 2007–08.* Washington, DC: U.S. Department of Education. Retrieved from http://nces.ed.gov/pubs2012/2012160.pdf

Worthington, R. L., Dillon, F. R., & Becker-Schutte, A. M. (2005). Development, reliability, and validity of the Lesbian, Gay, and Bisexual Knowledge and Attitudes Scale for Heterosexuals (LGB-KASH). *Journal of Counseling Psychology, 52,* 104–118.

Worthington, R. L., Navarro, R. L., Savoy, H. B., & Hampton, D. (2008). Development, reliability, and validity of the Measure of Sexual Identity Exploration and Commitment (MoSIEC). *Developmental Psychology, 44,* 22–33.

Worthington, R. L., Savoy, H. B., Dillon, F. R., & Vernaglia, E. R. (2002). Heterosexual identity development: A multidimensional model of individual and social identity. *Counseling Psychologist, 30,* 496–531.

Wright, B. (1988). "For the children of the infidels"? American Indian education in the colonial colleges. *American Indian Culture and Research Journal, 12*(3), 1–14.

Yosso, T. J., & Benavides Lopes, C. (2010). Counterspaces in a hostile place: A Critical Race Theory analysis of campus culture centers. In L. D. Patton (Ed.), *Culture centers in higher education: Perspectives on identity, theory, and practice* (pp. 83–104). Sterling, VA: Stylus.

Yosso, T. J., Smith, W. A., Ceja, M., & Solórzano, D. (2009). Critical Race Theory, racial microaggressions, and campus racial climate for Latina/o undergraduates. *Harvard Educational Review, 79,* 659–690.

Young, D. G., & Janosik, S. M. (2007). Using CAS standards to measure learning outcomes of student affairs preparation programs. *Journal of Student Affairs Research and Practice, 44,* 341–366.

Yourke, M., & Thomas, L. (2003). Improving the retention of students from lower socio-economic groups. *Journal of Higher Education Policy and Management, 25,* 63–74.

Zamudio, M., Russell, C., Rios, F., & Bridgeman, J. (2011). *Critical Race Theory matters: Education and ideology.* New York: Routledge.

Zeller, W. J. (2005). First-year student living environments. In M. L. Upcraft, J. N. Gardner, B. O. Barefoot, & Associates (Eds.), *Challenging and supporting the first-year student: A handbook for improving the first year of college* (pp. 410–427). San Francisco: Jossey-Bass.

Zhang, L., & Ness, E. D. (2010). Does state merit-based aid stem brain drain? *Educational Evaluation and Policy Analysis, 32,* 143–165.

Zhang, Y., & Chan, T. (2007). *An interim report on the student support services program: 2002–2003 and 2003–2004, with select data from 1998–2002.* Washington, DC: U.S. Department of Education.

Zimbroff, J. A. (2005). Policy implications of culturally based perceptions in college choice. *Review of Policy Research, 22,* 811–840.

NAME INDEX

SUBJECT INDEX

Page references followed by *fig* indicate an illustrated figure; followed by *t* indicate a table.